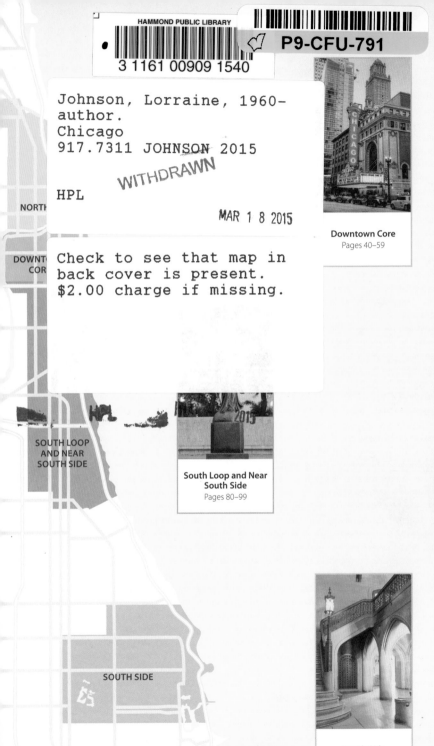

NORTH

DOWNTOWN
CORE

Downtown Core
Pages 40–59

SOUTH LOOP
AND NEAR
SOUTH SIDE

**South Loop and Near
South Side**
Pages 80–99

SOUTH SIDE

South Side
Pages 100–111

EYEWITNESS TRAVEL

CHICAGO

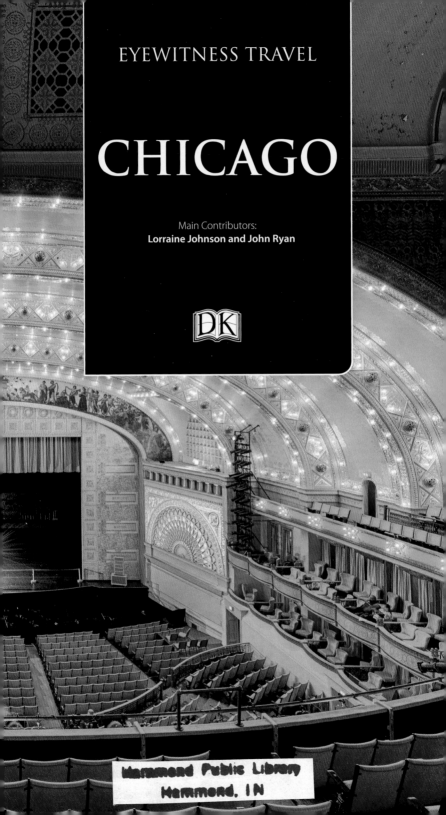

EYEWITNESS TRAVEL

CHICAGO

Main Contributors:
Lorraine Johnson and John Ryan

DK

DK

LONDON, NEW YORK,
MELBOURNE, MUNICH AND DELHI
www.dk.com

Produced By International Book Productions,
Part of Denise Schon Books Inc.
Toronto, Canada

Project Editor And Art Director Barbara Hopkinson
Editor Judy Phillips
Designers Dietmar Kokemohr, Stella Powelczyk
Editorial And Map Assistance Terri Rothman
Picture Research
Karen Taylor Permissions and Photo Research

Main Contributors
Lorraine Johnson, John Ryan

Photographer
Andrew Leyerle

Illustrator
William Band

Printed and bound by L. Rex Printing Company Limited, China

First American edition, 2001

14 15 16 17 10 9 8 7 6 5 4 3 2 1

Published in the United States by
Dorling Kindersley Limited,
345 Hudson Street, New York 10014

**Reprinted with revisions 2003, 2004, 2006, 2008,
2010, 2012, 2015**

Copyright 2001, 2015 © Dorling Kindersley Limited, London
A Penguin Random House Company

A Catalog Record is available from the Library of Congress

ISSN 1542-1554

ISBN 978 1 46541 207 2

MIX
Paper from
responsible sources
FSC
www.fsc.org FSC™ C018179

Front cover main image: View of Lake Shore Drive

◀ The Auditorium Theatre of Roosevelt University in Chicago

Nuclear Energy by Henry Moore at
University of Chicago *(see p102)*

Contents

How to Use
this Guide
6

Introducing
Chicago

Twisted Columns by Ricardo Bofill,
R.R. Donnelley Building *(see p57)*

South Michigan Avenue, one of Chicago's grandest streets *(see p85)*

Raptor perched on a tree branch in Washington Park *(see p106)*

Painted-glass window in St. James Episcopal Cathedral *(see p69)*

Street-by-street map of South Loop *(see pp82–3)*

HOW TO USE THIS GUIDE

This DK Eyewitness travel guide helps you get the most from your stay in Chicago. *Introducing Chicago* locates the city geographically, sets modern Chicago in its historical context, and describes events through the entire year. *Chicago at a Glance* highlights the city's top attractions. The main sightseeing section of the book is *Chicago Area by Area*. It describes the city sights, with photographs, maps, and drawings. It also offers suggestions for day trips outside the city center. *Beyond Chicago* delves into destinations in the region ideal for either day trips or longer sojourns, such as weekend getaways. Restaurant and hotel recommendations, as well as specially selected information about shops and entertainment, are found in *Travelers' Needs*. The *Survival Guide* gives practical information on everyday needs, from using Chicago's medical system and public transportation to the telephone system.

Finding your way around the Sightseeing Section

Each of the sightseeing areas in Chicago is color-coded for easy reference. Each chapter opens with a description of the area and a list of sights to be covered, located by numbers on an area map. This is followed by a Street-by-Street map, illustrating an interesting part of the area. Finding your way around the chapter is made simple by the numbering system used throughout. Sights outside Chicago have a regional map.

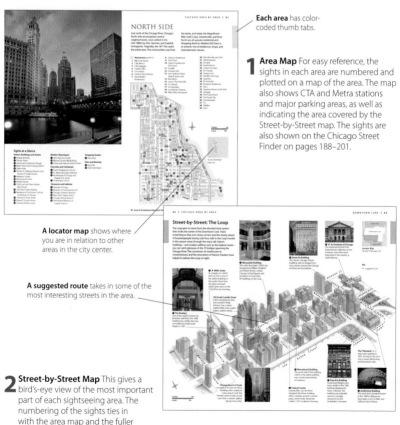

Each area has color-coded thumb tabs.

1 Area Map For easy reference, the sights in each area are numbered and plotted on a map of the area. The map also shows CTA and Metra stations and major parking areas, as well as indicating the area covered by the Street-by-Street map. The sights are also shown on the Chicago Street Finder on pages 188–201.

A locator map shows where you are in relation to other areas in the city center.

A suggested route takes in some of the most interesting streets in the area.

2 Street-by-Street Map This gives a bird's-eye view of the most important part of each sightseeing area. The numbering of the sights ties in with the area map and the fuller descriptions on the pages that follow.

Chicago Area Map

The colored areas shown on this map *(see inside front cover)* are the four main sightseeing areas – each covered by a full chapter in *Chicago Area by Area (see pp38–111)*. The four areas are highlighted on other maps throughout the book. In *Chicago at a Glance (see pp22–33)*, for example, they help locate the top sights.

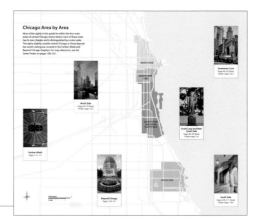

Numbers refer to each sight's position on the area map and its place in the chapter.

Practical information provides all you need to know to visit each sight, including a map reference to the *Chicago Street Finder (see pp188–201)*.

3 Detailed information All the important sights in Chicago are described individually. They are listed in order, following the numbering on the area map. Practical information such as address, telephone number, and opening hours is provided for each sight. The key to the symbols used is on the back flap.

The visitors' checklist provides all the practical information needed to plan your visit.

Façades of important buildings are often shown to illustrate their architectural style, and to help you recognize them quickly.

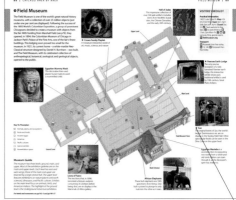

4 Chicago's major sights These are given two or more full pages in the sightseeing area where they are found. Museums and galleries have color-coded floor plans to help you find important exhibits.

Stars indicate the features no visitor should miss.

INTRODUCING CHICAGO

GREAT DAYS IN CHICAGO

Chicago is a city full of things to see and do, and is well-known for its influential architecture, excellent shopping, renowned museums, and many cultural institutions. The following itineraries, that take in a variety of sights and activities, are aimed at helping you make the most of your time here. They are listed first by

theme and then by duration of stay. The sights and activities included are cross-referenced to detailed entries in the guide and are easily accessible by foot or public transportation. Prices mentioned on pages 10–11 cover travel, food, and admission fees. Family prices are for two adults and two children.

Chicago's skyline, dominated by the John Hancock Center, from the lake

Fun for the Family

Family of four allow at least $100

- **Funfair at Navy Pier**
- **Animal adventures at Lincoln Park Zoo**
- **Butterfly heaven at Peggy Notebaert Nature Museum**

City of Skyscrapers

Two adults allow at least $50

- **Breakfast at Lou Mitchell's**
- **Be awestruck by the stunning Willis Tower**
- **Admire the city's historic architecture**
- **Enjoy the view from the top of John Hancock Center**

Morning

Start your day with pancakes at the legendary diner **Lou Mitchell's** at 565 W. Jackson Blvd. Two blocks east, the glass-and-steel **Willis Tower** (*see p44*) is the second-tallest building in the US at 1,450 ft (442 m); go up to the 103rd-floor Skydeck and The Ledge for views of four states on a clear day. The **Monadnock Building** (*see p46*), a few blocks west, is a lesson in 19th-century architectural history. Finished in 1891, its north half is a traditional structure with 6-ft-(1.85-m) thick walls; the south half, finished three years later, has a more modern steel-frame construction. A five-minute

walk north, the 1895 **Reliance Building** (*see p52*), is an airy, terra-cotta-clad gem – forerunner of the modern skyscraper. North on State Street towards the river you will see more modern architecture. Built in 1964, the two towers of **Marina City** (*see p68*) rise like twin corn cobs, and to the east is Mies van der Rohe's stark **IBM Building** (*see p68*). Facing each other are the more Classical **Wrigley Building** (*see p64*), clad in white terra-cotta and **Tribune Tower** (*see p64*), a Neo-Gothic structure.

Afternoon

After a quick bite on North Michigan Avenue, stroll up to the **Water Tower and Pumping Station** (*see p65*), a Gothic, limestone survivor of the Great Chicago Fire of 1871. The interior showcases Chicago-themed photographs. One block ahead, looms the **John Hancock Center** (*see p66*), for now the city's fourth tallest at 1,127 ft (343 m). Try the screened skywalk, or enjoy the view for the price of a drink in the Signature lounge.

Morning

Jutting out into Lake Michigan just east of downtown, **Navy Pier** (*see p67*) is the city's most popular attraction and a great place to start a day out with the kids. From interactive exhibits at the **Chicago Children's Museum** (*see p67*) to IMAX movies, boat cruises and a 15-story-high Ferris wheel, there's enough at this 50-acre (20-hectare) park to keep the family busy all morning. Stop for lunch at the food court or check out the scene in Joe's Be-Bop Café and Jazz Emporium where there's live music daily.

Landing point for Navy Pier, in front of the Ferris wheel

◀ Lithographic depiction of the view of Chicago from Lake Michigan (1860-69)

Afternoon

For an animal-themed afternoon, take the bus to the free **Lincoln Park Zoo** *(see pp114–15)*, which houses rhinos, giraffes, gorillas, snakes, polar bears, and more than 1,000 other animals from the world over. Be sure to visit the Pritzker Family Children's Zoo, which simulates a walk in the woods with exhibits of wolves, bears, beavers, otters and other woodland creatures.

If you still have the energy, pay a visit to the **John G. Shedd Aquarium** *(see pp98–9)*, for a close-up view of sea otters, dolphins, whales, and over two dozen sharks. The Underwater Viewing gallery of the Oceanarium will captivate the kids.

The impressive tyrannosaurus rex skeleton at the Field Museum

Museums and Culture

Two adults allow at least $80

- A morning at the Art Institute of Chicago
- T. rex at the Field Museum
- An interactive planetarium

Morning

Spend the morning at the **Art Institute of Chicago** *(see pp48–51)*, one of the world's finest museums, just south of **Millennium Park** *(see p55)* on the east side of Michigan Avenue. It has some exquisite works of American art such as Grant Wood's *American Gothic*, Edward Hopper's *Nighthawks*, and several iconic pieces by Georgia O'Keeffe. Admire its French Impressionist collection, the centerpiece of which is Seurat's *A Sunday on La Grande Jatte–1884*. Also worth checking out is the Modern Wing, opened in 2009 and designed by Pritzker Prize-winning architect Renzo Piano. For lunch, grab a bite in the lower-level café or pop out to an eatery on Michigan Avenue nearby.

Afternoon

Catch the No. 146 bus from State Street to the Museum Campus and head for the **Field Museum** *(see pp88–91)*. Inside, you will come face-to-face with the largest and best-preserved T. rex skeleton ever discovered. Walk through "Evolving Planet," which tells the story of the Earth's 4 billion-year history. The adjacent lakeside **Adler Planetarium** *(see pp94–5)* has a really good interactive exhibit of America's space program.

Shop till you Drop

Two adults allow at least $30 (cost of transport and food)

- **Wonderful stores on Michigan Avenue**
- **Boutiques on Oak Street**
- **Upscale elegance on Armitage Avenue**

Morning

Start your day on Michigan Avenue, one of the world's greatest retail areas, where names such as Crate & Barrel, Gap, and Banana Republic

Michigan Avenue, a magnet for shoppers and tourists alike

compete with department stores and shopping centers such as the famous **Water Tower Place** *(see p63)*, the nation's first vertical mall. An all-white interior packed with iPods and iMacs makes the Apple Store a stylish must-stop for the high-tech set. Farther north, Nike Town shows off the latest in shoes and sportswear. Alternatively, take in the elegant scene of **Oak Street** *(see p66)*, where upscale boutiques such as Hermès, Prada, Kate Spade, and Tod's reside. Lunch in style (Italian-American cuisine) around the corner at Fred's (15 E. Oak St., 312-596-1111) within Barneys department store.

Afternoon

Take the El to the Armitage Brown Line stop to browse the boutiques of Armitage Avenue district where it's all top-quality, from truffles at Vosges Haut-Chocolat (951 W. Armitage Avenue) to hand-made stationery at Paper Source (No. 919). Or catch the No. 73 bus west to Damen Avenue and stroll south to trendy **Wicker Park** *(see p116)* for some great shopping as well as interesting galleries and cafés.

Exhibits at the Adler Planetarium

2 Days in Chicago

- Admire Impressionist masterpieces at the Art Institute of Chicago
- Get a bird's-eye view of four states from the Skydeck of Willis Tower
- Window shop on the Magnificent Mile

Day 1
Morning Start the day with the **Chicago Architecture Foundation** *(see p47)* tour, which offers a first-hand orientation to the city's landmark architecture. Follow it up with the amazing view from the Skydeck at **Willis Tower** *(see p44)*. Next, head over to **Millennium Park** *(see p55)* to see the skyline reflected in the mirrored surface of Anish Kapoor's jellybean-like *Cloud Gate* sculpture, and appreciate the brushed steel headdress of Frank Gehry's J. Pritzker Pavillion.

Afternoon Spend at least two hours viewing the Impressionist collection of the **Art Institute of Chicago** *(see pp48–51)*. Don't miss Edward Hopper's *Nighthawks* and Grant Wood's iconic *American Gothic*. From here go south through **Grant Park** *(see pp86–7)* for a photo op at **Buckingham Fountain** *(see p87)*. Then make a beeline for State Street, entering the theater district as you head north. That done, walk across to State Street and head north to the Theater District. Continue on to the State Street Bridge for terrific views of the Chicago River.

Day 2
Morning The **Michigan Avenue Bridge** *(see pp56–7)* is ground zero for the **Magnificent Mile** *(see pp62–3)*. As you pass the **Tribune Tower** *(see p64)*, look for the collage of labeled fragments from the Taj Mahal, the Parthenon and the Great Pyramid that are embedded in its Neo-Gothic façade. Head east on to Grand Street, which has the **Navy Pier** *(see p67)*, with its five-story Ferris wheel, an IMAX theater, and several shops and restaurants.

Afternoon Window shop on the Mag Mile. Look out for the castle-like **Water Tower and Pumping Station** *(see p65)*, the only downtown Chicago building predating the Great Chicago Fire. North of the Water Tower, the serene **Fourth Presbyterian Church** *(see p65)* is the second oldest building on Michigan Avenue. Across the street, visit the **John Hancock Center** *(see p66)* – it has the best panoramic views of the city.

3 Days in Chicago

- Explore the collections of world-class museums at the Museum Campus
- Have brunch and wander through Chinatown
- Cruise along the Chicago River for a panoptic view of the landmark architecture

Day 1
Morning Spend a couple of hours looking at the lovely Impressionist collection and the new Modern Wing of the **Art Institute of Chicago** *(see pp48–51)*. Move on to contemporary art in **Millennium Park** *(see p55)*, including the reflective *Cloud Gate*, the Pritzker Pavillion with Frank Gehry's sweeping bandshell, and Juan Plensa's Crown fountain.

Afternoon Begin with the two-hour **Chicago River Architecture tour** *(see p59)* that allows you to sit back and appreciate the landmark buildings as you float by. Back

on dry land, stroll down State Street and check out the marquee at the landmark **Chicago Theatre** *(see p56)*.

Day 2
Morning Enjoy breathtaking views of four states from the **Willis Tower Skydeck** *(see p44)*. Then, visit **Chinatown** *(see p96)* for a wholesome dim sum brunch and some window shopping.

Afternoon The museum campus houses three of Chicago's cultural gems: the **Field Museum** *(see pp88–91)*, the **John G. Shedd Aquarium** *(see pp98–9)*, and **Adler Planetarium** *(see pp94–5)*. After spending time at the museum of your choice, enjoy the gorgeous harbor views from the campus lawn. At sunset, catch the sound and light show at **Buckingham Fountain** *(see p87)*.

Day 3
Morning Meander up the **Mag Mile** *(see pp62–3)*, and enjoy the interesting juxtaposition of modern complexes with historic buildings. Take in the castle-like Neo-Gothic architecture of the historic **Water Tower and Pumping Station** *(see p65)*. Shop at fashionable **Oak Street** *(see p66)* boutiques if so inclined or else, climb up to the observation deck of the **John Hancock Center** *(see p66)* for mesmerizing views of the city.

Afternoon Spend the afternoon exploring **Navy Pier** *(see p67)*. If traveling with children, be sure to visit the hands-on **Chicago Children's Museum** *(see p67)* or catch a movie at the IMAX theater.

Sunset in Chicago, with a view of the Marina Towers on the right

5 Days in Chicago

- Visit the animals at the Lincoln Park Zoo
- Discover the University of Chicago's myriad cultural attractions
- Tour a captured U-Boat at the Museum of Science and Industry

Wrigley Field, the world-famous home of the Major League Baseball Chicago Cubs

Day 1

Morning Begin your day at **Navy Pier** *(see p67)*, browsing shops and visiting tourist attractions. If you have kids on board, make a trip to the **Chicago Children's Museum** *(see p67)* or, catch an IMAX movie. With or without kids, a Lake Michigan boat excursion is a must.

Afternoon Stroll the **Mag Mile** *(see pp62–3)* from the **Michigan Avenue Bridge** *(see pp56–7)*, past the **Wrigley Building** *(see p64)* and **Tribune Tower** *(see p64)* towards the historic **Water Tower and Pumping Station** *(see p65)* – Chicago's oldest building, which houses a cafe and a theater. Also visit **Water Tower Place** *(see p159)* – a mall with a fabulous food court.

Day 2

Morning Get schooled in Chicago's architecture with a two-hour **Chicago Architecture Foundation** *(see p47)* walking, Segway, or river tour. Afterward, visit Anish Kapoor's jellybean-like *Cloud Gate* sculpture and the other public art in **Millennium Park** *(see p55)*. Later, head south to take in the spectacle that is **Buckingham Fountain** *(see p87)*.

Afternoon A couple of hours at the **Art Institute of Chicago** *(see pp48–51)* is essential to explore its Impressionist galleries and the Modern Wing, opened in 2009. Then, State Street is great for some retail therapy; take a detour to see the Picasso sculpture at **Daley Plaza** *(see p163)*, and the futuristic **James R. Thompson Center** *(see p58)*. At dusk, ascend **Willis Tower** *(see p44)* for an amazing view of the sunset.

Day 3

Morning With acres of exhibits and a petting zoo, a few hours at the **Lincoln Park Zoo** *(see pp114–15)* is a great way to start the day. Later, visit the Lincoln Park Conservatory which has on display thousands of botanical specimens, as well as the dazzling butterfly exhibits at **Notebaert Nature Museum** *(see p125)*.

Afternoon Get a sense of the city's turbulent history at the **Chicago History Museum** *(see p76)*. A few blocks further down on Clark Street is the site of the notorious gangland St. Valentine's Day massacre. Continue north to the historic **Wrigley Field** *(see p116)*, the famous home of Chicago Cubs baseball team.

Day 4

Morning Take a pleasant stroll around the **University of Chicago** campus *(see pp102–103)*, looking

The interiors of the massive James R. Thompson Center

out for Frank Lloyd Wright's **Robie House** *(see p104)*, an excellent example of Prairie School architecture. Visit the **Oriental Institute Museum** *(see pp104–105)* to see remnants from ancient civilizations and the **Smart Museum of Art** *(see p105)* for its master artworks. Later, see the second-largest bell tower in the world at the **Rockefeller Memorial Chapel** *(see p104)*.

Afternoon Plan on about two hours to explore the **Museum of Science and Industry** *(see pp108–11)*. The collection includes a U-Boat, the Apollo 8 command module, and a fairy castle dollhouse. Afterwards, enjoy the expansive skyline from **Jackson Park** *(see p107)*, site of the 1893 World's Fair.

Day 5

Morning The Museum Campus is home to three world-class museums. Take your pick of the **Field Museum's** *(see pp88–91)* dinosaurs, **John G. Shedd Aquarium's** *(see pp98–9)* aquatic life, or the **Adler Planetarium** *(see pp94–5)* starscapes.

Afternoon Golden-age industrialists made their homes in the **Prairie Avenue Historic District** *(see p92)*, and a tour of **Clarke House and Museum** *(see p93)* or **Glessner House** *(see p92–3)* lends insight to that era. A short stroll away, Chicago's **Chinatown** *(see p96)* is the largest in the Midwest. Browse the shops and stay for dinner.

Putting Chicago on the Map

Chicago, a city of almost 3 million people, covers 228 sq miles (591 sq km) of the US's Midwest. Situated at the southwest edge of Lake Michigan, the world's fifth-largest freshwater body, Chicago claims 26 miles (42 km) of lakefront. Two airports handle international and internal flights. There are also interstate highways and rail links serving both the East and West Coasts and other parts of the country, and Canada.

Key

- ▬▬ Interstate highway
- ▬▬ Major road
- ┄┄ Minor road
- ─── Major railroad
- ▬ ▬ International border
- ─ ─ State/provincial boundary

For keys to symbols *see back flap*

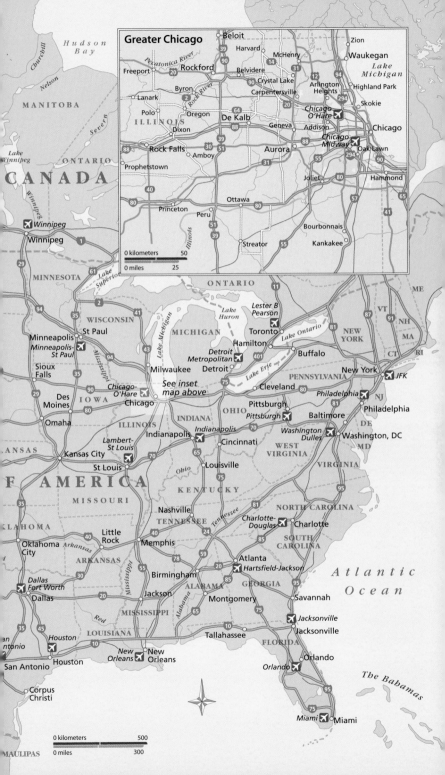

THE HISTORY OF CHICAGO

The third-largest city in the US is world famous for magnificent and innovative architecture, its colorful and turbulent political history and significance as a national transportation hub, the now-vanished stockyards, as well as its educational institutes and vibrant cultural venues.

The French missionary Jacques Marquette and French-Canadian explorer Louis Jolliet were the first Europeans to record a visit to this spot at the foot of Lake Michigan, in 1673. The peaceful, friendly local Potawatomi Indians called the low-lying swampy area "Checaugou," which likely means "wild onion" or "skunk cabbage." Jolliet and Marquette used this Indian name on the maps they drew, which were then used by later explorers.

More than 100 years passed before the first permanent settlement was established in 1779 by Jean Baptiste Point du Sable, an African-American trader from the Caribbean. Du Sable and his Indian wife built a house on the north bank near the mouth of the Chicago River.

A treaty negotiated with local Indian tribes in 1795 gave US citizens access to most of Ohio and a 6-sq-mile (15.5-sq-km) area of land where the Chicago River emptied into Lake Michigan – now the heart of Chicago's downtown.

In 1803, the US Army built Fort Dearborn along the river to protect settlers from the Indians, the British, and the French. Fort

Dearborn was destroyed during the War of 1812 between the US and Britain; soldiers and their families were slaughtered by the Indians, allies of the British, as they fled the fort. Although the fort was rebuilt in 1816 and Illinois became a state in 1818, the area remained Indian territory until it was ceded in 1833 and the Indians were relocated to reservations by the federal government. That year, Chicago became a town.

Early Chicago

With the land open for development, the rivers gained importance as shipping routes. In 1837, Chicago, its population now over 4,000, received city status. The expansion of the lake ports, completion of the Illinois and Michigan Canal connecting the Great Lakes with the Mississippi River, and arrival of the railroads spurred rapid growth. Public schools were established in 1840, and by 1847 the new city had two daily newspapers. From 1855 to 1858, Chicago literally pulled itself out of the mud, jacking up the downtown buildings and filling in the swamp muck with soil (see p59).

1673 Explorers Jacques Marquette and Louis Jolliet arrive at "Checaugou"

1779 First settlement in Chicago established by trader Jean Baptiste Point du Sable

Jean Baptiste Point du Sable

1803 Fort Dearborn built

1848 Illinois & Michigan Canal completed (see pp120–21)

| 1650 | 1700 | 1750 | 1800 | 1850 |

1682 Frenchman La Salle explores area and establishes forts

A Potawatomi chief

1783 British cede land that is now Chicago to the newly established US government

1825 Erie Canal opens

1837 Chicago incorporates as a city

1858 Chicago becomes US's chief railroad hub

1847 *Chicago Tribune* newspaper founded

◄ A contemporary lithograph depicting the Great Chicago Fire of 1871

Chicago's proximity to both the Mississippi River and the Great Lakes confirmed it as the nation's transportation hub. By 1860, 15 railroad companies had terminals here. Christmas Day 1865 saw the opening of the gigantic Union Stock Yards, the city's largest employer for decades. (It eventually closed in 1971.) Meatpacking laws, along with the Food and Drug Administration, were created after Upton Sinclair's stirring 1906 book, *The Jungle,* revealed the poor conditions of such stockyards.

Detail of cow (1879) on the archway to Union Stock Yards

Although meat processing remained Chicago's major industry, positioning the city as the US's primary supplier, the grain-handling and manufacturing industries were also strong in 19th-century Chicago.

The Great Fire

The Great Chicago Fire of 1871 burned for 36 hours, October 8 to 10, destroying most of the buildings in downtown Chicago, all of which were made of wood. At least 300 people died, and about 100,000 – one-third of the population – were left homeless. A cow, belonging to a certain Mrs. O'Leary, was blamed for kicking over a lantern and starting the fire. Although an inquiry confirmed that the blaze started in the O'Leary shed, the cause of the fire was not determined, and the O'Leary family was later given public pardon. An 1874 bylaw prohibited the building of wooden structures downtown. Consequently, Chicago architect William Le Baron Jenney *(see pp28–9)* designed the Home Insurance Building (1884), a nine-story structure supported by a steel skeleton, regarded by many to be the first skyscraper. Jenney's design paved the way for the canyons of tall buildings found in city centers today.

Social Unrest, Social Reform

As Chicago's downtown rebuilt and the city continued to expand – to 500,000 inhabitants by 1880 – social divisions grew. In the 1873 Bread Riot, police trapped thousands of protesting hungry workers under a bridge, clubbing many to death. Four years later, during the 1877 national railroad strike, Chicago police fired on demonstrators, killing 30. On May 4, 1886, workers rallied at Haymarket Square to protest the police killing of two laborers

The aftermath of the Great Fire, as seen from Chicago Harbor

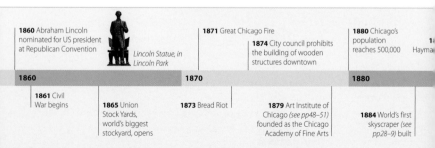

1860 Abraham Lincoln nominated for US president at Republican Convention

Lincoln Statue, in Lincoln Park

1871 Great Chicago Fire

1874 City council prohibits the building of wooden structures downtown

1880 Chicago's population reaches 500,000

Hayma

1860

1870

1880

1861 Civil War begins

1865 Union Stock Yards, world's biggest stockyard, opens

1873 Bread Riot

1879 Art Institute of Chicago *(see pp48–51)* founded as the Chicago Academy of Fine Arts

1884 World's first skyscraper *(see pp28–9)* built

Protesters clash with police in the 1873 Bread Riot

demanding the shortening of the workday to eight hours. A bomb exploded in the midst of the police officers, starting a riot that eventually killed seven officers. It was never determined who threw the bomb, and the ensuing trial, in which eight men were charged with murder and four subsequently executed, is considered one of the worst miscarriages of justice in the US.

Into this social tumult stepped Jane Addams (see p33) and Ellen Gates Starr. In 1889, they founded Hull-House to help settle immigrants (see p118). It would soon become a leader in US social welfare and reform.

Progress, and the 1893 World's Columbian Exposition

Downtown, other initiatives were underway. The Art Institute of Chicago (see pp48–51) was founded in 1879, and the Chicago Symphony Orchestra (see p166) and the University of Chicago (see pp102–103) in 1890. The first elevated tramway opened in 1892, and in 1897 a circle around the commercial core opened, giving downtown

Guidebook for the 1893 World's Columbian Fair

the nickname "The Loop." Chicago celebrated the 400th anniversary of Christopher Columbus' journey to the Americas with the 1893 World's Columbian Exposition, held in Jackson Park (see p107). Over 25 million visitors came to it, the largest fair yet to be held in the Americas. Despite a deep national economic depression, the city built a fabulous fairground, dubbed the "White City" because of its Neo-Classical white plaster buildings. It was to have a huge impact on US architecture. Most of the buildings burned down or were vandalized after the fair.

Growth and Growing Pains

By 1890, the population climbed past one million. Awareness of public health issues led to concern that the city discharged, directly or indirectly, most of its waste into the Chicago River, and from there into Lake Michigan, the source of drinking water. In 1900, the Chicago Sanitary and Ship Canal opened, and the direction of the Chicago River was reversed so that the river flowed away from the lake, not into it (see p59).

In 1903, a disaster affected both urban design and bylaws nationwide. Nearly 600 people died when a fire tragically destroyed the Iroquois Theater (see p53). Investigators blamed the fatalities on the doors. Many opened inward: impossible to open with a frantic crowd pressed against them. Most US cities now require that doors of all public buildings open outward.

1890 Chicago becomes second-largest US city, its population over 1 million

1892 Elevated tramway ("The Loop") opens

1900 Chicago Sanitary and Ship Canal opens, reversing flow of Chicago River

1907 University of Chicago's Albert Michelson is first US scientist to win a Nobel Prize in Physics, for measurement of the speed of light

1890 **1900** **1910**

Hull-House (see p118) founded

1893 Chicago hosts World's Columbian Exposition

1890 University of Chicago (see pp102–103) founded

Opening of the new canal

1909 Plan of Chicago (see p32), the first civic blueprint for a city, published

Speakeasy directions written in chalk

By 1914, waves of immigrants from Europe had arrived in Chicago. Industrialization now brought another wave: African Americans from the South, seeking work after being displaced from farm work by the cotton gin and other new machinery. Chicago's Black population increased by about 14,000 in 1910 to almost 110,000 by the early 1920s. Previous arrivals did not always welcome the new migrants. A 1919 race riot that started at a segregated South Side beach raged for several days, leaving 38 dead and nearly 300 injured.

Speakeasies, illicit social clubs offering liquor despite the prohibition of alcohol, flourished in the 1920s and made way for the bootlegging gangster. The most famous gangster – and the one most closely linked to Chicago in the public mind – was Al Capone, who arrived in 1919 from New York. Capone is legendary for his bloody gang war. In the notorious 1929 St. Valentine's Day Massacre, seven mobsters from a rival gang were killed execution-style by mobsters loyal to Capone.

Almost as famous were Eliot Ness and his team, who collected the evidence of income-tax evasion that put Capone in prison in 1931. He was released on parole eight years later.

Chicago Milestones: 1920s–60s

The Chicago Municipal Airport (now Midway Airport) opened in 1927. From 1945 to 1958, it was the world's busiest airport, before being replaced by O'Hare, which was equipped to handle the new jetliners and is today one of the world's busiest airports.

The old airport brought visitors to the 1933–4 World's Fair. Showcasing innovative uses of electricity, the fair attracted 39 million people. Another kind of energy came to the fore when, in 1942, physicist Enrico Fermi from the University of Chicago conducted the world's first controlled atomic reaction *(see p102)*.

Physicist Enrico Fermi

After World War II, the city's economy boomed, its population peaking at 3.6 million. New arrivals included musicians from the Mississippi Delta and by 1950, they were recording a new form of blues.

Chicago's O'Hare Airport, one of the world's busiest

					1968 Democratic National
	1933 Chicago		**1942** First controlled	**1953** Hugh Hefner	Convention riot
1928 Chicago River	hosts Century		atomic chain reaction,	publishes first	
straightened to allow for	of Progress		at University of Chicago	issue of *Playboy*	
expansion of downtown	World's Fair			magazine	

1920	**1930**	**1940**	**1950**	**1960**

			1955 Richard J. Daley	**1966** Martin
1929 St. Valentine's			elected mayor	Luther King Jr.
Day Massacre	**1931** Eliot Ness			brings civil rights
	succeeds in			movement
1919 Mobster	convicting Al	**1943** Chicago's	**1959** White Sox win	to Chicago
Al Capone	Capone	first subway opens	American League	
arrives	*Eliot Ness*		baseball pennant	

Richard J. Daley, mayor of Chicago for 21 years

The 1950s saw many milestones: Carl Sandburg won the Pulitzer Prize for Poetry in 1951; and Ray Kroc's first McDonald's opened in 1955 in Des Plaines, just outside Chicago.

Turbulent Politics

In 1955, Chicago elected Democrat Richard J. Daley as mayor, a position he held until his fatal heart attack in 1976. In 1966, Martin Luther King Jr. brought the civil rights movement to Chicago, challenging Daley's political machine and the segregation of the Black population. Daley's administration survived the West Side riots, prompted by the assassination of King in Memphis, and the confrontations between police and demonstrators outside the Democratic National Convention, both in 1968. Daley was equally well known for his commitment to a clean city.

Daley's successors include Jane Byrne, Chicago's first female mayor (1979–83), and Harold Washington, Chicago's first Black mayor (1983–7), called "the people's mayor" because he was in touch with the grassroots. Washington made significant structural changes in city operations before dying of a heart attack at his desk, shortly after his re-election as mayor in 1987. Richard M. Daley, son of former mayor Richard J. Daley, was Chicago's longest serving mayor (1989–2011). In 2011, Rahm Emanuel was elected mayor.

Chicago Today

In 1990, Chicago's title of "Second City" became an honorific, as the population of Los Angeles surpassed that of Chicago to become the second largest in the US. Chicago remains the US's largest transportation center and the financial capital of the Midwest. Chicago Board of Trade, founded in 1848, continues to be the most important grain market in the nation. Willis Tower (see p44) recaptured the title of World's Tallest Building in 1997. The Chicago Bulls won six NBA championships. In 2004, Millennium Park opened as Chicago's "front yard," serving as Mayor Richard J. Daley's multi-million dollar legacy.

Chicago has had its share of disasters. In 1992, the Chicago River poured into a hole in a tunnel in the Loop. Water filled downtown basements, threatening to sink the city center below the level of the original swampland.

Today, Chicago has a lot to offer, with superb public art and architecture, and an impressive cultural scene.

Willis Tower, one of the iconic sights of Chicago

1971 Union Stock Yards close	**1979** Jane Byrne elected mayor of Chicago		**2004** Millennium Park opens (see p55)		**2008** Chicago resident Barack Obama becomes US president	
		1986 Refurbished Chicago Theatre reopens (see p56)				
'0	**1980**	**1990**	**2000**		**2010**	**2020**
1973 Willis Tower (see p44) opens as tallest building in world	**1983** Harold Washington elected mayor of Chicago	**1992** Chicago River leaks into abandoned freight tunnel, threatening to collapse downtown		**2005** White Sox win the World Series	**2013** Chicago Blackhawks win Stanley Cup for the second time in four seasons	
	Willis Tower				**2011** Rahm Emanuel takes office as mayor	

CHICAGO AT A GLANCE

More than 100 places of interest are described in the *Area by Area* and *Beyond Chicago* sections of this book. They range from the Gothic–style Rockefeller Memorial Chapel *(see p104)* to the Post-Modern James R. Thompson Center *(see p58)*, from the trendy neighborhood of Wicker Park *(see p116)* to tranquil Washington Park *(see p106)*. To help make the most of your stay, the following ten pages are a time-saving guide to the best Chicago has to offer. The guide highlights the city's best museums and architecture, as well as the people and cultures that have given Chicago its unique character over the years. Below are the top ten tourist attractions that no visitor to Chicago should miss.

Chicago's Top Ten

Museum of Science and Industry
See pp108–111

Magnificent Mile
See pp62–3

Art Institute of Chicago
See pp48–51

Millennium Park
See p55

Willis Tower
See p44

Tourist Attractions

John G. Shedd Aquarium
See pp98–9

Navy Pier
See p67

Lincoln Park Zoo
See pp114–15

Adler Planetarium
See pp94–5

Field Museum
See pp88–91

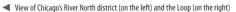
◀ View of Chicago's River North district (on the left) and the Loop (on the right)

Chicago's Best: Museums

Chicago has some of the world's finest museums, and the buildings in which they are housed are often works of art themselves. The Art Institute of Chicago, world-renowned for its Impressionist and Post-Impressionist paintings, and Museum Campus – consisting of the Field Museum, Adler Planetarium, and Shedd Aquarium – are prominent on any visitor's itinerary. There are many smaller museums, too, celebrating Chicago's heritage and giving insight into the people and events that have left their mark on the city.

North Side

WEST GRAND AVEN

Downtov Core

Chicago History Museum
This museum traces Chicago's rich history, beginning with its first explorers and settlers, through the development of the city, to major events in modern-day Chicago *(see p76)*.

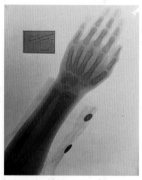

Chicago Cultural Center
The great hall is one of many highlights in this much loved center. Visitors can also enjoy theater, film, dance, and music. Most productions are free *(see p54)*.

International Museum of Surgical Science
The history of medicine and surgery, from blood-letting to X-rays, is brought to life at this fascinating museum *(see p77)*.

Spertus Museum
This Torah cover is part of the outstanding collection of art and artifacts reflecting 5,000 years of Jewish culture and ritual exhibited at this museum *(see p86)*.

0 kilometers		2
0 miles	1	

Museum of Contemporary Art

Cutting-edge modern works by European and American artists such as sculptor Alexander Calder are featured in permanent and rotating exhibits *(see p67)*.

Art Institute of Chicago

One of the largest holdings of Impressionist and Post-Impressionist paintings outside France can be found here *(see pp48–51)*.

Lake Michigan

Field Museum

An encyclopedic collection of objects relating to the earth's natural and cultural history are explored in vivid displays at this museum *(see pp88–91)*.

Adler Planetarium

One of the world's foremost planetariums, the Adler has a webcam atop its dome – offering a superb view of Chicago – and over 2,000 astronomical artifacts *(see pp94–5)*.

South op and Near outh Side

5TH STREET

SOUTH LAKE SHORE DRIVE

S COTTAGE GROVE AVENUE

E HYDE PARK BOULEVARD

South Side

Smart Museum of Art

The specialties within the wide-ranging collection of this compact museum are antiquities and Old Masters *(see p105)*.

Museum of Science and Industry

Many of the technological inventions and scientific discoveries that have changed our world are on display at this very popular museum, a leader in interactive exhibits *(see pp108–11)*.

Chicago's Best: Architecture

Chicago's downtown skyline is characterized by high-rises, both modern and historic, while a range of residential architecture styles, such as Queen Anne and Prairie, are found in the city's neighborhoods. After the 1871 fire *(see p18)* and subsequent ban on wood as a building material, the use of terra-cotta and cast-iron – both fire resistant and durable – became prevalent. Terra-cotta was also an excellent material for decorative carving and so sheaths many of the city's steel-frame buildings. A detailed overview of Chicago's architecture is found on pages 28–9.

North Side

WEST / GRAND AVEN

Downtown Core

Crilly Court
The Crilly Court row houses *(see p73)*, with their turrets and bays, are one of the finest examples of Queen Anne style in the city.

Newberry Library
Henry Ives Cobb, master of the Richardsonian Romanesque style, designed the library in 1890–93 *(see p69)*. Its heavy stone walls and recessed, arched windows are typical of this style, popular in the second half of the 19th century.

Gage Group
These three buildings reflect different approaches to the Chicago School: two, designed by Holabird and Roche, have minimal exterior decoration; the third, with a facade designed by Louis Sullivan, is more ornate.

333 West Wacker Drive
A Post-Modern structure designed by the architect firm Kohn Pedersen Fox, this building *(see pp58–9)* was met with critical acclaim and local approval when constructed in 1983.

Harold Washington Library Center
This Neo-Classical giant *(see p84)* alludes to Chicago's many historic buildings through its varied architectural features.

John Hancock Center
The towering glass walls and horizontal beams of the John Hancock Center *(see p66)* are characteristic of the International Style.

Water Tower
The Gothic Revival-style castellated tower is one of the city's best-loved landmarks *(see p65)*.

Lake Michigan

Field Museum
Designed in white marble by Daniel H. Burnham, this monumental Neo-Classical building (1921) features a long colonnaded facade with Greek-style caryatids *(see pp88–91)*.

th Loop
d Near
th Side

TH STREET

0 kilometers   2
0 miles   1

SOUTH LAKE SHORE DRIVE

S COTTAGE GROVE AVENUE

E HYDE PARK BOULEVARD

South Side

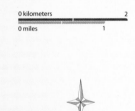

Christopher Bouton House
This villa-like residence, with its tall windows and dominant cornice, was built in 1873 in the Italianate style popular in 19th-century Chicago.

Robie House
Built 1908–1910, this house is considered by many to be Frank Lloyd Wright's Prairie School masterpiece *(see pp104–105)*.

Exploring Chicago's Architecture

Chicago is world famous as a center of architectural innovation, a city where new building techniques have been developed and where architects have pushed the boundaries of creative expression. This reputation had its beginnings in the defining event of Chicago's history – the tragic fire of 1871. With a blank slate on which to build, architects rose to the challenge, transforming devastation into opportunity and reshaping the city. It was in Chicago that the world's first skyscraper was built, and here that Frank Lloyd Wright developed his distinctive Prairie School of architecture.

Gothic Revival

Popular in the 1830s and 1840s, Gothic Revival was inspired by the medieval architecture of Europe, particularly of England. Steeply pitched roofs, pointed arches, turrets, and buttresses are typical features. One of Chicago's best examples of this style is the **Water Tower** (1869). Interest in Gothic continued through the 19th century and is reflected in many of the city's most impressive buildings, such as the **Fourth Presbyterian Church** (1914) and those of the **University of Chicago**.

Italianate Style

Popular from the mid- to late 1800s, the Italianate design style is based on the historic architecture of Italy: the villas of northern Italy and the palaces of the Italian Renaissance. Characteristic features include asymmetrical balancing, low-pitched flat roofs, projecting eaves, and ornate door and window designs, the windows often grouped into arcades. One such example is the **Richard H. Driehaus Museum** (1883), home of banker Samuel M. Nickerson (1830–1914).

Richardsonian Romanesque

Richardsonian Romanesque, or Romanesque Revival, was popularized in the US in the latter half of the 19th century by Bostonian Henry Hobson Richardson (1838–86). His architectural legacy is represented in Chicago by the severe yet subtly ornamented **Glessner House** (1887). Typical features of this style are heavy rough-cut stone, round arches, and deeply recessed windows. Richardson's influence can be seen in the work of Henry Ives Cobb, particularly Cobb's design of **Newberry Library** (1890–93) and the former home of the Chicago History Museum (*see p76*) at Dearborn and Ontario streets.

Queen Anne

Mainly used in residential architecture, Queen Anne style was highly influential in Chicago from the mid- to late 1800s. The name does not reflect a historical period but was coined by English architect Richard Shaw. Queen Anne homes are built on a human scale. A mix of Classical, Tudor, and Colonial elements lead to a hybrid look. Victorian detailing, such as curlicue cutouts on the trim, is often prominent. **Crilly Court** (1885) and the **Olsen-Hansen Row Houses** (1886) are fine examples of Queen Anne style. There are also many Queen Anne houses to be found in the **Pullman Historic District**.

Crilly Court, the name of Crilly's son carved above the door

Chicago School

Named after the city in which it developed, the commercial style of the Chicago School led to both an engineering and aesthetic revolution in architecture. William Le Baron Jenney created the first skyscraper when he designed the nine-story Home Insurance Building (1884; demolished 1929), using skeletal steel frames rather than the conventional

Balloon Frame

Balloon-frame construction was first developed in Chicago by Augustine D. Taylor, in 1833 (though some credit George Washington Snow's 1932 Chicago warehouse as the first such construction). The name refers to the ease of construction: it was as simple as inflating a balloon, although critics said it referred to the ease with which the wind would blow away such structures. Raising a balloon-frame house required simply joining machine-cut lumber with machine-made nails, rather than interlocking time-consuming joints. Various interior and exterior surfaces could then be applied. Chicago's early balloon-frame houses fed the flames of the 1871 fire, but some built after the fire still exist in Old Town (*see pp72–3*).

The elegant Richard H. Driehaus Museum built in the Italianate style

height-limiting, masonry load-bearing walls.

Jenney trained many of Chicago's celebrated architects, including Louis Sullivan, William Holabird, Daniel Burnham, and John Wellborn Root, whose architect firm designed several Chicago School buildings, such as the **Rookery** (1885–8) and the **Reliance Building** (1891–95). The new window style of these buildings, made possible by Jenney's structural innovation,

Reliance Building, Chicago School

became known as Chicago windows. Each consists of a large central glass pane, flanked by two slender windows that open.

Neo-Classical or Beaux-Arts

Neo-Classical, or Beaux-Arts, style became popular in Chicago once it was chosen as the design style for the 1893 World's Fair. Based on classical Greek and Roman architecture, with its columns, pilasters, and pediments, these buildings are often monumental in scale. Many of Chicago's most notable cultural institutions, such as the **Chicago Cultural Center** (1893–7), are housed in Neo-Classical buildings.

Prairie School

In the first two decades of the 20th century, Frank Lloyd Wright developed a truly indigenous American architectural style. Reflecting the sweeping lines of the Midwestern landscape, Prairie style is characterized by low horizontal lines, projecting eaves, and rectangular windows. It is used mostly in residential architecture.

Oak Park is a treasure-trove of Wright-designed houses. Notable Wright buildings elsewhere in Chicago are **Robie House** (1908–1910) and **Charnley-Persky House** (1892).

Prairie School is considered a part of the Chicago School.

International Style

The international style developed primarily at Germany's Bauhaus School. Luminary Ludwig Mies van der Rohe immigrated to Chicago in 1938, after the Nazis closed the Bauhaus, and his ideas took root in the US. Simple, severe geometry and large expanses of glass are typical elements. One of the best places to see examples of Mies'"less is more" philosophy is at the **Illinois Institute of Technology** campus. Another landmark Mies building is the austere but beautifully proportioned **IBM Building** (1971).

Chicago firm Skidmore, Owings and Merrill, architects of the **John Hancock Center** (1969), **Willis Tower** (1974), and **Trump International Hotel & Tower** (2009), is famous for its International-style designs.

Where to Find the Buildings

Charnley-Persky House *pp78–9*
Chicago Cultural Center *p54*
Crilly Court *p73*
Fourth Presbyterian Church *p65*
Glessner House *p92*
IBM Building *p68*
Illinois Institute of Technology *p96*
James R. Thompson Center *p58*
John Hancock Center *p66*
Newberry Library *p69*
Oak Park *pp116–17*
Olsen-Hansen Row
    Houses *p73*
Pullman Historic District *p121*
Reliance Building *p52*
Richard H. Driehaus
    Museum *p68*
Robie House *pp104–105*
The Rookery *p44*
Trump International Hotel &
    Tower *p79*
333 West Wacker Drive *pp58–9*
Willis Tower *p44*
University of Chicago *pp102–105*
Water Tower *p65*

The Post-Modern Harold Washington Library Center *(see p84)*

Post-Modern

Post-Modern architecture developed in the 1970s primarily in response to – and as a rejection of – the formal ideals of the International style. It is an eclectic style without strict rules or unified credo, although playful references to architectural styles of the past are typical features of Post-Modern structures.

The building at **333 West Wacker Drive** (1983), designed by the firm Kohn Pedersen Fox, and the **James R. Thompson Center** (1985), designed by architect Helmut Jahn, are notable examples of Post-Modern design.

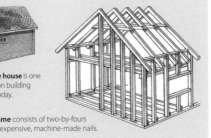

A balloon-frame house is one the most common building types in the US today.

The balloon frame consists of two-by-fours fastened with inexpensive, machine-made nails.

Multicultural Chicago

Chicago prides itself on being one of the most ethnically diverse cities in the US. In the 1840s, the Irish, fleeing their country's potato famine, arrived in droves in the young city of Chicago. Since then, successive waves of immigrants from countries around the world have shaped the city's many neighborhoods. These varied ethnic communities continue to celebrate their cultures at various festivals that are held throughout the year *(see pp34–7)*.

Spanish sign welcoming visitors to Pilsen, once a Czech community

Irish police officers joining the St. Patrick's Day celebrations

The Irish

The first Irish immigrants to Chicago worked as laborers, helping build the Illinois and Michigan Canal *(see p120)* in the mid-1800s. By 1870, the Irish represented over 13 per cent of the city's population. Settled mostly in the South Side industrial town of Bridgeport, they soon became a powerful force in city politics. Over the years, there have been eight Irish mayors.

An Irish tradition not to be missed is a foaming glass of Guinness beer at one of the city's many Irish pubs.

The Western Europeans

Germans were some of the earliest immigrants to Chicago. Settling primarily in the North Side neighborhood of Old Town, by the 1870s they were Chicago's largest ethnic group. Today, the core of Germantown is Old Town's Lincoln Square, teeming with delicatessens and dance halls.

In the mid-1800s a small community of Swedes was established just north of the Chicago River. They later moved to Clark Street and Foster Avenue, an area now known as Andersonville. The community, with its bakeries and shops, retains its original character. Midsommarfest is celebrated here each June.

Prosperous Italians arrived in Chicago in the 1860s. By 1900, they were joined by poorer Italian farmers, some of whom settled between Van Buren and 12th streets. Taylor Street, between Madison and Halsted streets, on Chicago's West Side, used to be regarded as the nucleus of Little Italy, but most Italians have now left the neighborhood to live in different suburbs.

Greek immigration was spurred by the 1871 fire, when laborers came to help rebuild the city. By 1927, 10,000 shops, mainly selling fresh produce and flowers, were operated by Greeks. A short stretch of Greek restaurants lies along South Halsted Street near Van Buren Street, on the West Side.

Traditional German maypole at the corner of Linden in Lincoln Square

South Side neighborhoods such as Hyde Park and Kenwood *(see pp106–107)* were populated by wealthy German Jews. Over 125 Jewish congregations worshipped in the city by the late 1920s, with the Jewish population and synagogues spread throughout the city.

The Eastern Europeans

The political unrest in Czechoslovakia in 1848 led to the first wave of Czech immigrants to the US, many settling in the Midwest. By the 1870s, Chicago had a Little Prague along DeKoven Street on the West Side. Over the next few decades, a thriving Czech community developed nearby, along Blue Island Avenue from 16th Street to Cermak Road (then known as 22nd Street). Named Pilsen, after the west Czechoslovakian city Plzeň, the neighborhood today is predominantly Hispanic. Remnants of the Czech community, however, can be seen in buildings such as Thalia Hall *(see p118)*.

The Polish community, which is the largest outside Warsaw, is also the largest White ethnic group in Chicago after the Hispanics. Poles began arriving in large numbers during the 1870s. By the turn of the century, the Polish Downtown had been established at Division Street and along Milwaukee Avenue.

Ukrainians arrived in Chicago during the early 1900s, settling Ukrainian Village, an area bounded by Division Street and Chicago, Damen, and Western avenues, northwest of the Loop. Two interesting museums in the community celebrate Ukrainian culture. The

Lithuanian community, in the suburban village of Lemont, also has a strong presence in Chicago, as does the smaller Latvian community, west of Lakeview.

Eastern European Jews settled the West Side's Maxwell Street at Halsted Street from the 1880s until the 1910s. Community life focused around the Maxwell Street Market *(see p161)*, which was once the world's largest flea market, with stalls selling their reasonably priced wares.

Jazz legend Nat "King" Cole, son of a Chicago Baptist minister

The African Americans

Despite Chicago's first settler being mulatto *(see p17)*, racist practices significantly affected African-American settlement throughout Chicago's history. By 1850, the city was home to a small population of fugitive slaves from the South. From 1915 all the way to the 1970s, the Great Migration brought African Americans seeking to escape the oppressive conditions in the South, and hoping to secure factory work and a better life in the North. Many settled in the area known as the Black Belt, a 30-block stretch along State Street that at one point housed half the city's African American population. A lively cultural scene developed, establishing Chicago as a hub for jazz, blues, and gospel.

In the 1940s and 1950s, the Chicago Housing Authority replaced South Side tenements with public-housing projects, which soon became notorious for crime. But by the 1960s and 1970s, Chicago also had several

middle-class Black communities, such as Park Manor, as well as somewhat racially integrated areas, such as Hyde Park. The Black Metropolis Historic District (35th Street and Indiana Avenue) is commonly known as Bronzeville and was created in 1984 to commemorate the vibrant Black Belt community. Today, African Americans represent around 33 per cent of Chicago's population.

The Hispanic Americans

The first flood of Mexican immigrants was early in the 20th century, as laborers came to Chicago to help build the city's railroad. A second wave came after World War II, again as laborers. This time they were accompanied by Puerto Ricans. Cubans, fleeing from the 1959 revolution, joined Chicago's Hispanic community. Today, the Hispanic Americans – nearly 30 per cent of the city's population – continue to have an enormous impact on the cultural fabric of Chicago.

In the two southwest neighborhoods of Pilsen *(see p118)* and Little Village (south of Cermak Road between Western Avenue and Pulaski Road), the colorful streets are alive with Latin music, and inviting aromas waft from the numerous eateries.

Menu and graffiti on the wall of Mi Barrio Taqueria, in Pilsen

The Asians

Chinese immigrants first arrived in Chicago in the 1870s, working on building roads and canals. By the turn of the century, a Chinese community was growing in the South Side vice

Colorful Vietnamese and Chinese signs on bustling Argyle Street

district known as the Levee. That Chinatown dissolved in the early 1900s once the vice lords left. Chinese immigrants, faced with anti-Chinese sentiment reflected in excessive rent increases, found themselves forced to the fringes of the district. They settled at 22nd (now Cermak Road) and Wentworth streets, an area that is now the heart of Chicago's Chinese community *(see p96)*. Marked by a pagoda on Argyle CTA stop on the North Side, "New Chinatown," which is also known as "Little Saigon," is home to a large Vietnamese population, as well as Cambodian, Laotian, and Thai communities.

Chicago's Asian population swelled considerably in the 1980s with the arrival of Vietnamese, Cambodian, and Thai political refugees, as well as Filipino, Indian, Korean, and Japanese immigrants. Many settled in various pockets on the North Side.

The Melting Pot

Other cultures are represented in Chicago but are not as distinctly defined. Chicago's American Indian population of approximately 17,000, concentrated in Uptown, north of Lakeview, is the highest of any US city after San Francisco and Los Angeles. Chicagoans of Middle Eastern origin are scattered throughout the city.

Remarkable Residents

Chicago has always been a city at the forefront. It has nourished leaders in diverse fields, from music to industry, from architecture to sports. Some have been drawn to Chicago from other parts of the US and abroad; others were born and bred in Chicago. All have left their mark on the city and, indeed, on the world, including, most notably, the current President of the United States, Barack Obama. As the city where the skyscraper was developed in the late 1800s, Chicago has long been a center for architectural innovation, with many of North America's influential architects based here for at least part of their careers. Having nurtured outstanding musicians since the 1910s, the city is also famous for its jazz and blues.

Blues legend Muddy Waters playing his electric guitar

Frank Lloyd Wright, one of the world's most influential architects

Architects

Chicago architects have literally shaped the city. Daniel Burnham (1846–1912) was one of Chicago's most successful architects. His partnership with John Wellborn Root (1850–91) led to buildings such as the Rookery (see p44), a stunning early skyscraper. His later partnership with designer Charles Atwood (1849–95) resulted in the groundbreaking Reliance Building (see p52).

Burnham was in charge of designing the 1893 World's Fair. However, it is for the 1909 Plan of Chicago, which he coauthored that he is best known. This document of civic planning became the vision for Chicago, proposing a series of riverfront public spaces and the widening of major roads to make the downtown easily accessible.

Louis Sullivan (1856–1924) has been called the first truly American architect. Celebrated for his organic style of ornamentation, as seen on the windows of Carson Pirie Scott

(see p52), Sullivan declared that form follows function. Indeed, the detailing allowed the architect artistic license while drawing in passers-by.

Sullivan nurtured a young draftsman with whom he worked, Frank Lloyd Wright (1867–1959). Over the next 70 years, Wright played a significant role in modern architecture, fathering the Prairie School (see p29) and designing such masterpieces as Robie House (see pp104–105).

Ludwig Mies van der Rohe (1886–1969) moved to Chicago in 1937. The impact of his International style (see p29) was profound.

Musicians

Louis Armstrong (1901–1971) lived in Chicago from 1922 to 1929. He launched a revolution with his trumpet playing, popularizing the new art of jazz.

If Armstrong was the king of jazz, Benny Goodman (1909–1986) was the king of swing. His Russian parents settled in Chicago's West Side, where Goodman joined the Hull-House (see p118) youth band. Later, he led the US's first racially integrated band, inviting Black pianist Teddy Wilson to join his orchestra. Jelly Roll Morton (1890–1941), the great pianist from New Orleans, came to Chicago in 1922. Morton claimed to have invented jazz. Muddy Waters (1915–83) didn't claim to have invented blues, but he did bring the sound of the Mississippi

Delta to Chicago, where his use of electric guitar was seminal.

Nat "King" Cole (1919–65), with his unique and velvety vocals, broke several color barriers in the 1950s. He was the first African American to have a radio and TV show.

The electronic dance music genre House originated here, and the 90s rock scene erupted with bands like Smashing Pumpkins and Wilco. Hip-hop star Kanye West is from Chicago.

Actors and Comedians

Paul Sills and Bernie Sahlins opened Chicago's renowned improvisational comedy spot Second City in 1959. Many comics, including Gilda Radner (1946–89), Stephen Clobert, Tina Fey, Bill Murray, Dan Aykroyd, and Joan Rivers, got their start here. Comic genius Jack Benny (1894–1974) and Saturday Night Live star John Belushi (1949–82) both lived in Chicago suburbs.

Several Chicago-based actors, including John Cusack and John Malkovich, have

Chicago's Oprah Winfrey, a national TV personality

gone on to international fame. One of the city's best-known TV personalities is talk-show host Oprah Winfrey, whose show was watched by nearly 15 million Americans each weekday. It was in Chicago that the concept of the TV talk show was born, in 1949, with NBC's *Garroway at Large*.

Athletes

Sports teams in Chicago are not known for their winning streaks, but they do boast a number of superstars. Former Chicago Bulls basketball player Michael Jordan is perhaps most famous, known as much for his product endorsements as for his scoring.

Hockey legend Bobby Hull, as the star of the 1961 Chicago Blackhawks team, helped bring the Stanley Cup to the city – the team's only cup win in more than half a century.

Johnny Weissmuller (1904–1984) may be best known as the star of 18 Tarzan movies; however, the boy who swam at Oak Street Beach *(see p79)* became the man who held every world freestyle swimming record of the 1920s.

Michael Jordan, the Chicago Bulls' No. 1 basketball player

Writers

Chicago's most famous literary figure is Ernest Hemingway (1899–1960), who grew up in Oak Park *(see pp116–17)*. He

rejected the conservative mindset of this Chicago suburb at that time, saying it was full of "wide lawns and narrow minds."

Theodore Dreiser (1871–1945), considered the father of American literary naturalism, wrote about Chicago, his home city, in his masterpiece *Sister Carrie*.

African-American novelist Richard Wright (1908–1960) moved to Chicago at age 19, though he wrote his bestselling novel *Native Son*, about a man raised in a Chicago slum, in New York.

Illinois-native poet Carl Sandburg (1878–1967) moved to Chicago in 1912, where he worked as a literary critic. His 1914 poem "Chicago" describes it as the "City of the Big Shoulders." Poet Gwendolyn Brooks (1917–2000) lived in Chicago her whole life, writing exclusively about it. She was, in 1950, the first African-American to win a Pulitzer Prize, for *Annie Allen*, her collection exploring the Black experience in Chicago.

Renowned poet Carl Sandburg

Gangsters and Criminals

The city's reputation for lawlessness was secured in the 1920s with the rise of the US's infamous crime lord, Al Capone (1899–1947). Prohibition set the stage for mob warfare as gangsters monopolized the lucrative market of banned alcohol. More than 300 gang-related murders occurred in the 1920s, including the Capone-orchestrated St. Valentine's Day Massacre *(see p20)*.

Bank robber John Dillinger's daring made him a folk hero of sorts. When he was killed by the FBI outside Lincoln Park's Biograph Theatre in 1934, onlookers dipped handkerchiefs in his blood for morbid mementos.

Entrepreneurs and Industrialists

Young Chicago attracted many enterprisers. Cyrus Hall McCormick (1809–1884) transformed wheat farming with his invention of the Virginia reaper. In 1848, he concentrated his farm-implement empire in Chicago. He died the richest man in Illinois.

Charles Wacker, city planner

Real-estate developer Potter Palmer (1826–1902) built luxury hotels and is credited with creating the wealthy Gold Coast area *(see pp74–9)*.

Marshall Field (1834–1906) built his fortune as a department store owner *(see pp52–53)*, funding some of Chicago's most important institutes.

Brewer Charles H. Wacker (1856–1929), son of Frederick Wacker *(see p73)*, helped shape the city as chair of the Chicago Plan Commission, overseers of the 1909 Plan of Chicago *(see p32)*.

Social Reformers

At the turn of the 20th century, Chicago was home to three of the most influential women in the US.

Black civil-rights activist Ida B. Wells (1862–1931) successfully sued a railroad company for racial discrimination. Her columns appeared in many of the nation's 200 Black papers during the 1890s *(see p97)*.

Jane Addams (1860–1935) was involved with almost every US social movement of the early 20th century, winning a Nobel Peace Prize for her work. In 1889, she co-founded Hull-House *(see p118)*.

Suffragist Frances Willard (1839–98) helped found the WCTU, the first international women's organization *(see Frances Willard House, p132)*.

A bank robber as folk hero, John Dillinger

CHICAGO THROUGH THE YEAR

Chicago's nickname "The Windy City" originally referred to its blustery politicians who lobbied to host the 1893 World's Columbian Exposition, but, Downtown Chicago or anywhere else by the lakefront is windy whatever the season – although it ranks only 14th for wind velocity in the country.

Springtime in Chicago begins in late March. The city bursts into bloom after a long winter, living up to its official motto, *Urbs in Horto*, or "City in a garden." In summer, Chicago's beaches offer cooling breezes and the sun-warmed waters of Lake Michigan. These same waters keep the city temperate during autumn. In winter, they lead to "lake effect" storms: plenty of snow and chilling breezes. Intrepid locals bundle up and take advantage of winter attractions such as the Winter Delights festival. City Visitor Centers and the mayor's office *(see p165)* provide event information.

Irish reveler at Chicago's annual St. Patrick's Day Parade

Spring

Chicagoans welcome the arrival of spring by jogging through Grant Park, enjoying Lincoln Park's magnificent flower displays, and cheering on the city's two baseball teams, the Chicago Cubs and the White Sox, whose seasons begin in April *(see pp166–7)*.

March

Pulaski Day Reception *(1st Mon in Mar)*, Polish Museum of America, 984 N Milwaukee Ave. Celebrations in honor of Polish freedom fighter and later US Civil War hero Casimir Pulaski.

St. Patrick's Day Parade *(Sat before Mar 17)*, the Loop. The Chicago River is dyed green in celebration.

South Side Irish Parade *(Sun before Mar 17)*, Western Ave. from 103rd to 114th streets. One of the largest Irish parades outside Dublin.

April

Chicago Park District Spring Flower Show *(early Apr–mid-May)*, Lincoln Park and Garfield Park conservatories. An exuberant display of colorful flowers.

Chicago Cubs and Chicago White Sox Home Openers *(early Apr)*. See both Major League Baseball teams start the season on their home turf.

May

Greek National Parade *(first Sun)*, Greektown. Annual parade commemorating the anniversary of the Greek Declaration of Independence.

Chicago Kids and Kites Fest *(early May)*, Montrose Harbor.

All Wright *(mid- or late May)*, Oak Park *(p116)*. Tour Frank Lloyd Wright-designed private residences and national historic landmarks in this annual housewalk.

Mayfest *(end May)*, Lakeside. This three-day community festival kicks off summer and includes local food vendors, live music, and games for kids.

Summer

Chicagoans throng to art fairs and outdoor concerts during the summer. A long-standing Chicago tradition is the free evening concerts – from opera to blues, from country to pop – at Millennium Park's *(see p55)* Pritzker Pavilion. Neighborhood festivals take place around the city virtually every weekend from May to September, and range from market days to street festivals.

June

Chicago Blues Festival *(early Jun)*, Grant Park. A three-day extravaganza of local blues musicians and southern artists.

Printer's Row Lit Fest *(early Jun)*, Dearborn Ave. between Congress Pkwy and Polk St *(p84)*. Book dealers, along-side papermaking and book-binding demonstrations.

Old Town Art Fair *(second weekend)*, N Lincoln Ave. and W Wisconsin. Artists from around the world display and sell their work.

Navy Pier, Chicago's amusement park for the entire family *(see p65)*

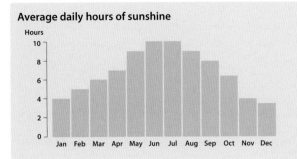

Average daily hours of sunshine

Hours

Sunshine
More than 50 days a year on average have clear skies, whereas 240 are overcast. Night descends early during the winter months, but the days can be brilliantly clear. December is the cloudiest month of the year, with an average of just four cloud-free days.

Wells Street Art Festival *(second weekend)*, Wells St. between Division and North aves. Crafts and fine art on display and for sale.

Ravinia Music Festival *(mid-Jun–mid-Sep)*, Ravinia Park. Dozens of performances in all musical styles *(p166)*.

Chicago Pride Parade *(fourth Sun)*, from Lakeview *(p116)* to Lincoln Park, celebrates the gay and lesbian community.

July
Chicago Gospel Festival *(first week)*, Millennium Park. A two-day free event featuring gospel composers, singers, and musicians.

Taste of Chicago *(first week)*, Grant Park *(pp86–7)*. Concerts and cooking lessons accompany the cuisine of some of the city's finest restaurants.

Kwanzaa Summer Festival *(first Sat)*, Abbott Park, 49 E 95th St. Musical entertainment, food, and activities for children.

Chicago Country Music Festival *(early Jul)*, Grant Park *(pp86–7)*. Part of the Taste of Chicago Festival.

Rock Around the Block *(mid-Jul)*, Lakeview *(p116)*. Annual weekend-long neighborhood festivities.

Chicago Folk and Roots Festival *(mid-Jul)*, Welles Park. A mix of musical styles from around the world.

La Fiesta del Sol *(late Jul)*, Pilsen *(p118)*. Carnival rides, arts and crafts, local and visiting musicians, and Mexican cuisine are featured at this festival, one of Chicago's largest.

Pitchfork Music Festival *(third weekend)*, Union Park. Three-day music festival featuring alternative bands and artists.

South Shore Jazzfest *(late Jul/ early Aug)*, South Shore Cultural Center, 7059 S Shore Dr. Top jazz musicians perform.

Chinatown Summer Fair *(mid-or late Jul)*, Wentworth Ave. between Cermak Rd and 24th St. Fabulous food, art, and dance displays to admire.

Celebrate Clark Street Festival *(end Jul)*, Rogers Park. Top world music acts and a diverse range of food vendors.

Taste of Lincoln Ave. *(end Jul)*, Lincoln Ave. The street is closed to traffic for a weekend street festival with live bands and a kids carnival.

August
Lollapalooza *(first weekend)*, Grant Park. Massive alternative rock festival held in Chicago since 2007.

Bud Billiken Day Parade *(second Sat)*, King Dr. from 35th to 55th sts. One of the US's oldest African-American parades culminates with a huge picnic in Washington Park *(p106)*.

Chicago Carifete *(mid-Aug)*, Midway Plaisance *(p106)*. Music, dance, and food from the islands of the Caribbean.

Air maneuvers over the North Side as part of the Air and Water Show

Northalsted Market Days *(mid-Aug)*, Halsted St. Gay festival, with market stalls, comedians, and pop groups.

Ukranian Festival *(mid-Aug)*, Ukranian Village. An authentic ethnic festival with crafts, food, and dancing.

Chicago Air and Water Show *(late Aug)*, North Ave. Beach. Planes perform maneuvers in the sky and boats do stunts on the water.

Bucktown Arts Fest *(late Aug)*, N Oakley Blvd *(p116)*. Local artists display their work.

Visitors sampling delicacies of dozens of restaurants at Taste of Chicago

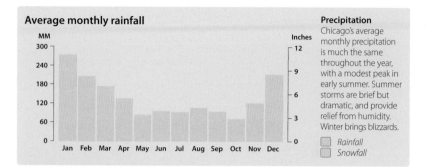

Average monthly rainfall

MM
300
240
180
120
60
0

Inches
12
9
6
3
0

Jan Feb Mar Apr May Jun Jul Aug Sep Oct Nov Dec

Precipitation
Chicago's average monthly precipitation is much the same throughout the year, with a modest peak in early summer. Summer storms are brief but dramatic, and provide relief from humidity. Winter brings blizzards.

☐ *Rainfall*
☐ *Snowfall*

Pumpkins at a local farmers' market, a telltale sign of autumn

Autumn

Autumn is an invigorating season in Chicago. September's comfortable weather provides an inviting backdrop to the numerous outdoor festivals held throughout the city.

Autumn is also the season when Chicagoans and visitors alike test their mettle and stamina during the internationally celebrated annual marathon.

Football season kicks off the first week of September with the Chicago Bears playing at Soldier Field. The city's many sports enthusiasts also flock to the United Center to see the Chicago Bulls play basketball and the Chicago Blackhawks play hockey (*see p167*).

In late autumn, the city gets a head start on the Christmas season, with many holiday traditions beginning immediately after Thanksgiving, in November.

September
Chicago Jazz Festival *(Labor Day weekend)*, Grant Park *(pp86–7)*. Swing to the lively sounds of renowned jazz musicians and singers.
North Coast Music Festival *(Labor Day weekend)*, Union Park. With electronic, hip-hop, and rock acts, this festival rivals Loopalooza.
Art on Harrison *(second weekend)*, Oak Park *(pp116–17)*. Showcasing Oak Park's artists, galleries, and studios, with displays, demonstrations, and food.
Renegade Craft Fair *(mid-Sep)*, Division St. between Damen and Ashland. Handmade goods, live music, craft workshops, and food stalls.
Mexican Independence Day Parade *(mid-Sep)*, Columbus Dr between Monroe and Columbus. Floats, bands, and dancers join to celebrate Mexico's 1820 independence from Spain.
World Music Festival *(mid-to late Sep)*, various locations. The eclectic sounds of music from Europe, Africa, and South America.

October
Annual House Tour *(second weekend)*, Pullman *(p121)*. A rare opportunity to see inside this historic district's 19th-century houses.
Chicago Marathon *(second Sun)*, downtown. One of the world's largest marathons, with thousands of participants, and spectators in the hundreds of thousands giving support and cheering runners along the 26.2-mile (43-km) course.

Oktoberfest *(early Oct)*, Lincoln and Southport Ave. Celebrates German culture with food and beer gardens.
Chicagoween *(month-long)*, Daley Plaza. An outdoor haunted village that kids will love.

November
Holiday Windows at Macy's *(Nov–Dec)*. Animated Christmas displays in the windows of the State Street store *(pp52–3)* are a Chicago tradition.
Christmas Around the World and Holidays of Light *(mid-Nov–Jan)*, Museum of Science and Industry *(pp108–111)*. Chicago's ethnic groups decorate trees in an "enchanted" forest and share holiday traditions.
Magnificent Mile Lights Festival *(third weekend)*, Michigan Ave. from the Chicago River to Oak St. Christmas lights are lit during this annual procession.
State Street Thanksgiving Day Parade *(Thanksgiving)*, State St. between Congress Pkwy and Randolph St. Santa and his elves delight children.

The Chicago Marathon, attracting athletes from around the world

Average monthly temperature

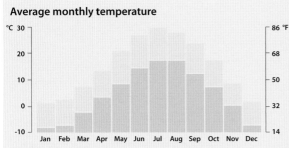

Temperature Chart
Spring is generally mild. Most summer days are comfortably warm, but there may be some very hot and humid periods. Autumn is crisp, with unpredictable temperatures. Winter winds are often bitingly cold. This chart shows the average minimum and maximum temperatures for each month.

☐ *Maximum Temperature*
☐ *Minimum Temperature*

Holiday Tree Lighting Ceremony *(day after Thanksgiving Day)*, Daley Plaza.
Christkindlmarket *(late Nov–Dec)*, Daley Plaza. Holiday shopping in a German marketplace, complete with an 80-ft (24-m) tree.
Zoo Lights *(last weekend Nov until Jan 1)*, Lincoln Park Zoo *(pp114–15)*. More than 1.5 million lights illuminate the zoo. Free admission.

Winter

The city sparkles during winter with elaborate decorations, and buildings and trees festooned with green and red lights. The Merchandise Mart, on the north bank of the river, looks like a massive wrapped gift.

December
Winter Wonderfest *(throughout Dec)*, Navy Pier. Family-friendly activities, a carousel, ferris wheel, and ice-skating.

Winter Flower and Train Show *(early Dec)*, Lincoln Park Conservatory. Model trains weave through colorful holiday poinsettia displays.
Night of the Luminaria *(third Sat)*, Galena *(pp136–7)*. Thousands of candle-lit luminaria line the streets of the town's Victorian historic district and surrounding neighborhoods.
New Year's Eve *(Dec 31)*, Navy Pier *(p67)* and Buckingham Fountain *(p87)*. An evening of celebration with laser-lights and fireworks.

January
New Year's Day *(Jan 1)*, Navy Pier *(p67)*. Family activities and fireworks to start off the New Year.
Winter Delights *(Jan 1–Mar 31)*. City-wide indoor and outdoor events, including music performances, themed weekends and the Magnificent Mile Crystal Carnival, with its giant ice sculptures.

Illuminated Christmas tree in front of the Tribune Building

February
Chinese New Year Parade *(date varies)*, Wentworth Ave. from Cermak Rd. to 24th St. Festivities include colorful floats, traditional music and dancing, and food.

Public Holidays
New Year's Day (Jan 1)
Martin Luther King Day (3rd Mon in Jan)
President's Day (3rd Mon in Feb)
Pulaski Day (1st Mon in Mar)
Memorial Day (last Mon in May)
Independence Day (Jul 4)
Labor Day (1st Mon in Sep)
Columbus Day (2nd Mon in Oct)
Veterans Day (Nov 11)
Thanksgiving Day (4th Thu in Nov)
Christmas Day (Dec 25)

Ice skaters enjoying a bright winter day outdoors

The glittering skyline of Chicago at night ▶

CHICAGO AREA BY AREA

DOWNTOWN CORE

Bordered on the north and on the west by the Chicago River, on the east by Lake Michigan, and on the south by the Congress Parkway, the Downtown Core is Chicago's historic and financial center. The downtown's nucleus is the Loop, named for the elevated train tracks encircling it. Even though the area was completely destroyed by the Great Fire of 1871, a mere two decades later it had been rebuilt with pioneering skyscrapers, including the Marquette Building. Along with this architectural legacy, the area is home to such famous museums as The Art Institute of Chicago. State Street is home to landmark department stores.

Sights at a Glance

Historic Buildings
2 The Rookery
3 Marquette Building
5 Monadnock Building
6 Auditorium Building
7 Fine Arts Building
8 Santa Fe Building
10 Sullivan Center
11 Reliance Building
12 Macy's
13 Oriental Theater
16 Chicago Theatre
18 35 East Wacker Drive

Modern Skyscrapers
1 Willis Tower
4 Federal Center
19 R.R. Donnelley Building
20 James R. Thompson Center
21 333 West Wacker Drive

Museums and Galleries
9 *The Art Institute of Chicago pp48–51*
14 Chicago Cultural Center

Bridges, Parks, and Streets
15 Millennium Park
17 Michigan Avenue Bridge
22 Wacker Drive

Restaurants *pp148–9*
1 Aria
2 Artist's Café
3 Atwood Café
4 Cafecito
5 Catch35
6 Frontera Fresco
7 Heaven on Seven
8 Henri
9 Italian Village
10 Lockwood
11 Miller's Pub
12 Morton's The Steakhouse
13 Native Foods Café
14 Park Grill
15 Pastoral
16 Petterino's
17 Pizano's Pizza
18 Plymouth Pub
19 Rosebud Prime
20 Russian Tea Time
21 The Gage
22 Trattoria No.10

See also Street Finder maps 3 & 4

◀ One of the city's most iconic landmarks, the Chicago Theatre

For keys to symbols *see back flap*

Street-by-Street: The Loop

The Loop gets its name from the elevated track system
that circles the center of the Downtown Core. Trains
screeching as they turn sharp corners and the steady stream
of businesspeople during rush hour add to the Loop's bustle.
In the canyon vistas through the many tall, historic
buildings – and modern edifices such as the Federal Center –
you can catch glimpses of the 19 bridges spanning the
Chicago River. The conversion of warehouses to
condominiums and the renovation of historic theaters have
helped to enliven the Loop at night.

❸ **Marquette Building**
This early skyscraper (1895) was
designed by William Holabird
and Martin Roche, central
Chicago School figures and
architects of more than
80 buildings in the Loop.

❶ ★ **Willis Tower**
At a height of 1,454 ft
(443 m), this is one of
the tallest buildings in
the world. Views from
the glass-enclosed
observation deck on the
103rd floor are stunning.

190 South LaSalle Street
(1987), designed by New
York architect Philip
Johnson, has a white-
marble lobby with a gold-
leafed, vaulted ceiling.

❷ **The Rookery**
One of the earliest designs by
Burnham and Root, this 1888
building has a lobby that was
remodeled by Frank Lloyd
Wright in 1907.

STREET

CLARK

ADAMS

FRANKLIN

WACKER

STREET

DRIVE

Chicago Board of Trade
occupies a 45-story Art Deco
building, with a statue of
Ceres atop its roof. The
frenetic action inside can be
seen from a viewers' gallery
(group tours only).

0 meters   100
0 yards   100

8 Santa Fe Building
This classic Chicago School
building, with an elegant two-
story atrium, houses the Chicago
Architecture Foundation.

9 ★ Art Institute of Chicago
The Impressionist and Post-
Impressionist collection at this
museum, one of the most
important in the country, is
world famous.

Locator Map
See Street Finder maps 3 & 4

Key

— Suggested route

MONROE ST

SOUTH

WABASH

STATE

STREET

AVENUE

JACKSON BLVD

MICHIGAN AVENUE

PKWY

CONGRESS

BUREN STREET

The **"Elevated,"** or "L,"
train tracks opened in
1897. Its loop in the city's
core is seven blocks long
and five blocks wide.

5 Monadnock Building
The north half of this building
(1891) is the tallest building
ever constructed entirely
of masonry.

7 Fine Arts Building
Frank Lloyd Wright once
had a studio in this 1885
building designed by
Solon S. Beman. The
building was originally
used as a carriage
showroom by the
Studebaker Company.

6 Auditorium Building
The lavish birch paneled theater
in this 1889 multipurpose
skyscraper, is one of Adler and
Sullivan's best interiors.

4 Federal Center
Ludwig Mies van der Rohe
designed this three-building
office complex around a central
plaza, which holds Alexander
Calder's 1973 sculpture *Flamingo*.

❶ Willis Tower

233 S Wacker Dr. **Map** 3 B2.
Tel (312) 875-9696. **M** Quincy.
Open Apr–Sep: 9am–10pm daily;
Oct–Mar: 10am–8pm daily; last adm
30 min before closing.
P **w** willistower.com;
theskydeck.com

In 2009 Sears Tower was renamed Willis Tower. It was the tallest building in the world from the time of its construction in 1973 until 1997 when the Petronas Twin Towers were built in Kuala Lumpur. In 2000 it regained its status as the world's tallest structure when one of its antennas was extended. The building held this record until early 2010 when Burj Khalifa in Dubai opened as the world's tallest building, with the highest occupied floor in the world. Willis Tower remained the tallest building in the western hemisphere until the 2013 completion of New York's One World Trade Center. It remains a significant landmark in Chicago.

The skyscraper was designed by Bruce Graham, a partner at the Chicago architectural firm of Skidmore, Owings and Merrill, with the assistance of chief engineer Fazlur Khan. Construction of the innovative building took three years, employing 1,600 people during the peak period. More than 110 concrete caissons anchored in bedrock support the tower's 222,500 tons.

Today, the tower contains 3.5 million sq ft (0.3 million sq m) of office space and more than 100 elevators. It also contains approximately 43,000 miles (69,000 km) of telephone cable, almost enough to encircle the Earth twice.

The elevator to the Skydeck travels at a stomach-churning 1,600 ft (490 m) per minute. During summer, there are often lengthy lineups for the Skydeck and The Ledge, an observation deck that extends onto a glass-floored platform for thrilling views. Diversions include a short movie and exhibits on Chicago.

The 110-story tower soars to 1,450 ft (442 m) – or 1,730 ft (527 m) if the higher of the two antennas is included.

The tower top sways 6 inches (15 cm) in strong wind.

The glass-enclosed, 103rd-floor Skydeck, and The Ledge, the world's third-highest observation deck, provides views of the far shores of Lake Michigan and four states on clear days.

The 16,000 bronze-tinted windows are cleaned by six automatic machines eight times a year.

Black aluminum clads the framework, which is made from 76,000 tons of steel.

Alexander Calder's mobile sculpture *Universe* (1974) is on display in the lobby.

View of the Willis Tower and Skydeck, looking northeast

❷ The Rookery

209 S LaSalle St.
Map 3 C2. **Tel** (312) 553-6100. **M** Quincy;
Jackson (Brown Line).
Open 8am–6pm Mon–Fri; 8am–2pm Sat.
Closed major public hols.

When the Rookery opened in 1888, it was the tallest building in the world. The 12-story building, designed by the influential firm Burnham and Root in the Richardsonian Romanesque style (see p28), has a dark red brick facade with terra-cotta trim and a rough granite base. The building, now housing offices, was constructed on a foundation of crisscrossing rails – necessitated by the clay soils unable to support the weight of the massive structure. While its thick masonry walls are load bearing, the iron framing of the lower stories allows for the use of large windows – a welcome innovation when artificial lighting technology was in its infancy.

Framing the main entrance is a monumental arch with geometric carvings, including eponymous rooks. Inside is a two-tiered court, remodeled in 1907 by Frank Lloyd Wright, who covered the original iron columns and staircases with white marble, inlaid with gold leaf. The central staircase, framed with Wright's signature urns, leads to a mezzanine enclosed by a domed skylight. A magnificent, cantilevered cast-iron staircase leads from

The Rookery's spectacular light court

❹ Federal Center

Dearborn St, between Adams and Jackson sts. **Map** 3 C2. **M** Jackson (Blue Line). **Open** 7am–6pm Mon–Fri. **Closed** major public hols. ♿

The three-building Federal Center complex, designed by Ludwig Mies van der Rohe and completed in 1974, expresses the pared-down functionalism of Mies' International style *(see p29)*. There is little ornamentation to distract from these austere curtain-wall structures made of glass and steel.

The 30-story Dirksen courtroom building stands on the east side of the complex; the 42-story Kluczynski office tower and one-story post office are to the west. The center is interesting for the expert arrangement of its buildings around the plaza and with each other. The granite grid of the pavement forms a unity between these three structures

The sterile plaza is graced with Alexander Calder's 53-ft (16-m) vermilion sculpture *Flamingo (see p46)*, which seems almost to be dancing – its steel organic form a surprising complement to the rigid geometry of the buildings.

Federal agencies located in this building include the Air Force Recruiting Service, Department of Labor, Internal Revenue Service, and the Consumer Product Safety Commission. Barack Obama briefly had offices here following his election as President of the USA in 2008.

the second floor to the top. The building was made a National Historic Landmark in 1988, 100 years after its opening.

❺ Marquette Building

140 S Dearborn St. **Map** 3 C2. **Tel** (312) 422-5500. **M** Monroe (Blue Line). **Open** 24 hrs daily. ♿ 🅦 **marquette. macfound.org**

Considered the premier remaining example of the Chicago School of architecture *(see pp28–9)*, the Marquette Building was designed by Holabird and Roche in 1895. Commissioned by the owners of the Rookery, the architects faced the demanding task of equaling the Burnham and Root original sophisticated design of that building.

The grid of this early commercial 17-story high-rise's steel-frame skeleton is easily seen in the terra-cotta and brick exterior.

The building's ground-breaking expansive horizontal windows became known as Chicago windows *(see p29)*. They are one of the few remaining examples of this innovative window design.

Bronze bas-relief panels over the entrance doors, designed by Hermon Atkins MacNeil, illustrate Jesuit missionary Father Jacques Marquette's 1673–4 expedition to the area. Marquette was the first European settler in Chicago.

In the two-story lobby, mosaic panels of mother-of-pearl and glass designed by J.A. Holzer of Tiffany and Company depict scenes of the French exploration of Illinois. Sculpted heads inset above the elevators on the first and second floors pay tribute to the Native American chiefs and early French explorers of the Chicago area *(see p17)*. The revolving doors of the lobby show exquisite metalwork, including forged peace pipes, which Father Marquette gave to the Native Americans as a gesture of goodwill.

The building underwent restoration in 1980, and a four-year renovation was also completed in 2006. An exhibit located just past the lobby outlines the building's history.

Originally built for an insurance company, the Marquette Building is now home to the MacArthur Foundation, started by John MacArthur, once one of the wealthiest men in America.

Entrance to the Marquette Building

The Monadnock Building's filigree wrought-iron staircase

❺ Monadnock Building

53 W Jackson Blvd. **Map** 3 C2.
Tel (312) 922-1890. Ⓜ Jackson (Blue Line). **Open** 7am–6pm Mon–Fri.
Closed public hols. ♿
🔲 monadnockbuilding.com

Constructed in two parts two years apart (and by two different architectural firms), the interestingly bisected Monadnock Building looks both to the past and to the future. The northern half of this office building, designed by Burnham and Root, was built first, in 1891. Sixteen stories tall and with masonry load-bearing walls (the building method at the time), it is the tallest commercial masonry building ever constructed. The southern section, designed by Holabird and Roche, has a steel skeleton sheathed in terra-cotta, an innovation that in the 1890s allowed skyscrapers to soar. Upon completion, it was the largest office building in the world.

The building is named after one of New Hampshire's White Mountains. "Monadnock" is also a geological term for a mountain surrounded by a glacial plain – an appropriate name, as its walls are 6 ft (2 m) thick at the base. The interior was restored in the 1980s: the mosaic floor is a replica; the white-marble ceiling and ornate staircase are original. At the north entrance and at the south elevator banks, you can see, under glass, part of the original marble floor. A corridor bordered by shops and restaurants runs the length of the building, much like an interior street.

❻ Auditorium Building

430 S Michigan Ave. **Map** 4 D3.
Tel (312) 341-3500. Ⓜ Library.
🚌 3, 145, 147, 151. **Open** 7:30am–10:30pm Mon–Thu; 7:30am–6pm Fri; 10:30am–5pm Sat, Sun. **Closed** major public hols. ♿ 🔲 Building: (312) 341-3555; Theater: (312) 922-2110.
See Entertainment: p164.

Designed by Dankmar Adler and Louis Sullivan, their first major commission together, the Auditorium Building (1889), with its walls of smooth limestone typical of the Richardsonian Romanesque style *(see p28)* rising above the rough granite base, broke many records and achieved a number of firsts. Combining a 400-room hotel, a 17-story office tower, and a 4,300-seat theater, it was the tallest building in Chicago and the first building of its size to be electrically lighted and air-conditioned. Not surprisingly, it was also the most expensive, costing over $3 million to build. At 110,000 tons, it was the heaviest building in the world, and the most fireproof.

The building's crowning jewel is the lavish Auditorium Theatre, the first home of the Chicago Symphony Orchestra. After many years of neglect

Roosevelt University admissions office in the Auditorium Building

(World War II servicemen used the stage as a bowling alley), it was restored in the 1960s and is now a venue for performing arts events. Four elliptical arches span the width of the theater, which is ornamented with stenciling, stained glass, and gold-leaf plaster reliefs. Its excellent acoustics enable guests in the last row to hear an unamplified whisper on stage, six stories below. The grand lobby, with its onyx walls and ornate staircase,

Stained-glass detailing in the Auditorium Building

contains an exhibition on the building's history. The tenth-floor library, originally the hotel's dining room, has a dramatic barrel-vaulted ceiling and superb lake views.

The building also houses Roosevelt University.

Facade of the Auditorium Building, with cows from a past public-art project in the foreground

The Artist's Café on the ground floor of the Fine Arts Building

❼ Fine Arts Building

410 S Michigan Ave. **Map** 4 D2.
Tel (312) 566-9800. Ⓜ Library.
🚌 3, 4, 145, 147, 151. **Open** 7am–
10pm Mon–Fri; 7am–9pm Sat;
10am–5pm Sun. **Closed** major
public hols. ♿

Although now closely associated with fine art and culture, the Fine Arts Building was originally commissioned by Studebaker Brothers Manufacturing to house a wagon carriage showroom. (The name "Studebaker" inscribed outside in stone is still visible above the first floor.)

Designed by Solon S. Beman and completed in 1885, the building, with its columns, rough stone, and arched entranceway and windows, is typical of the Romanesque style.

When the Studebaker Company moved to a new location, Beman was commissioned to renovate the building as a cultural center. The facade of the eighth floor was removed and replaced with a three-story addition. Inside, studios, shops, and offices were added, and the building quickly became a hub of artistic activity. The literary magazines *Dial, Poetry,* and *Little Review* were published here; the Little Theater staged dramas; and painters, sculptors, and architects (including Frank Lloyd Wright, *see p32*) had their studios on the tenth floor. In 1892, resident artists, including Frederic Clay Bartlett and Ralph Clarkson, formed a group called the Little Room and produced eight murals, which still can be seen on the walls of the tenth floor.

Today, the building, which has been given national historic landmark status, has a slightly frayed, run-down charm. Many arts-related enterprises remain in the building, including the Fine Arts Building Gallery in Suite 433, which showcases Chicago artists with a new exhibition each month. There are also two movie theaters.

The sound of singers practicing scales can be heard echoing through the halls, and a ride in the old elevator (with an operator) is an experience not to be missed.

❽ Santa Fe Building

224 S Michigan Ave. **Map** 4 D2.
Tel (312) 341-9431. Ⓜ Adams.
Open 24 hrs daily. **Closed** major
public hols.

The Santa Fe Building gleams – inside with white marble, and outside with white-glazed terra-cotta. Designed by D.H. Burnham and Co. in 1904 and originally known as the Railway Exchange Building, it is now called the Santa Fe because of the rooftop sign, erected in the early 1900s by the Santa Fe Railroad.

Porthole windows line the top floor; terra-cotta reliefs of ancient goddesses decorate the vestibule. The atrium's balustraded mezzanine, marble staircase, and elevators with grillwork are all notable. The building also houses the Chicago Architecture Foundation, which has a "mini-museum" detailing the history of Chicago architecture and offers guided tours of the city.

White-marble lobby of the Santa Fe Building

⓿ The Art Institute of Chicago

The extensive collections at the Art Institute of Chicago represent nearly 5,000 years of human creativity through paintings, sculptures, textiles, photographs, cultural objects, and decorative artifacts from around the world. The museum was founded by civic leaders and art collectors in 1879 as the Chicago Academy of Fine Arts, changing its name to The Art Institute of Chicago in 1882. Outgrowing two homes as wealthy patrons donated collections, it finally settled in a Neo-Classical structure built for the 1893 World's Fair. The Modern Wing devoted to modern and contemporary art, designed by Renzo Piano, opened in 2009, increasing gallery space by one third.

Kartikeya sculpture, 12th century
This gray granite sculpture of Kartikeya, Ganesha's brother, is the Hindu God of War.

Key

- American Art
- Eastern & Islamic Art
- Architecture & Design
- Modern Art 1900–1950
- African Art
- Greek, Roman & Byzantine Art
- Photography
- Indian Art of the Americas
- Prints and Drawings
- Contemporary Art after 1945
- European Art before 1900

First floor

McKinlock Court

McKinlock Court

Indra Statue, 16th century
Originating from Kathmandu Valley, this gilded bronze statue is a fine example of Nepalese handicraft. Indra, the Hindu god of warriors and thunder, was said to ride Airavat, a four-tusked white elephant. Traditionally, followers of Indra would honor him by sacrificing animals.

Lower level

Main Entrance

The Child's Bath (1891–2)
American artist Mary Cassatt
employed a raised vantage point and
cropped figures in her work – artistic
devices uncommon at the time. This
painting is influenced by the realistic
style prominent in Japanese prints.

Third floor

McKinlock
Court

★ **American Gothic**
Grant Wood's 1930
portrait of an Iowa
farmer and his spinster
daughter, initially
criticized as satire,
has become an
American classic.

McKinlock
Court

Second floor

★ **A Sunday on La Grande Jatte – 1884**
Post-Impressionist Georges Seurat
composed this image of promenading
Parisians using tiny dots of color.

The Assumption
of the Virgin

Museum Guide

*First-floor galleries range from ancient Greek
artifacts to Asian collections, American art, and
the Modern Wing's film, video and new media,
and photography galleries. The second floor is
devoted mostly to European works from the 15th
to 20th centuries and to art after 1960. The third
floor houses modern art from 1900 up to 1950.*

★ **Old Man with
a Gold Chain**
Rembrandt van
Rijn's interest in
the wisdom of
age can be seen
in this character
study (c.1631).

Exploring the Art Institute of Chicago

The museum's holdings span the globe as well as centuries, from 3rd-millennium BC Chinese artifacts to modern American and European art. Almost every major artistic movement of the 19th and 20th centuries is represented. The museum's Early Modernism collection is very strong; its Impressionist and Post-Impressionist collection – one of the most significant in the world – is outstanding. Important Renaissance and Baroque paintings complement these exhibits.

Flower gardens in the grounds of the Art Institute

Visitor to the European gallery appreciating the old masters on display

Asian Art

Some of the museum's most exquisite pieces are in its distinguished Asian collection, which comprises 35,000 works of archeological and artistic significance.

The galleries of Chinese, Japanese, and Korean art include celebrated collections of ancient Chinese bronzes and jades, 18th- and 19th-century Japanese woodblock prints, and early Korean ceramic vases.

The art from the Golden Age of the Tang Dynasty (AD 618–907) is the prize of this exhibit, in particular, the magnificent brightly glazed earthenware funerary horses.

Indian, Himalayan, and Southeast Asian art dating from the 2nd to 19th centuries encompasses artifacts of the Hindu and Buddhist faiths. Among the gems here are the nearly life-sized 2nd- and 3rd-century bodhisattva sculptures from Gandhara (present-day Pakistan), and a carved 13th-century stone statute of Saraswati, the Hindu goddess of learning, from Southern India.

The Art Institute also houses Persian 16th-century illuminated manuscripts and miniature paintings, though these are not currently on view.

Arms and Armor

Remarkable works of late medieval and Renaissance metal-craft are showcased in the George F. Harding Collection. One of the finest such collections in North America, it consists of 3,000 pieces of arms and armor. These include finely etched helmets, chain mail, equestrian equipment, historic weaponry, and decorated breastplates.

One of the earliest pieces in the collection is a breastplate from northern Italy. Dating from 1380, its original fabric covering is still intact. Also striking is a 1575 northern Italian suit of armor, used for foot combat. Made of etched and gilded steel and brass, the suit is decorated with large medallions depicting allegorical figures.

Decorative Arts

For unparalleled insight into the ever-changing taste of Western society, visit the decorative arts galleries. Their broad array embraces household items, including furniture and tableware, jewelry, and religious artifacts.

The impressive European collection contains 25,000 objects crafted from wood, metal, glass, ceramics, enamel, and ivory dating from 1100 to the present. It also includes sculpture from the medieval period to 1900.

The American collection includes an excellent selection of Arts and Crafts furniture, including a beautiful oak library table (1896) designed by Frank Lloyd Wright (see p32).

The fine European and American textile collection spans 15 centuries and features vestments, tapestries, and embroideries. Highlights are a 19th-century William Morris-designed carpet and two rare

The grand staircase and foyer of the Art Institute

fragments of Coptic cloth dating from between the 5th and 8th centuries.

Two of the quirkiest – and most renowned – collections are the Arthur Rubloff Paperweight Collection and the Thorne Miniature Rooms. The museum's holdings of more than 1,000 French, English, and American glass paperweights, popular in the mid-19th century, are one of the largest in the world.

The Thorne Miniature Rooms consist of 68 model rooms, painstakingly constructed to a scale of 1 inch (2.5 cm) to 1 foot (30 cm). The intricate European and American furnished interiors, ranging from the 16th to 20th centuries, are made with extraordinary technical precision.

The Londonderry Vase (1813), inspired by Roman imperial art

20th-Century Art

The museum's collection of more than 1,500 20th-century and contemporary paintings and sculptures provides a comprehensive and provocative survey of the development of modern art. Representing every significant artistic movement in Europe and the US, the works are arranged in groupings that highlight stylistic affinities between varied artists.

The collection is divided into pre-1950 and post-1950 works, housed in the Modern Wing. Particularly strong are the examples of Cubism, the

precursor of all abstract art forms; German Expressionism, the embodiment of the search for a strong emotional language in art; and Surrealism, the liberation of the irrational.

Post-World War II art is also well-represented by works of such influential artists as Willem de Kooning and Jackson Pollock.

The Basket of Apples (c.1895) by Paul Cézanne

Architecture

When the 1894 Chicago Stock Exchange (Adler and Sullivan) was demolished in 1972, its Trading Room was salvaged and reconstructed at the museum. Its ornate glory can still be seen in the stenciled ceiling and art-glass skylights. There are also pieces from other demolished Chicago buildings.

Special exhibits and a library with a comprehensive collection on Louis Sullivan complement the installations, housed in the Modern Wing.

Impressionist and Post-Impressionist Art

Gifts from wealthy patrons such as Bertha Palmer (see p79) and Frederic Clay Bartlett, who astutely began collecting works by Monet, Degas, and Seurat in the late 19th century, led to the Art Institute becoming the first in the US to include a gallery of Post-Impressionist art. Today, it is one of the foremost centers of Impressionist and Post-Impressionist paintings outside France.

United only by their fiercely held belief in artistic experimentation, the French Impressionists were a diverse group who exhibited together in the 1870s and 1880s.

Dedicated to a new form of art – one that eschewed the constraints of the prevailing formal style – these artists attempted to capture the textures and moods of fleeting moments, or impressions. Their final exhibition was in 1886.

The artists who followed in the Impressionists' footsteps – labeled Post-Impressionists by English art critic Roger Fry – created works of art exploring evocative color relationships and rules of composition.

Highlights of the museum's holdings include the highly estimable Helen Birch Bartlett Memorial Collection, featuring Paul Cézanne's *The Basket of Apples* (c.1895) and Henri de Toulouse-Lautrec's *At the Moulin Rouge* (1895).

No better illustration of Impressionist and Post-Impressionist principles can be found than Claude Monet's six versions of a wheat field, which combines the basic doctrine of Impressionism – capturing nature's temporality – with the Post-Impressionist concern for reconstructing nature according to art's formal, expressive potential.

On the Seine at Bennecourt (1868) by Claude Monet

❿ Sullivan Center

1 S State St. **Map** 3 C2. **Tel** (312) 675-5363. Ⓜ Monroe; Washington (Red Line). **Open** 10am–8pm Mon–Sat. **Closed** Easter, Thanksgiving, Dec 25. Ⓦ thesullivancenter.com

It is appropriate that such an architectural gem as the Sullivan Center (formerly known as the Carson Pirie Scott Building), which, until 2007, housed one of Chicago's oldest department stores, rests at Chicago's ground-zero address of State and Madison, the starting point for the city's street-numbering system. In 2012, the City Target store chain opened shop in the building.

The upper floors of the building are finished in white terra-cotta, but it is the ornamental metalwork on the first two floors that give this building, designed by Louis Sullivan in 1899, its distinctive character.

A particularly noteworthy feature of the exterior is the corner entrance pavilion, which extends 12 stories to the top of the building and has ornamental cast-iron motifs. Along with intricate botanical and geometric forms, Sullivan's initials, L.H.S., can be seen above the corner entrance. While this is the showy heart of the building, it is worth taking a walk east along Madison Street to take time to admire the metalwork and Chicago windows from a far less busy vantage point.

The Reliance Building, precursor to the modern skyscraper

⓫ Reliance Building

32 N State St. **Map** 3 C1. **Tel** (312) 782-1111. Ⓜ Washington (Red Line). **Open** 24 hrs daily. Ⓐ Ⓟ See Where to Stay, Hotel Burnham: *p144*.

The Reliance Building's two-stage construction (1891–95) was as unusual as were the structural-support techniques used. The leases for the upper floors of the original building on the site did not expire until 1894, so when work on the new Reliance Building began in 1890,

the upper floors of the old building were supported on jack screws and the lower stories demolished. The ground floors of the Reliance Building were completed and in 1894, when the leases expired, the upper floors were demolished and the steel framing for 13 more stories completed, in 15 days.

The new building, officially opened in March 1895, was considered revolutionary because of its steel frame and unusual two-story-column design, allowing for the masses of windows which give the building its modern look. The building's design was undertaken by John Root of Burnham and Root. Charles Atwood completed it upon Root's death in 1891.

The building was in serious disrepair in the mid-1990s, until the City of Chicago purchased it and began an exterior renovation, which involved the replacement of 2,000 pieces of terra-cotta. In 1995, it was designated a Chicago landmark. In 1998, a hotel company bought the building, undertaking a $27.5-million refurbishment before opening the Hotel Burnham in 1999. Root's original bronze and granite design of the first floor has been re-created and the 20-ft- (6-m-) high elevator lobby reconstructed using Italian marble, ornamental metal elevator grills, and elaborate mosaic floor tiles.

⓬ Macy's

111 N State St. **Map** 4 D1. **Tel** (312) 781-1000. Ⓜ Washington (Red Line). **Open** 10am–8pm Mon, Thu–Sat; 9am–9pm Tue & Wed; 11am–6pm Sun. **Closed** Easter, Thanksgiving, Dec 25. Ⓐ Ⓒ Ⓩ Ⓟ See Shops and Markets: *p159*. Ⓦ visitmacyschicago.com

No other retail establishment is, perhaps, as important to Chicago's cultural history as Marshall Field's department store, which became part of the Macy's chain in 2006. The original Marshall Field plaques remain on the building but, despite protests

The red bull's eye logo represents City Target, a popular store at the Sullivan Center

Christmas window display at Macy's

by loyal customers, the name Macy's remains ubiquitous elsewhere. Originally a dry-goods shop begun by wealthy businessman Marshall Field *(see p79)*, the store now occupies an entire city block. Built in five stages as the company grew, the original building, a Renaissance Revival-style design by Charles B. Atwood of D.H. Burnham, still stands at Washington and Wabash.

Field is credited with transforming State Street into the retail heart of Chicago in the early 1900s and for coining the commercial credo "Give the lady what she wants." When the store opened in 1907, it was considered the largest in the world, with 1,339,000 sq ft (124,400 sq m) of retail space, including the basement (such use was until then unheard of in US merchandising), 35,000 electric lights, 50 elevators, and 12 street-front entrances.

The store's most spectacular feature is its Tiffany mosaic vaulted dome. With more than 1.6 million pieces of iridescent glass covering 6,000 sq ft (557 sq m), it took 18 months and 50 artisans, supervised by designer Louis Comfort Tiffany, to complete.

1925, when it was demolished. The Oriental, built on the site, opened in 1926. The 22-story building, with its 3,238-seat auditorium, was designed by renowned theater architects Cornelius W. and George L. Rapp.

The theater was used as a movie palace back when live performances accompanied screenings. Judy Garland, Jackie Gleason, and Bob Hope all performed here.

Inspired by the East Indian carnival-festival Durbar, the theater's interior is full of fantastic decorative elements, such as the elephant-head light fixtures in the foyer.

The Oriental is in what, for more than a century, was Chicago's bustling theater district: Randolph Street between Michigan Avenue and Wacker Drive. The Rice Theatre was the first to open in the area, in 1847 (since it has burned down). By the 1880s, more than 25 entertainment palaces were offering vaudeville, musicals, opera, and drama. Although few of the original theaters remain, the district has been revitalized, spurred by the restoration of the Oriental, which reopened as the Ford Center for the Performing Arts Oriental Theater. Restoration of the theater was completed in 1998 after a 17-year closure; 62,500 sq ft (5,800 sq m) of gold leaf were used in the theater's renovation.

Superb Tiffany glass dome in Macy's southern atrium

⑬ Oriental Theater

24 W Randolph St. **Map** 3 C1. **Tel** (312) 782-2004. Ⓜ Washington (Red Line). ♿ 🎫 11am Sat. See Entertainment: *pp166–7.* Ⓦ **broadwayin chicago.com**

The Oriental Theater occupies the site of one of the worst theater fires in US history: just weeks after opening in 1903, fire broke out in the Iroquois Theater, claiming almost 600 lives *(see p19)*. The theater was rebuilt and operated until

Signs such as this mark the Loop's theatrical district

Facade of Chicago Cultural Center's Randolph Street entrance

⑭ Chicago Cultural Center

78 E Washington St. **Map** 4 D1. **Tel** (312) 744-6630. Ⓜ Randolph. **Open** 8am–7pm Mon–Thu; 8am–6pm Fri; 9am–6pm Sat; 10am–6pm Sun. **Closed** public hols. ♿ via Randolph St. entrance. 🎫 1:15pm Wed, Fri, Sat. 🖥 🏛 ℹ Weekly arts events: call (312) 346-3278. 🅦 **chicagoculturalcenter.org**

Built between 1893 and 1897 as the city's main library, the building was dedicated in 1991 as the Chicago Cultural Center to showcase and celebrate the performing, visual, and literary arts.

Designed by the Boston firm Shepley, Rutan and Coolidge, this massive Neo-Classical (see p29) edifice features soaring arches of white marble and classical Greek columns. The 3-ft- (1-m-) thick masonry walls, clad with Bedford limestone, rise 104 ft (32 m) above a granite base. The elegant building cost almost $2 million to construct.

There are two entrances to the building. The north entrance, at 77 East Randolph Street, with Doric columns and a massive portico, serves the four-story north wing; the deeply arched Romanesque portal with bronze-framed doors at the south entrance, at 78 East Washington Street, serves the five-story south wing. The Garland Court corridor connects the wings.

The interior of the building, which includes a grand Carrara marble staircase just inside the Washington Street entrance, is a monument to elegant ornamentation. Inset in the staircase are small medallions made from a rare Irish emerald marble. On the underside of the staircase, seen by looking up from each landing, are intricate mosaics.

Two spectacular glass domes complete the opulent detailing. At the south end of the building, on the third floor in Preston Bradley Hall, is a huge Tiffany dome. This 38-ft (11.5-m) jewel of sparkling colored glass, stone, and mother-of-pearl is valued at an incredible $35 million. It is the largest stained-glass Tiffany dome in the world. At the north end of the building, in the second-floor G.A.R. Rotunda, is a stained-glass dome in an intricate Renaissance pattern. It was created by the local firm Healy and Millet. Both domes were originally skylights but have since been sheathed with copper and backlit to protect and preserve the glass.

On the fourth floor is the Sidney R. Yates Gallery, a replica of an assembly hall in Venice's 14th-century Doge's Palace. Arched, bronzed doorways are inlaid with antique marble, and the ceiling is coffered. The stairway leading to the fifth floor is modeled on the Bridge of Sighs in Venice.

Although the building itself deserves many hours of architectural exploration, allow enough time to view the center's many exhibits that reflect the city's rich cultural heritage and showcase local and international artists. Along the western corridor on the same floor is the Landmark Chicago Gallery, displaying photographs of the city's architectural heritage.

The center also contains two concert halls, two theaters, and a dance studio. Hundreds of programs and exhibitions are presented annually. Each week, there are many concerts, literary readings, and cultural events held here.

One of two Visitor Information Centers operated by the Chicago Office of Tourism is on the first floor of the Chicago Cultural Center, near the Randolph Street entrance.

Grand staircase leading to the third-floor Preston Bradley Hall

Stained glass dome by Healy and Millet in the G.A.R. Rotunda

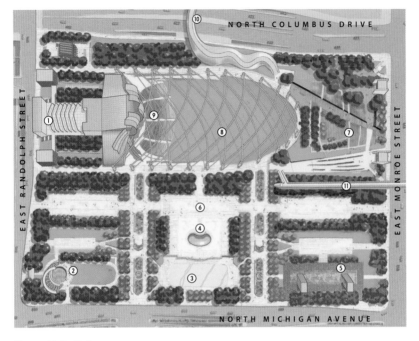

Key to Main Sights

① Harris Theater for Music & Dance
② Wrigley Square
③ McCormick-Tribune Ice Rink
④ AT&T Plaza

⑤ South Terrace and Crown Fountain
⑥ Chase Promenade
⑦ Lurie Garden

⑧ Great Lawn
⑨ Jay Pritzker Pavillion
⑩ BP Bridge
⑪ Nichols Bridgeway

ⓑ Millennium Park

Bounded by Randolph & Monroe sts., Michigan Ave., & Columbus Dr.
Map 4 D1. **Tel** (312) 742-1168.
Ⓜ Madison; Randolph. 🌳 Park: 6am–11pm daily. 📷 📶 Concerts.
🔲 **millenniumpark.org**

A project to celebrate the 21st century, Millennium Park has provided year-round recreational opportunities since it opened in summer 2004. A northern expansion of Grant Park (see pp86–7), it covers more than 1 million sq ft (93,000 sq m). This park-within-a-park has transformed an unsightly rail yard and parking lot into a world-class cultural destination for families, tourists, and convention-goers.

The showpiece is the outdoor **Jay Pritzker Pavilion**, which was designed by internationally acclaimed architect Frank Gehry in association with the park's own designers. The bandshell includes a special sound system that reaches the whole audience. The Pavilion is the home of several summer music festivals. It can accommodate up to 14,000 people, while its stage allows for up to 120 musicians and a chorus of 150 singers to perform at the same time. Nearby, connecting the **Great Lawn** with the third floor of the Art Institute's Modern Wing, is the **Nichols Bridgeway**.

The 1,500-seat **Harris Theater for Music and Dance** was built mostly below ground so as not to obscure views through the park. Designed by Hammond Beeby Rupert Ainge, the theater offers ballet and other dance performances, in addition to classical, chamber, opera, and folk music.

Designed to pay homage to the city's motto *Urbs in Horto* (City in a Garden), the **Lurie Garden**, with its graceful wooden footbridge and groves of trees, is a pleasant landscape of plants and flowers. This 2.5-acre garden was the result of an international design competition and has become a popular meeting place.

The **Crown Fountain** consists of two 50-ft (15-m) towers that project video images of Chicago citizens, whose mouths open to spout water on those visitors splashing below.

The **McCormick-Tribune Ice-rink** converts to an outdoor restaurant and activity plaza in the summer, becoming a venue for Chicago's summer dance program (see p164).

Beside the Ice Rink is the **AT&T Plaza**, featuring the huge *Cloud Gate* sculpture by renowned British artist Anish Kapoor. This giant elliptical structure (nicknamed *The Bean*) has a highly polished surface, which is designed to reflect the park and surroundings. It is Kapoor's first public work installed in the US.

⓰ Chicago Theatre

175 N State St. **Map** 4 D1. **Tel** (312) 462-6300. Ⓜ Lake (Red Line), State and Lake (Brown, Green, & Orange Lines). 🚌 29, 36, 62, 145, 146. **Open** 10am–6pm Mon–Fri. 🎭 Apr–Sep: noon Tue & Thu; Oct–Mar: noon Tue. 3rd Sat of month: 11am & noon. See Entertainment: pp166–7. 🌐 thechicagotheatre.com

Slated for demolition in the 1980s but reprieved, this grand 3,800-seat theater has been restored to its former glory. The oldest surviving theater in Chicago, it was designed by Rapp and Rapp in 1921 and originally was a vaudeville movie palace. It now hosts musicals and other live performances.

Chicago Theatre's marquee and sign

Along with its Beaux-Arts white terra-cotta facade, the theater has the last cast-iron building front in Chicago. In 1902, architects Hill and Woltersdorf remodeled the west facade and added another floor. The decoration of the entranceway, triumphal arch (inspired by Paris' Arc de Triomphe), and palatial lobby reflect the opulence of early theater design. The six-story-high sign above the marquee has become a city symbol.

⓱ Michigan Avenue Bridge

Map 2 D5. **Tel** (312) 977-0227. Ⓜ Lake/State (Red Line), State and Clark/Lake (Blue Line). 🚌 11, 33, 125, 145, 146, 147, 151. Museum **Open** 10am–5pm Thu–Mon.

Linking the loop with the Magnificent Mile, this bridge, the first double-deck trunnion bascule bridge ever built, was completed in 1920. Spanning the Chicago River, the two leaves, each weighing 3,340 tons (3,030 tonnes), open by turning on enormous trunnion bearings on the banks. The bas-relief sculptures, one on each of the four bridge-houses, commemorate important events in Chicago's history. A plaque on the south-west corner marks the site of Fort Dearborn (1803–12).

Henry Hering's *Defence* **depicting the 1812 massacre, on the bridgehouse**

At the bridge's north end, in the 401 North Michigan Avenue plaza, a plaque marks the homestead of Jean Baptiste Point du Sable, Chicago's first permanent non-American Indian resident. On the northwest end is the McCormick Bridgehouse & Chicago River Museum, which reveals the inner workings of the bridge, and the man-made transformations of the Chicago River.

Michigan Avenue Bridge is one of 20 downtown bridges spanning the Chicago River, in a city that has the greatest

The opulent interior of the restored Chicago Theatre

number of movable bridges of any city in the world. Visitors can also stroll along nearby Riverwalk, parallel to Wacker Drive from Wabash Avenue to Wells Street.

⑱ 35 East Wacker Drive

Map 4 D1. **Tel** (312) 726-4260.
Ⓜ Lake; State. **Open** 24 hrs daily. ♿
Ⓦ 35eastwackerdrive.com

This sandy-colored terra-cotta office building, which became a Chicago landmark in 1994, has been described as a "confection" – the dome at the top really does resemble a birthday cake! The building, designed by Thielbar and Fugard, opened in 1926. During Prohibition, the dome housed mobster Al Capone's notorious speakeasy, the Stratosphere Club.

The building once had private parking garages on each of the first 22 floors; jeweler tenants, concerned about security, drove into the elevator and were lifted up to their floors. A 1988 renovation restored the marble interior. Outside, a 6-ton (5.4-tonne) clock with the gilded bronze figure of Father Time overhangs the Wacker Drive sidewalk.

Corberó's *Three Lawyers and a Judge* in the R.R. Donnelley Building

35 East Wacker Drive, seen from across the Chicago River

⑲ R.R. Donnelley Building

77 W Wacker Dr. **Map** 3 C1.
Tel (312) 917-1177. Ⓜ Clark.
Open 24 hrs daily. ♿

The R.R. Donnelley Building, a modern 50-story office tower overlooking the Chicago River, was built in 1992 in the Downtown Core.

Designed by Chicago architect James DeStefano, with famed Catalan architect Ricardo Bofill as the design consultant, the building combines classical aesthetic with Chicago School (*see pp28–9*) functionality. The many classical references to ancient Greece and Rome include the four-pedimented roof, a contemporary take on a classically proportioned Greek temple. The building materials likewise conjure the classics: a grid of Portuguese white granite frames the exterior curtain wall of silver reflective glass.

The ground-floor marble lobby, with its 42-ft- (13-m-) high ceiling and huge, classical windows, is a monumental space housing two sculptural groupings: Ricardo Bofill's *Twisted Columns* (1992), a set of three Modernistic columns hand-carved from white Italian marble, and Catalan sculptor Xavier Corberó's *Three Lawyers and a Judge* (1992), rough-hewn basalt figures suggesting human forms.

At night, 540 high-intensity lamps dramatically illuminate the building in a lighting scheme designed by Pierre Arnaud, who also illuminated the Pyramids, the Parthenon, and the Louvre Museum.

The towering atrium in the James R. Thompson Center

⓴ James R. Thompson Center

100 W Randolph St. **Map** 3 C1.
Tel (312) 814-6660. Ⓜ Clark/Lake.
Open 6:30am–6pm (atrium
8am–6pm) Mon–Fri. ♿
🎨 Art exhibits

The James R. Thompson
Center (1985) is a refreshing
change from the rectangular
skyscrapers that make up
Chicago's Downtown. Architect
Helmut Jahn designed the
center as a symbol of open
democratic government,
one with no barriers between
it and the people. The all-glass
walls and roof in this multi-
shaped structure provide a
monumental, dazzling – and
some say, chaotic transparency.

Originally called the State
of Illinois Building, and often
still referred to as such, the
building was later renamed
after the former Illinois governor
who commissioned it. The
tricolor (patriotic but often
criticized salmon, silver, and
blue) center is home to almost
70 government offices and
numerous restaurants and
shops. Performances and fairs
are often held in the atrium.

The interior rotunda, at
17 stories and 160 ft (49 m) in
diameter, is one of the largest
enclosed spaces in the world.
A cylindrical skylight soaring
75 ft (23 m) above the roofline
caps the rotunda. Its steel
frame weighs almost 10,500
tons (9,525 tonnes).

Exposed escalator and
elevator machinery echo the
building's no-barriers theme.
Elevators run up glass shafts
to a viewing platform on the
16th floor. Here, visitors brave
enough to look down will
have a stunning view of the
marble rosette in the granite
concourse floor marking the
building's center.

Throughout the building are
14 specially commissioned
artworks showcasing Illinois
artists, and selections from the
building's permanent art
collection are also on view.
Ask for a directory at the
information desk.

On the main floor is the
Illinois Artisans gallery, where
local artisans frequently sell
artworks and crafts.

Not on view to the public
are eight ice banks – each
40 ft (12 m) long, 12 ft (3.5 m)
wide, and 14 ft (4 m) tall – in
the sub-basement. In summer,
up to 400 tons (363 tonnes)
of ice are frozen each night
in these giant cubes, then
used to cool the building.

Outside the building,
located at the Randolph Street
entrance, sits Jean Dubuffet's
29-ft (9-m) lighthearted
fiberglass sculpture *Monument
with Standing Beast* (1984)
(*see p127*).

㉑ 333 West Wacker Drive

Map 3 B1. Ⓜ Washington (Brown,
Orange, Purple Lines). **Open** 7am–
6:30pm Mon–Fri. ♿ 🅿

Located at a bend in the
Chicago River, this prominent
Post-Modern, 36-story edifice
echoes the curving form of its
natural neighbor. Designed in
1983 by the architectural firm
of Kohn Pedersen Fox, the

The massive James R. Thompson Center, *Standing Beast* in foreground

office tower is sheathed with reflective, green-tinted glass that changes shade depending on the levels of sun and water. Broad horizontal bands of brushed stainless steel run every 6 ft (2 m). Green marble and gray granite form the base of this elegant, wedge-shaped building, materials used again in the two-story lobby.

A cityscape reflected on 333 West Wacker Drive's convex surface

㉒ Wacker Drive

From N Wacker Dr to N Michigan Ave.
Map 3 C1. Ⓜ Clark.

Wacker Drive's east-west segment offers one of the loveliest downtown walks of any US city. Running alongside the south bank of the main branch of the Chicago River and connecting to 17 of the city's bridges, this two-tiered street was the first of its kind in the world.

Named in honor of Charles Wacker, one of Chicago's civic planners *(see p73)*, the drive was built in 1926 to replace the run-down South Water Street Market.

The lower level is reserved for through traffic, but the upper level consists of a roadway, sidewalks, and a pleasant riverwalk, lined with public art.

Wacker Drive affords a splendid view across the river of impressive architecture, including the massive Merchandise Mart. Built for Marshall Field in 1930, it is, at 4.2 million sq ft

The fortresslike Merchandise Mart, best viewed from Wacker Drive

(390,000 sq m), the world's largest commercial building.

State Street Bridge Gallery, in the bridge's mechanical room (open daily, no admission charge), offers visitors a rare opportunity to see the machinery at work behind this famous movable bridge. The gallery also displays local artwork.

At 75 East Wacker Drive is the city's thinnest skyscraper. This Gothic-style, 1928 building is clad in white terra-cotta.

The Chicago Architecture Foundation's river cruise tours, departing from Michigan Avenue Bridge at Wacker Drive, offer fantastic views of Chicago's towers.

Chicago River

No other natural feature played as important a role in the early development of Chicago as did the Chicago River. For Native Americans and settlers alike, the river served as a trade route connecting the Great Lakes and the heart of the continent. By the mid-1800s, as shipping became a major economic activity in the area, the Chicago River was the main thoroughfare of a growing metropolis.

One unsanitary result of such growth was that the Chicago River also served as the city's sewer, a dumping ground for waste. The swampy conditions, with the surface of the land near to the level of standing water, made it impossible to construct an underground sewer system.

In the mid-1800s, a Boston engineer, Ellis Chesbrough, was hired to fix the problem. Chesbrough developed the country's first comprehensive sewer system – above ground.

The streets, along with the buildings on them, were raised above the new system, sometimes by as much as 12 ft (3.5 m). The city's largest hotel at the time, the Tremont, was raised while still open for business, without breaking a pane of glass or cracking a plaster wall.

This new sewer system did not entirely eradicate the city's unsanitary conditions, however. In 1885, a devastating cholera and typhoid epidemic killed thousands of Chicagoans (12 per cent of the population by some estimates) when sewage flowed into Lake Michigan, the city's source of drinking water.

In response to this tragedy, the city initiated the largest municipal project in the US at the time – the construction of the 28-mile- (45-km-) long Sanitary and Ship Canal. Built between Damen Avenue and the town of Lockport, the canal

connected the Chicago River to the Des Plaines and Illinois Rivers and involved the digging out of more rocks, soil, and clay than was excavated for the Panama Canal. This massive project reversed the flow of the main and south branches of the river, which now drain away from Lake Michigan and into the Sanitary and Ship Canal.

Drawbridge spanning the Chicago River opening for water traffic

Sunset at the downtown distict by the Chicago River

Sights at a Glance

NORTH SIDE

Just north of the Chicago River, Chicago's North Side encompasses several neighborhoods, most settled in the mid-1880s by Irish, German, and Swedish immigrants. Tragically, the 1871 fire razed the entire area. The communities rose from the ashes, and today the Magnificent Mile, Gold Coast, Streeterville, and River North are all upscale residential and shopping districts. Modest Old Town is an eclectic mix of residences, shops, and entertainment venues.

See also Street Finder maps 1& 2

0 meters 500
0 yards 500

For keys to symbols see back flap

Street-by-Street: The Magnificent Mile

The magnificent mile, a stretch of Michigan Avenue north of the Chicago River, is Chicago's most fashionable street. Although almost completely destroyed in the 1871 fire, by the early 1900s, Michigan Avenue had become a major traffic artery. The 1920 opening of Michigan Avenue Bridge led to a retail boom. In 1947, developer Arthur Rubloff, predicting that the street would be Chicago's premier shopping district, dubbed it the Magnificent Mile. His prediction came true and the name stuck. Exclusive shops line the wide boulevard, while modern retail complexes and mixed-use skyscrapers rub shoulders with historic buildings.

900 North Michigan Shops
Anchored by Bloomingdales department store, this contemporary mall houses over 400 retailers, including specialty shops and high-end designers such as Coach and Gucci.

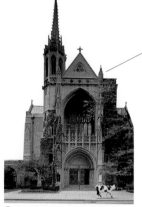

❻ Fourth Presbyterian Church
Fourteen carved stone angels, each holding a musical instrument, adorn the nave of this Gothic Revival-style church, the oldest structure on the Magnificent Mile after the Water Tower. A large fountain sparkles at the center of its inner courtyard.

❺ ★ Water Tower and Pumping Station
These two historic castellated structures, the station housing a café, theater and visitors' center, sit on an island in the street – a relaxing, shady retreat from busy Michigan Avenue.

❼ ★ John Hancock Center
This tower offers spectacular views from its open-air skywalk and a thrilling TILT experience, both on the 94th floor. The ground-level plaza has a fountain, cafés, and, occasionally, live music.

Key

— Suggested route

Water Tower Place
The shopping area of this 1970s tower block is centered around an eight-story terraced atrium and includes upscale boutiques, numerous restaurants, and two major department stores.

Locator Map
See Street Finder map 2

❸ ★ Hotel InterContinental Chicago
An eclectic mix of detailing – from Mesopotamian-inspired carvings to knights in armor – vie for attention in this 1929 hotel. It underwent major renovation in 2013.

❷ Tribune Tower
Rock fragments from famous sites around the world, including St. Peter's Basilica in Rome, are embedded in the exterior of this Gothic-style tower.

NORTH MICHIGAN AVENUE

The Shops at North Bridge
development houses shops, restaurants, a movie theater, and several hotels.

❶ Wrigley Building
This structure, one of Chicago's most beloved, boasts a giant four-sided clock and a quiet courtyard, which is open to the public. The building is particularly dazzling at night, when it is illuminated.

| 0 meters | 200 |
| 0 yards | 200 |

View of the two-part Wrigley Building, to the left of Tribune Tower

❶ Wrigley Building

400–410 N Michigan Ave. **Map** 2 D5.
Tel (312) 923-8080. Ⓜ Grand (Red
Line). 🚌 3, 145, 146, 147, 151. North
lobby: **Open** 24 hrs daily; South lobby:
Open 7am–6pm Mon–Fri. South
building: **Closed** public hols. ♿
Ⓦ thewrigleybuilding.com

The Wrigley Building rests on a
historical site: it was to here that
Jesuit missionary Jacques
Marquette and explorer Louis
Jolliet made their first portage
west of the Great Lakes in the
1670s, and here that La Salle
planted the flag of France (see p17).

The wealthy chewing-gum
manufacturer William Wrigley, Jr.
commissioned the architectural
firm Graham, Anderson,
Probst and White to design
the building. The 30-story south
tower was built in 1920, the
21-story north tower in 1924.
They are connected by three
arcades. The circular temple and
cupola rising above a massive
four-faced clock were inspired
by Seville's Giralda Tower.

Six shades of white enamel,
from gray to cream, were baked
onto the terra-cotta cladding; at
night, it shimmers.

❷ Tribune Tower

435 N Michigan Ave. **Map** 2 D5.
Tel (312) 981-7200. Ⓜ Grand (Red
Line). **Open** 24 hrs daily. ♿ 📷

The 36-story limestone Tribune
Tower is the winning design
of a 1922 international
competition sponsored by the
Tribune Company to celebrate

the 75th anniversary of
the *Chicago Tribune*, the
newspaper whose offices still
occupy the building. Architects
were challenged to create the
most beautiful office building
in the world. From 263
submissions, that of New York
firm Howells and Hood was
chosen. Their Gothic design,
reflected in the flying
buttresses of the crowning
tower, echoes France's
Rouen Cathedral.

The building's ornate three-
story arched entrance is carved
with figures from Aesop's
fables. Gargoyles, such as the
monkey symbolizing human
folly (below the south-side
fourth-floor windows),
embellish the facade. More
than 100 rock fragments from
famous sites, including Beijing's
Forbidden City and London's
Westminster Abbey, are

embedded in the exterior walls,
as is a 3.3-billion-year-old piece
of moon rock, collected by the
Apollo 15 mission.

❸ Hotel InterContinental Chicago

505 N Michigan Ave. **Map** 2 D5.
Tel (312) 944-4100. Ⓜ Grand (Red
Line). **Open** 24 hrs daily. ♿ 🍴 🏊
🖥 Ⓟ See Where to Stay: p144.

Originally the Shriners'
Medinah Athletic Club, this
magnificent building was
renovated at a cost of $130
million, reopening in 1990 as
the Hotel InterContinental
Chicago. Designed in 1929 by
Walter W. Ahlschlager, it is
topped with a large onion-
shaped gilt dome.

Many of the building's
exterior and interior details
reflect the Shriners' interest in
all things Egyptian, medieval,
and Renaissance. Ask the
concierge for the free self-
guided tour audiotape, which
explains historic features.

Carved in stone on the
2nd-floor staircase to the Hall
of Lions, two lions guard the
intricate terra-cotta fountain.
Inside the King Arthur Foyer
and Court on the 3rd floor,
colorful paintings on the
ceiling beams depict King
Arthur's life. On the 5th floor,
classical Renaissance paintings
adorn the walls of the
Renaissance Room Foyer.

The Johnny Weissmuller Pool at Hotel InterContinental Chicago

For hotels and restaurants see pp142–5 and pp148–57

The Spanish Tea Court features a fountain lined with Spanish Majolica tiles.

A gem is the 11th-floor swimming pool, named after the swimmer and actor Johnny Weissmuller. A renovation in 2000 created a common entrance for the north and south towers, which were both updated in 2013.

Sign for the giant chocolate store on Magnificent Mile

❹ Hershey's Chicago

822 North Michigan Ave. **Map** 2 D4. **Tel** (312) 337-7711. Ⓜ Chicago (Red Line). **Open** 10am–8pm Sun–Thu (to 10pm in summer); 10am–10pm Fri & Sat.

When candy-maker Milton Hershey visited the city of Chicago in 1893, he purchased the equipment that he would use to revolutionize the chocolate industry. With mass production he was able to lower the cost of manufacturing milk chocolate, once a luxury item, making it affordable to all. Today, the Hershey Foods Corporation is the largest North American producer of confectionary.

Hershey's Chicago is a huge themed store located in a Loyola University building on Magnificent Mile. It stocks all the well-known brands such as Hershey's, Reese's, and Kit Kat, as well as the latest products and goods unique to the Chicago store. Sugar-free versions of the most popular products are also available. The store's interactive "bake shoppe", where visitors can customize cookies, cupcakes, and brownies, is popular with children.

The Chicago store is the latest addition to the world-famous chain which includes Hershey's Time Square in New York and the Hershey's Chocolate World in Hershey Pennsylvania.

❺ Water Tower and Pumping Station

806 N Michigan Ave. **Map** 2 D4. Ⓜ Chicago (Red Line). Tower: **Tel** (312) 742-0808. **Open** 10am–6:30pm Mon–Sat; 10am–5pm Sun. **Closed** public hols. Station: **Tel** (312) 744-2400. **Open** 7:30am–7pm daily. **Closed** Thanksgiving, Dec 25. Ⓖ station only. 🅿 📷 ℹ

Built just before the fire of 1871, the Water Tower (1869) and the Pumping Station (1866), housing Chicago's original waterworks, were two of the few buildings in the city to survive the conflagration.

Designed by William W. Boyington, these structures look like Gothic castles. The 154-ft (47-m) tower consists of limestone blocks rising in five sections from a square base. The tower originally housed a standpipe that stabilized the mains water pressure. It is now home to a City Gallery which specializes in photography. The Lookingglass Theatre is also based here.

In addition to housing a Visitor Information Center (163 E. Pearson St.), the Pumping Station fulfills its original purpose, pumping up to 250 million gallons (946 million liters) of water per day.

The Water Tower survived Chicago's Great Fire of 1871

❻ Fourth Presbyterian Church

866 N Michigan Ave. **Map** 2 D4. **Tel** (312) 787-4570. Ⓜ Chicago (Red Line). 🚌 143, 144, 145, 146, 147, 151. **Open** 9am–6pm Mon–Fri; 8am–7:30pm Sun. 🕆 8am, 9:30am, 11am, 6:30pm Sun. Ⓖ via 126 E Chestnut St. Concerts: 12:10pm Fri. 🆆 fourthchurch.org

The 1871 fire destroyed the original Fourth Presbyterian Church, at Wabash and Grand, the night it was dedicated. The current building is the oldest surviving structure (after the Water Tower) on Michigan Avenue, north of the river.

Designed by Ralph Adams Cram, architect of New York's Cathedral of St. John the Divine, the church is Gothic Revival in style (*see p28*). Its exposed buttresses, stone spire, and recessed main window all reflect the influences of medieval European churches.

Angels, 7 ft (2 m) tall, stand just below the illuminated timber ceiling; the stained-glass windows are magnificent.

A covered walkway leads to a tranquil courtyard designed by Howard Van Doren Shaw.

Weekly Friday concerts, some including the church's magnificent organ, are free.

The peaceful courtyard of the Fourth Presbyterian Church

Upscale boutiques lining Oak Street

❼ John Hancock Center

875 N Michigan Ave. **Map** 2 D4. 360
Chicago: **Tel** (312) 751-3680.
Ⓜ Chicago (Red Line).
Open 9am–11pm daily. ⛪ to 360
Chicago (children under 5 free). ♿
♻ Ⓟ Ⓦ 360chicago.com

The John Hancock Center
stands out as a bold feature of
the Chicago skyline. The 100-
story building has 18-story-
long steel braces crisscrossing
the tapering obelisk tower like
stacked Xs.

The center's major attraction
is 360 Chicago, formerly known
as the Hancock Observatory,
located on the 94th floor.
Here, 1,127 ft (343 m) above
the Magnificent Mile, you
can actually go outside,
onto Chicago's only open-air
(screened) skywalk, or experience
a physically tilting observation
deck dubbed as the "TILT".
Designed by architect Bruce

Graham of Skidmore, Owings
and Merrill and engineer Fazlur R.
Khan, the John Hancock Center
opened in 1969, and houses
offices, condominiums, and
shops in 2.8 million sq ft
(0.26 million sq m) of space.
The elevator ride to the top is
touted as the fastest in
North America. At a
speed of 20 miles (32
km) per hour, you reach
the observatory in just
40 seconds. On a clear
day, you can see for up
to 80 miles (130 km).
The view is especially
dazzling during the late-
afternoon when the
sun falls on the
downtown buildings.
A wall-to-wall exhibition
in the observatory
traces Chicago's history.
The center's lower
courtyard has several
cafés, with patios
in summer.

The John Hancock
Center

❽ Oak Street

Between Rush St. & N Michigan Ave.
Map 2 D3. Ⓜ Chicago (Red Line).
See Shops and Markets: pp158–9.

Tree-lined Oak Street at the
north end of the Magnificent
Mile is home to many upscale
boutiques such as
Prada, Hermès, Sonia
Rykiel, Luca Luca, and
Jil Sander.

Along with its chic
fashion boutiques, Oak
Street has numerous
art galleries, such as
the Colletti Antique
Poster Gallery,
specializing in original
works from 1880
to 1940. Perhaps
the grandest one-stop
shop in Oak Street
is Barneys New York,
which opened its
spacious store
here in 2009.
Luxury brands and Barneys'
in-house label attract
distinguished shoppers.

The 20-story apartment
building (1929) at No. 40
was designed by Ben Marshall,
architect of the Drake Hotel.

❾ Drake Hotel

140 E Walton Pl. **Map** 2 D3.
Tel (312) 787-2200. Ⓜ Chicago
(Red Line). ♿ ♻ ⬛ See Where
to Stay: p144.
Ⓦ thedrakehotel.com

The essence of the golden age
in the heart of the Magnificent
Mile, the 537-room Drake Hotel
opened in 1920. Designed by
Marshall and Fox, and inspired

Entrance to the 1920s Drake Hotel

For hotels and restaurants see pp142–5 and pp148–57

by the Italian Renaissance, this 13-story hotel is clad in limestone.

The lobby, paneled in marble and oak, is graced with grand chandeliers, elegant red carpets, and a magnificent fountain.

The elegant Palm Court, in the lobby, offers traditional afternoon tea and is also a fashionable place for refreshing cocktails, with live jazz Fridays and Saturdays. The Cape Cod Room has an extensive seafood menu to choose from.

The hotel's splendid piano bar, the Coq d'Or, has live music every night. When Prohibition ended in 1933, this bar served the second drink in Chicago.

⑩ Museum of Contemporary Art

220 E Chicago Ave. **Map** 2 D4. **Tel** (312) 280-2660. Ⓜ Chicago (Red Line). 🚌 10, 66. **Open** 10am–8pm Tue; 10am–5pm Wed–Sun. **Closed** Jan 1, Thanksgiving, Dec 25. 🚻 ♿ 🚫 🎧 🖥 📷 🅿
Ⓦ mcachicago.org

Founded in 1967, the Museum of Contemporary Art offers innovative exhibits that interpret and present contemporary art. Designed by Berlin architect Josef Paul Kleihues, the sleek building has four floors of naturally lit exhibition space. On display are selections from the museum's extensive collection of works by internationally acclaimed artists, including Andy Warhol, René Magritte, Cindy Sherman, and Alexander Calder. Don't miss Richard Long's *Chicago Mud Circle* (1996), an exuberant application of mud on the gallery wall. The museum also hosts evenings of dance, theater, and live music.

⑪ Navy Pier

600 E Grand Ave. **Map** 2 F5. **Tel** 800-595-7437. 🚌 29, 65, 66, 124. **Open** 10am; closing times vary by day and season. **Closed** Thanksgiving, Dec 25. ♿ 🚫 🖥 🅿 ℹ Lake cruises. Ⓦ **navypier.com**

Navy Pier is a bustling recreational and cultural center. Designed by Charles S. Frost, the 3,000-ft- (915-m-) long and 400-ft- (120-m-) wide pier was the largest in the world when built in 1916. Over 20,000 timber piles were used in its construction.

Originally a municipal wharf, the pier was used for naval training during World War II. After a four-year renovation, Navy Pier opened in its present incarnation in 1995.

Jane Addams Memorial Park has a 150-ft- (45-m-) Ferris wheel (offering fine lake views in the daytime); old-fashioned carousel; outdoor amphitheater; ice skating rink; miniature golf course; and IMAX 3D theater. The Smith Museum displays stained glass.

Tranquil fountains and palms at Navy Pier's Crystal Gardens

⑫ Chicago Children's Museum

700 E Grand Ave. at Navy Pier. **Map** 2 F5. **Tel** (312) 527-1000. 🚌 29, 56, 65, 66, 124. **Open** 10am–5pm daily; 10am–8pm Thu. **Closed** Thanksgiving, Dec 25. 🎨 (free 5–8pm Thu). ♿ 📷 🅿 Special activities daily. Ⓦ **chicago childrensmuseum.org**

Chicago Children's Museum, focusing on activating the intellectual and creative potential of children aged 1 to 12, is an activity center for the whole family. All exhibits are hands-on. Kids can build a fort in the Under Construction exhibit, climb three stories of rope-rigging on the Kovler Schooner, or make a flying machine in the Inventing Lab. In the WaterWays, they can channel water with dams and locks. The Dinosaur Expedition is where children can dig for bones in an excavation pit. Along with educational exhibits, it is a space where kids can simply have fun.

Chicago Children's Museum

⓭ Marina City and IBM Building

Marina City: 300 N State St.
Map 1 C5. Ⓜ State and Lake.
Open 24 hrs daily. ♿ 🚲 Ⓟ IBM
Building: 330 N Wabash Ave.
Map 2 D5. Ⓜ State and Lake.
Open 24 hrs daily. ♿

The two towers of Marina City pay symbolic tribute to the Midwest's farming economy – they look like giant corncobs. Designed by Bertrand Goldberg Associates and opened in 1967, these twin circular towers function like a city within a city, with apartments, offices, shops, parking, a marina, and even a bowling alley.

To the east of Marina City, and in stark contrast to its organic form, rises the IBM Building, a sleek modern monument. Designed by Mies van der Rohe (see p32) with C.F. Murphy Associates and opened in 1971, the 52-story office tower has an exposed steel frame and dark bronze-tinted glass walls.

A small bust of Mies van der Rohe, who died before construction of the building was complete, is located in the lobby. In winter, the exterior plaza can be quite bleak and frigid. There are ropes strung to prevent people from being blown into the Chicago River.

Shops and galleries lining the streets of the River North Gallery District

⓮ River North Gallery District

Between N Wells & N Orleans Sts.,
from W Erie St to W Chicago Ave. **Map**
1 B4. Ⓜ Chicago (Brown, Purple
Lines). ☎ 649-0065. See Shops and
Markets: pp158–63.

River North is home to more than 65 art galleries – the largest concentration outside New York City. Some of Chicago's finest antique and home-furnishing shops are also located here.

West Superior Street is the center of the district. Galleries here and on adjoining streets offer a wide range of artwork by both international and local artisans. Unusual pieces by American folk artists, African-American art, glass sculpture, photography, and contemporary paintings are just some of the treasures to be found. Most galleries are closed Sundays and Mondays.

⓯ Richard H. Driehaus Museum and Ransom R. Cable Houses

40 & 25 E Erie St. **Map** 2 D4.
Ⓜ Chicago (Red Line); Grand (Red
Line). Nickerson House: **Open**
10am–5pm Tue–Sun. Cable House:
Closed major public hols.
ⓦ driehausmuseum.org

The Richard H. Driehaus Museum offers a glimpse into the wealthy world of late-1800s Chicago high society. Commissioned by Samuel Nickerson, a distillery owner and banker, this Italian Renaissance palazzo was designed in 1883 by Chicago church-architects Burling and Whitehouse and, after restoration, is now a museum.

The mansion has 23 rooms on its three floors, each room seemingly more opulent than the next. More than 20 varieties of marble, along with onyx and alabaster, were used to build the main hall and great staircase. Even the ceiling is marble. The largest room is the first-floor Picture Gallery, illuminated by a domed, Tiffany leaded-glass skylight.

Across the street, the Ransom R. Cable House now quarters a securities and capital management corporation. Designed by Cobb and Frost, the 1886 Richardsonian Romanesque (see p28) mansion was built for the president of the Chicago, Rock Island and Pacific Railway Company. It features rough-hewn rusticated masonry. Both houses are designated as Chicago landmarks.

Marina City's twin towers, flanked on the right by the IBM Building

Charming coach house belonging to the Ransom R. Cable House

For hotels and restaurants see pp142–5 and pp148–57

⓰ St. James Episcopal Cathedral

65 E Huron St. **Map** 2 D4. **Tel** (312) 787-7360. Ⓜ Chicago (Red Line). **Open** for mass only. Cathedral: ⓣ 10:30am Sun; Chapel: ⓣ 12:10pm Thu–Fri; 5:30pm Wed. & ⓐ Concerts. ⓦ **saintjames cathedral.org**

The parishioners of St. James have worshiped at this site since 1857. After their original building was destroyed in the Great Fire of 1871 (only the 1867 bell tower survived), architects Burling and Adler were hired to design a new building. The St. James Episcopal Cathedral, a Gothic Revival *(see p28)* structure of Joliet limestone, was completed in 1875.

Inside is a fine example of Victorian stencil work (1888), designed by Edward J. Neville Stent, a student of British designer William Morris. The stencils were restored in 1985 by the Chicago architects Holabird and Root.

The Chapel of St. Andrew is at the north end of the cathedral. Designed by Bertram G. Goodhue in 1913, it is said to be based on a private oratory in an ancient Scottish abbey. The painted-glass windows portray the figures of St. Paul, Mary Magdalene, and St. Francis.

The majestic altar and stained-glass windows in the Chapel of St. James

Statue of Archbishop Quigley outside Quigley Seminary

⓱ Archdiocese of Chicago and Chapel of St. James

835 N Rush St. **Map** 2 D4. **Tel** (312) 534-8200. Ⓜ Chicago (Red Line). Archdiocese office: **Closed** to public. Chapel: ⓒ mandatory: noon, 2pm Tue, Thu–Sat. Concerts

The Archdiocese of Chicago is in the process of moving into the former Quigley Seminary, which closed in 2007. Designed by Zachary T. Davis (architect of Wrigley Field) and Gustave E. Steinback and completed in 1919, this Gothic building has carved buttresses and spires.

Ten statues in the niches along the north wall represent saints, such as St. Cecilia, patron of music, and St. Elizabeth, patron of pregnant women. On the spire of the library tower is a statue of St. George, his iron spear serving as the building's lightning rod. A statue of Archbishop James E. Quigley (1854–1915), known for his commitment to building Catholic schools in Chicago, is at the northwest corner of the grounds.

Also on the site is the Chapel of St. James, inspired by the Gothic Sainte-Chapelle in Paris. The spectacular Rose Window, 28 ft (9 m) in diameter, depicts the life of the Virgin Mary. Smaller windows relate stories from the Bible and the pictorial scheme represents 245 events of scriptural and church history. More than 700,000 pieces of glass are set in limestone frames. The magnificent 50-ft- (15-m-) tall limestone altar, adorned with sculptures, was hand-carved in France.

⓲ Newberry Library

60 W Walton St. **Map** 1 C3. **Tel** (312) 943-9090. Ⓜ Chicago (Red Line). **Open** Hrs for lobby, book rooms, and exhibits vary; call ahead. **Closed** public hols. & ⓒ 3pm Thu; 10:30am Sat. ⓐ Exhibits, lectures, concerts. ⓦ **newberry.org**

At the north end of Washington Square Park is the impressive Newberry Library. Founded in 1887 by Walter Newberry, a merchant and banker, this independent research library for the humanities – one of the best in the US – opened to the public in 1893. Henry Ives Cobb, master architect of the Richardsonian Romanesque style, was the designer.

Strengths of the collection include cartography, Native American history, Renaissance studies, and geneology. Rarities include a 1481 edition of Dante's *Divine Comedy*, first editions of Milton's *Paradise Regained*, and the King James Version of the Bible.

Through the triple-arched entrance, the lobby has a grand staircase, terrazzo flooring, galleries, and a bookstore.

Jeweled cover of the first edition of Milton's *Paradise Regained*

⑲ St. Michael's Church

1633 N Cleveland Ave. **Map** 1 B1.
Tel (312) 642-2498. **M** Sedgwick.
✝ 9am, 11am, 7pm Sun; 5:30pm
Mon, Wed–Sat. ♿ weekends or by
arrangement. **P** **W** **st-mikes.org**

The original St. Michael's Church was a small brick building built in 1852. As St. Michael's small congregation expanded, it outgrew the building. The cornerstone for a new church was laid in 1866. In just three years the building's construction, overseen by builder August Wallbaum, was complete. Later, the Great Fire of 1871 destroyed the roof and interior of the church. However, the thick, brick walls survived and remain to this day.

The steeple, added to the bell tower in 1888, rises 290 ft (88.5 m) above the ground.

Angel in St. Michael's

The bell tower is adorned with a large four-faced clock. Each of the five bells in the tower weighs between 2,500 and 6,000 lbs (1,135 and 2,720 kg). By tradition, if you can hear the bells of St. Michael's, you are in Old Town.

Restoration of the church began in the 1990s. The first phase involved removing a ton of pigeon excrement from inside the bell tower. The colorful, vaulted interior features Mayer stained glass, frescoes, and sculptures depicting the life of Christ and the Virgin Mary. The carved high altar and its four subsidiary altars illustrate St. Michael, flanked by the archangels Gabriel and Raphael, triumphant over Lucifer.

Located on the church grounds is a small memorial dedicated to Catholic war veterans.

335 Menomonee Street, a wooden cottage typical of Old Town

⑳ Menomonee Street

From N Sedgwick St. to Lincoln Park W. **Map** 1 B1. **M** Sedgwick.

Menomonee Street lies in the heart of Old Town Triangle Historic District (bounded by Cleveland Street and North and Lincoln avenues), a delightful area of vintage cottages and Queen Anne-style (see p28) row houses settled in the mid-1800s by working-class German immigrants.

In the 1940s, community concern over the area's falling fortunes led to one of the city's earliest neighborhood revitalization efforts. Today, the Old Town Triangle's narrow tree-lined streets are home to picturesque houses and numerous interesting shops and restaurants.

Walk along Menomonee Street to view the residences that typify mid- to late-19th-century Old Town. Most of the original houses in the area were small cottages built using the method of balloon framing, so-called because such structures were reportedly as easy to construct as blowing up a balloon (see p29). The lightweight wooden frames provided ample kindling when the 1871 fire swept through the area.

The whitish gray clapboard house at No. 350 is a rare surviving example of the fire-relief shanties the Chicago Relief and Aid Society built for people made homeless by the fire.

The high-domed interior and main altar of St. Michael's Church

◀ Giant Ferris wheel and merry-go-round at Navy Pier, illuminated at night

These one-room structures, costing the City about $100 each, were transported on wagons to charred lots, providing fire victims with instant lodging.

The shanties were later replaced with permanent wooden cottages, constructed before an 1874 city ordinance prohibited the building of wooden structures. The high basements and raised front staircases typical of these cottages were designed to accommodate the above-ground sewage system *(see p59)*. The cottages at Nos. 325–45, although built after 1871, are typical of those in the neighborhood before the ravages of the Great Fire.

㉑ Wacker Houses

1836 & 1838 N Lincoln Park W. **Map** 1 B1. **Ⓜ** Sedgwick. **Closed** to public.

Both the Charles H. Wacker House and the Frederick Wacker House, designed in the early 1870s by an unknown architect, are highly ornate examples of the Chicago cottage style.

Commissioned by Frederick Wacker, a Swiss-born brewer, No. 1836 was built as a coach house but served as the Wacker's temporary home until No. 1838, a wood-frame structure built just before the ban on wood as a building material, was completed.

Frederick Wacker House, with its alpine-style overhanging porch

The elaborate Queen Anne-style Olsen-Hansen Row Houses

Charles Wacker, Frederick's son and the city planner after whom Wacker Drive is named *(see p59)*, remodeled the coach house after moving it to its present location beside the main family home.

No. 1838's elaborately carved trim is an excellent example of the handcrafted details on many houses in the Old Town neighborhood.

㉒ Crilly Court and Olsen-Hansen Row Houses

Crilly Court: north of W Eugenie St. between N Wells St. & N Park Ave.; Olsen-Hansen Row Houses: 164–172 W Eugenie St. **Map** 1 C1. **Ⓜ** Sedgwick. **Closed** to public.

Representing two different approaches to Queen Anne-style row-house design are Crilly Court and the Olsen-Hansen Row Houses.

Crilly Court was created in 1885 by real-estate developer Daniel F. Crilly, when he bought a city block and cut a north-south street through it, which he named after himself. Over the next ten years, Crilly built a residential and retail development, creating what is now one of the quaintest streets in Chicago.

Two columns frame the entrance to the court. On the court's west side are two-story stone row houses. On the east side is a four-story apartment building, the names of Crilly's four children carved above the doors.

The renovation of the development in the 1940s, led by Crilly's son Edgar, included closing off alleys behind the residences to create private courtyards and replacing wooden balconies with wrought-iron ones, giving the complex a New Orleans-like atmosphere. This redevelopment of Crilly Court initiated the renewal of the Lincoln Park neighborhood.

The Olsen-Hansen Row Houses, on West Eugenie Street, are more elaborate expressions of the Queen Anne style *(see p28)*. The row houses were designed by Norwegian-born architect Harald M. Hansen in 1886 for Adolph Olsen. Only 5 of the original 12 remain.

Turrets, various window styles, Victorian porches, irregular rooflines, and a mixture of building materials – ranging from red brick to rough stone – give each of the row houses a distinctive identity. Hansen himself lived here, at No. 164.

Daniel F. Crilly, developer of Chicago's handsome Crilly Court

Astor Street

For more than 100 years, Astor Street, named for fur tycoon and real-estate magnate John Jacob Astor, has been the heart of fashionable Gold Coast. Wealthy Chicagoans flocked to the area in the 1880s and built over the next 60 years the striking houses in myriad architectural styles that line the street, though interspersed today with more modern buildings. Just six blocks long, the charming Astor Street district, designated a Chicago landmark in 1975, is ideal for leisurely strolling.

VISITORS' CHECKLIST

Practical Information
From North Ave. to W Division St.
Map 2 D1–D2.

Transport
Ⓜ Clark/ Division.

John Jacob Astor

German-born John Jacob Astor (1763–1848) made his fortune in the fur trade. In 1808 he chartered the Chicago-based American Fur Company, creating a monopoly in the Great Lakes area. Astor's successful fur business helped fund later, highly profitable, real-estate ventures. When he died, he was the richest man in the US.

ASTOR STREET EAST SIDE ◁◁

May House (No. 1443) is a granite Romanesque Revival-style mansion designed in 1891 by celebrated residential architect J.L. Silsbee, one of Frank Lloyd Wright's (see p32) first employers. The mansion's grand arched entranceway with ornate carving is one of its most striking features.

William D. Kerfoot
This real-estate businessman lived at No. 1425. The first Chicagoan to reopen for business in the Loop after the fire of 1871, he posted outside his hastily erected shanty a sign the day after the fire: "All gone but wife, children, and energy."

1400 Block North Astor Street
The buildings lining this handsome block of the Gold Coast reflect an eclectic mix of architectural styles, ranging from a Tudor Revival country-style house at No. 1451 to a Gothic-influenced chateau at No. 1449.

John L. Fortune House
(No. 1451)

ASTOR STREET WEST SIDE ▷▷▷▷▷▷▷▷▷▷▷▷▷▷▷▷▷▷▷▷▷▷▷▷▷▷▷

Key

◄ ◄ East side walking south

► ► West side walking north

28 ★ Edward P. Russell House

Carvings in a floral motif decorate the Art Deco facade and window metalwork of this 1929 Holabird and Root-designed townhouse (No. 1444).

25 ★ Residence of the Roman Catholic Archbishop of Chicago

Built in 1880 of red brick, this massive Queen Anne-style mansion is the oldest home in the area. Decorative exterior features include floral carvings and lime-stone trim.

Patterson-McCormick Mansion (No. 1500; *see p78*)

29 ★ Charnley-Persky House

This superb house (No. 1365) is, appropriately, now the national headquarters of the Society of Architectural Historians. The building reflects the architectural styles of its two collaborators, Louis Sullivan and Frank Lloyd Wright, and is a masterpiece of Prairie School design *(see p29)*.

Astor Court

This Georgian-style mansion (No. 1355) was designed in 1914 by Howard Van Doren Shaw for William O. Goodman, who also commissioned Shaw to design the Goodman Theatre. A decorative iron gate opens to a courtyard. The building now contains luxury apartments.

Edwin J. Gardiner House (No. 1345)

⏀ Chicago History Museum

1601 N Clark St. **Map** 1 C1. **Tel** (312) 642-4600. ⌷ 11, 22, 36, 72, 151, 156. **Open** 9:30am–4:30pm Mon–Sat, noon–5pm Sun. **Closed** Jan 1, Thanksgiving, Dec 25. ⏀ (free Mon, children under 12 free) ⏀ ⏀ (call for times). ⏀ ⏀ ⏀ Concerts, lectures. ⏀ chicagohistory.org

Founded in 1856, the Chicago History Museum, formerly known as the Chicago Historical Society, is the city's oldest cultural institution. A major museum and research center, it boasts more than 22 million objects, images, and documents relating to the history of Chicago and Illinois.

Permanent exhibits, supplemented with temporary displays, trace the early recorded history of the Chicago area, beginning with the expeditions of 17th-century French explorers such as Father Jacques Marquette.

Among the highlights of the collection are the Chicago history dioramas on the first floor. Behind glass in a darkened room, eight miniature scenes show Chicago's rapid growth in the 18th and 19th centuries. The dioramas illustrate great events, such as the Great Fire of 1871 and the 1893 World's Columbian Exposition, as well as historic scenes, such as bustling LaSalle Street in the mid-1860s.

American-history buffs shouldn't miss the American Wing, on the second floor, which features 1 of only 23 surviving copies of the Declaration of Independence (the version printed in

The original, Neo-Georgian entrance to the History Museum

Philadelphia on July 4, 1776). As well, there is a rare copy of the American Constitution first printed in a Philadelphia newspaper, alongside the Bill of Rights drafted in 1789. Abraham Lincoln's deathbed is also on display. The Chicago History Museum also has a Research Center library, which is open for public research.

Along with the fascinating exhibits, the building itself is noteworthy, as it presents two dramatic faces to the world. The original Neo-Georgian structure, designed by architects Graham, Anderson, Probst and White in 1932, is best appreciated from Lincoln Park. The 1988 addition faces North Clark Street with a three-story, glass-and-steel atrium entrance. The most dramatic feature is the curving glass section at the south end.

In 2006, the museum completed extensive renovations and celebrated its 150th anniversary with a permanent exhibit entitled "Chicago: Crossroads of America." Offering a fresh perspective on the city, it interprets Chicago as a dynamic hub of commerce, industry, and culture that shaped modern America. A centerpiece is Chicago's first "L" car, which transported riders to the 1893 World's Columbian Exposition. As the title suggests, its galleries focus on Chicago first as a crossroads of commerce and industry, from fur to meatpacking. It also portrays Chicago as a city in crisis, from the fire of 1871 to the Democratic National Convention of 1968, and as a home for many generations of every race, ethnicity, and class; as a breeding ground for such innovations as skyscrapers, the Prairie School, Marshall Field's, Wrigley gum, and Weber grills; and finally, as a cultural hub, offering baseball to jazz, blues, and classical music.

1550 North State Parkway, once the epitome of Gold Coast luxury

⏀ 1550 North State Parkway

Map 1 C1. ⏀ Clark/Division. **Closed** to public.

When it opened in 1912, this apartment building overlooking Lincoln Park epitomized the luxury of the Gold Coast. Designed by Marshall and Fox (architects of the Drake Hotel, *see p66*), the 12-story Beaux-Arts (*see p29*) structure is faced with white terra-cotta.

Depiction of the 1871 Great Fire from the museum's excellent collection

Originally, each of the floors comprised a separate apartment with 15 rooms (5 for servants) and 9,000 sq ft (835 sq m) of living space – more than four times the size of the average modest home. The luxurious apartments have since been subdivided.

The black grillwork of the iron balconies, bowed windows, and the large urns on top of the balustrade are all interesting features.

The imposing home of Chicago's Roman Catholic archbishop

㉕ Residence of the Roman Catholic Archbishop of Chicago

1555 N State Pkwy. **Map** 2 D1.
Ⓜ Clark/Division. **Closed** to public.

Built in 1880 on the site of an early Catholic cemetery, the building is home to the archbishop of Chicago's Roman Catholic diocese. Archbishop Patrick A. Feehan was the first resident of this, the area's oldest home.

The two-and-a-half-story Queen Anne-style (see p28) mansion was designed by Alfred F. Pashley. Although not highly ornamented, its decorative features include Italianate windows and 19 chimneys rising from a peaked and gabled roofline, a landmark of the area.

The property surrounding the archbishop's residence was subdivided in the late 1800s by the Chicago Archdiocese and sold to Chicago's wealthy, who built their houses on the lots.

Today, the archbishop's residence has attractive landscaped grounds, complete with papal flag.

㉖ International Museum of Surgical Science

1524 N Lake Shore Dr. **Map** 2 D1.
Tel (312) 642-6502. Ⓜ Clark/Division (Red Line), Sedgwick (Brown and Purple Lines). 🚌 151. **Open** May–Sep: 10am–4pm Tue–Fri, 10am–5pm Sat & Sun (last adm 1hr before closing). **Closed** Mon, public hols. 🎫 (free Tue) 📷 Ⓟ ⓦ imss.org

The International Museum of Surgical Science, with its cranial saws and bone crushers, is an unusual museum and well worth a visit. Where else can one marvel at the variety, size, and intriguing shapes of gallstones and bladder stones?

Opened to the public in 1954, the museum is handsomely lodged in a historic (1917) four-story mansion designed by Howard Van Doren Shaw.

Fascinating exhibits from around the world trace the history of surgery and related sciences. Some of the earliest artifacts are 4,000-year-old Peruvian trepanning tools used to release evil spirits from the skull. Amazingly, some of the trepanned skulls on display show bony tissue growth,

Hope and Help, by Edouard Chaissing, at museum entrance

proof that patients survived the procedure. Less grisly exhibits include a recreation of a turn-of-the-20th-century apothecary, complete with medicine bottles with labels claiming to cure every ill.

The Hall of Immortals showcases 12 larger-than-life sculptures of important figures in medical history, such as the earliest-known physician, Imhotep (c.2700 BC), and Marie Curie.

An unusual exhibit is the 1935 Perfusion Pump created by Charles A. Lindbergh and Alexis Carrel, a device that enabled biologists to keep a human organ functioning outside of the body.

"Beyond Broken Bones," presents a historical overview of orthopedic treatments and prosthetics with a range of documents and artifacts, from ancient bone-cutting tools to artificial limbs and their histories.

A series of exhibitions called "Anatomy on The Gallery" displays contemporary art with medically-related themes. The library contains more than 5,000 books, including rare and antique volumes.

Turn-of-the-20th-century apothecary shop, Museum of Surgical Science

Facade of 1500 North Astor Street, with its Classical detailing

㉗ 1500 North Astor Street

Map 2 D1. **M** Clark/Division then bus 22, 36. **Closed** to public.

This opulent four-story Italian Renaissance palazzo was built in 1893 for *Chicago Tribune* publisher Joseph Medill as a wedding gift for his daughter. Designed by McKim, Mead and White, it is built of orange Roman brick, with terra-cotta trim. The most impressive feature of this house, the largest on Astor Street, is the two-story front porch with Doric and Ionic columns.

Cyrus Hall McCormick II, son of the inventor of the Virginia reaper *(see p33)*, bought the mansion in the 1920s. He then commissioned an addition to be built at the north end, doubling the building's size. It now contains luxury condominiums.

Art Deco window on the exterior of Edward P. Russell House

㉘ Edward P. Russell House

1444 N Astor St. **Map** 2 D2. **M** Clark/Division. **Closed** to public.

A unique, four-story townhouse, the Edward P. Russell House was designed in 1929 by the architect firm of Holabird and Root. Designed in the Art Deco style popular in the 1920s and 1930s, the house is, perhaps, the finest example of this architectural style in Chicago.

Graceful carvings in a floral motif decorate the building's smooth, white stone facade. These carvings are repeated in the metalwork on the windows. Although the shapes of the windows vary, they all unite to create a harmonious balance. The stone on the townhouse's facade, which was quarried in Lens, France, is trimmed with polished granite. A subtle three-story bay of black metal embodies the grace and elegance of this truly refined, much-admired, building.

㉙ Charnley-Persky House

1365 N Astor St. **Map** 2 D2. **Tel** (312) 573-1365. **Tel** (312) 915-0105. **M** Clark/Division. 🎥 mandatory; noon Wed, 10am & noon Sat. **Closed** public hols. 🏛️

Frank Lloyd Wright called Charnley-Persky House (1892) "the first modern house in America." Two of America's most influential architects collaborated on the design: Wright *(see p32)*, then a draftsman in the early stages of his career, and Louis Sullivan *(see p32)*, known for his architectural detailing. They were commissioned by lumberman James Charnley and his wife Helen.

Charnley-Persky House is a pivotal work in the history of modern architecture. Its design embraces abstract forms, every interior view providing a perfectly balanced composition. The house's relatively simple facade of brick and limestone contrasts with the elaborate fronts of the exclusive Astor Street neighborhood.

An atrium reaching from the oak-paneled entry hall to a skylight two floors above is the interior's focal point. Dramatic arches frame the rooms on the first floor.

Along with bold geometrical forms and organic abstractions there are surprising details, such as windows in the closets. One striking feature of the house is the elegantly tapering wooden screen on the second floor.

The elegant second-floor stairway screen at Charnley-Persky House

View of the Gold Coast skyline from Oak Street Beach

Restored in 1988 by the architect firm of Skidmore, Owings and Merrill, the house now headquarters the Society of Architectural Historians. It was renamed in honor of Seymour Persky, who bought it for the society.

㉚ Oak Street Beach

Between E Division & E Oak Sts, at N and E Lake Shore Dr. **Map** 2 D3. **Tel** (312) 742-7529 (Chicago Park District). Ⓜ Chicago (Red Line) then bus 36; Clark/Division. ▦ 145, 146, 147, 155.

Just steps from Chicago's Magnificent Mile is the fashionable Oak Street Beach, one of the city's several beaches that together form a sandy chain along the lakefront.

As well as providing a great view of Lake Michigan, the Gold Coast, and towering North Side buildings, Oak Street Beach presents a good opportunity to don swimsuit and sandals. Throngs of joggers, cyclists, dog walkers, and in-line skaters make the broad expanse of Oak Street Beach a lively place to enjoy the sun and watch the waves. At the southern end of the beach is a pleasant promenade and outdoor eatery.

To reach the beach, use the pedestrian tunnels at Oak or Division streets. There are washrooms at the beach, but the nearest changing rooms are at North Avenue Beach.

㉛ Trump International Hotel & Tower

401 N Wabash Ave. **Map** 1 D5. **Tel** (312) 588-8000. Ⓜ Grand (Red Line). ♿ 🏨 ✎ 🅿 See Where to Stay: p144.

Completed in 2009 as the second-tallest building in Chicago after Willis Tower, Trump Tower stands sleek and shiny on the edge of the Chicago River, reflecting the skyline in its stainless steel and glass facade. At 92 stories and 1,392 ft (425 m) tall, it is a significant addition to the Chicago skyline. It houses shops, a hotel, and condominiums, breaking the John Hancock Center's record as Chicago's tallest residence.

Non-residents can enjoy dinner at the hotel restaurant on the 16th floor, or the terrace lounge. Both offer spectacular panoramic vistas of Lake Michigan, the Chicago River, and the city.

Trump International Hotel & Tower by the Chicago River

Old Money

Chicago has a beautiful sound because Chicago means money – so the late actress Ruth Gordon reputedly said. By the turn of the century, 200 millionaires flourished in the city. One of the most prominent was dry-goods merchant and real-estate mogul Potter Palmer, who with his socialite wife Bertha Honore, had an enormous impact on the city's social, cultural, and economic life. Chicago's wealthy began to flock from the Prairie Avenue District, to the Gold Coast after Palmer built, in 1882, his opulent home (since demolished) at present-day 1350 North Lake Shore Drive. Department-store owner Marshall Field (see pp52–3), was less ostentatious in his display of wealth. Although he rode in a carriage to work, he always walked the last few blocks so people wouldn't see his transport. Likewise, he asked the architect of his $2-million, 25-room mansion not to include any frills. The influential Field also provided major funding to the Field Museum (see pp88–91) and the 1893 World's Fair.

Marshall Field

Sights at a Glance

Historic Buildings and Churches
❸ Dearborn Station
❺ Hilton Chicago
⓮ Glessner House
⓰ Clarke House and Museum
⓳ Pilgrim Baptist Church
㉑ Ida B. Wells-Barnett House

Historic Streets and Districts
❷ Printing House Row Historic District
❹ South Michigan Avenue
⓭ Prairie Avenue Historic District
⓱ Chinatown
⓴ Calumet-Giles-Prairie District

Modern Architecture
❶ Chicago Public Library, Harold Washington Library Center
⓲ Illinois Institute of Technology

Museums, Galleries, and Aquariums
❻ Spertus Museum
❼ Museum of Contemporary Photography
❿ *Field Museum pp88–91*
⓫ *John G. Shedd Aquarium pp98–9*
⓬ *Adler Planetarium pp94–5*
⓯ Willie Dixon's Blues Heaven Foundation

Parks and Fountains
❽ Grant Park
❾ Buckingham Fountain

◀ T. Thomas Memorial, Grant Park

SOUTH LOOP AND NEAR SOUTH SIDE

Two of Chicago's neighborhoods have always been areas of diversity, with dereliction and gentrification coexisting side by side. The South Loop developed as an industrial area in the late 1800s. But after World War II, manufacturers left and the area declined. Not until the 1970s did it again show signs of prosperity. The Near South Side also had cycles of boom and bust. After the 1871 fire, the city's elite created a wealthy enclave here that lasted until the early 1900s. Decay followed, as brothels and gambling houses formed the Levee vice district. In the 1940s, the Illinois Institute of Technology (IIT) transformed the area yet again. The contrasts remain striking. The oldest residence in the city, the Clarke House and Museum, is minutes by car from the sleek IIT campus; the city's teeming Chinatown borders the historic Black Metropolis.

See also Street Finder maps 3, 4, 5 & 6

| 0 meters | 500 |
| 0 yards | 500 |

For keys to symbols *see back flap*

Street-by-Street: South Loop

Just south of downtown, the South Loop has changed
dramatically in recent decades, from a run-down industrial
area to a residential and retail neighborhood. With the 1970s
conversion of the district's derelict warehouses to fashionable
lofts, businesses sprang up as Chicagoans took advantage of
the area's proximity to downtown. Today, the South Loop's
diversity is evident in its industrial heritage, the green
expanse of Grant Park, and the lively retail scene next door
to several outstanding museums.

**❶ ★ Harold Washington
Library Center**
Dominating the South Loop is
the world's largest public library
building, artwork displayed
throughout.

**❷ ★ Printing House
Row Historic District**
Many of this area's
historic warehouses,
built for the printing
trade, have been
converted into
fashionable apartments,
with numerous shops
and cafés at street level.

**The Transportation
Building** was one of
the earliest buildings
in Printers' Row to
be converted to
residential use
and helped start
the area's revival.

DEARBORN ST

PKWY

CONGRESS

HARRISON STREET

CLARK

STREET

POLK

STREET

LASALLE STREET

Details on the
Lakeside Press Building,
at 731 S Plymouth
Street, are typical of
the rich decoration of
buildings in this area.

The Second Franklin Building
Handsome tilework illustrates the history of printing
over its entranceway.

0 meters		100
0 yards		100

❼ Museum of Contemporary Photography

Focusing on American photography produced since 1959, the museum presents selections from its extensive collection and excellent temporary exhibitions.

❻ ★ Spertus Museum

This world-renowned collection of Judaic art highlights decorative objects and religious artifacts that span centuries of Jewish history.

Locator Map
See Street Finder maps 3 & 4

Key

— Suggested route

❹ South Michigan Avenue

Featuring a spectacular row of historic buildings, this is one of Chicago's grandest streets, an excellent place from which to admire the varied architectural styles for which the city is famous.

❺ Hilton Chicago

Decorated in the French Renaissance style, this 25-story building is one of Chicago's most opulent hotels and was the largest in the world when it opened in 1927.

Buddy Guy's Legends

This club presents both big-name and local blues acts. Proprietor and blues legend Buddy Guy can often be found among its patrons.

❸ Dearborn Station

Chicago's oldest surviving passenger train station building, an 1885 Richardsonian Romanesque design, has been converted into a multi-use building. Its square clock tower is a local landmark.

Harold Washington Library Center's ninth-floor Winter Garden

❶ Chicago Public Library, Harold Washington Library Center

400 S State St. **Map** 3 C2. **Tel** (312) 747-4300. Ⓜ Library. 🚌 2, 6, 29, 36, 62, 146, 147, 151. **Open** 9am–9pm Mon–Thu; 9am–5pm Fri–Sat; 1–5pm Sun. **Closed** major hols. 🅿 call (312) 747-4136. ⬛ 🎬 Exhibits, lectures, films. 🆆 chipublib.org/locations/15

This, the largest public library building in the world, was designed by Thomas Beeby – winner of a competition voted on by Chicagoans – and opened in 1991. It is named in honor of Chicago's first Black mayor.

Inspired by Greek and Roman structures – with five-story arched windows, vaulted ceilings, and decorative columns – the design also pays tribute to many of Chicago's historic buildings: the rusticated granite base recalls the Rookery (see p42), for example. Perched on each roof corner is a gigantic sculpted barn owl representing wisdom; over the main entrance, a great horned owl with a 20-ft (6-m) wingspan grips a book in its talons. The library holds close to two million books and periodicals on its 90 miles (145 km) of shelving. Artwork is displayed throughout the building, including work by Cheyenne

Carved detail on façade of the historic Lakeside Press Building

artist Heap of Birds. On the ninth floor is the beautiful light-suffused Winter Garden.

❷ Printing House Row Historic District

S Federal, S Dearborn, & S Plymouth sts.; between W Congress Pkwy & W Polk St. **Map** 3 C3. Ⓜ Harrison.

By the mid-1890s, Chicago was the printing capital of the US. The majority of this industry centered in a two-block area now known as Printing House Row Historic District. Nearby Dearborn Street railroad station (see p85) facilitated rapid industrial development in the neighborhood. However, by the 1970s, when the station closed, most of the printing companies had already moved out of the area.

Many of the massive, solid buildings erected to hold heavy printing machinery remain today. Their conversion into stylish condominiums and office lofts has led to the revitalization of the neighborhood and an influx of commercial activity.

The landmark Pontiac Building (542 South Dearborn Street; 1891) is the oldest surviving Holabird and Roche (see p29) building in Chicago. Several other noteworthy buildings line South Dearborn Street. The 1883 Donohue Building (Nos. 701–721) has an impressive arched entranceway, Romanesque Revival styling (see p28), and a birdcage elevator in the lobby. The Rowe Building (No. 714, c.1882) houses the excellent Sandmeyer's Bookstore, specializing in local authors and travel literature. The Second Franklin Building (No. 720) is significant for the ornamental tilework gracing its facade. Above the entrance is a delightful terra-cotta mural of a medieval print shop.

Rowe Building on Dearborn Street, in the Printing House Row District

❸ Dearborn Station

47 W Polk St. **Map** 3 C3. **Tel** 554-4408.
Ⓜ Harrison. **Open** 7am–9pm Mon–
Fri; 8am–5pm Sat. **Closed** major
public hols. 🖉 🖵

Dearborn Station, built in
1885, is the oldest surviving
passenger railroad station
building in Chicago, and
is a monument to the historic
importance of the nation's
coast-to-coast rail system.
By the turn of the century,
more than 100 trains (from
25 different railroad
companies) and 17,000
passengers passed through
the station each day.

Designed by Cyrus L.W.
Eidlitz, the station features
masonry walls and terra-cotta
arches in the Richardsonian
Romanesque style *(see p28)*.
A 1922 fire destroyed the roof,
attic, and upper story. The clock
tower was rebuilt and stands
today as the striking terminus
of Dearborn Street, visible from
the northern Loop.

The station closed its
passenger service in 1971. After
a period of neglect, in 1986,
amid much controversy, the
building's train shed was
demolished. The building was
subsequently converted into a
dynamic shopping mall and
office complex, which helped to
revitalize the area. Today, many
of its original features have since
been restored.

View along South Michigan Avenue looking north

❹ South Michigan Avenue

S Michigan Ave. from E Madison
St. to E Balbo Ave. **Map** 4 C2–C3.
Ⓜ Madison.

South Michigan Avenue is
the place to revel in the
monumental solidity of late
19th- and early 20th-century
architecture. This historic
street has been described
variously as a "cliff" and a "wall."
Be warned: you may strain
your neck gazing up to the
tops of these massive
structures. The longest span
of pre-1920 buildings in
Chicago, South Michigan
Avenue contains numerous
architectural styles, from
the Gothic-inspired *(see p28)*
Chicago Athletic Association
Building (No. 12) to the
Chicago School *(see pp28–9)*
Gage Building (No. 18), one
of three buildings making up
the Gage Group. The Gage
Building was designed by
Holabird and Roche; Louis
Sullivan designed the terra-
cotta facade.

At Nos. 24 and 30 are striking
examples of Chicago windows
(see p29), which allowed in plenty
of light and air for the milliners,
who once worked here.

The School of the Art
Institute of Chicago residence
(No. 112) contains a frieze
of the Greek god Zeus
overseeing athletic games,
a decorative detail that
reflects the original 1908
purpose of the building as
the home of the Illinois
Athletic Club.

❺ Hilton Chicago

720 S Michigan Ave. **Map** 4 D3.
Tel (312) 922-4400. Ⓜ Harrison.
Open 24 hrs daily. ♿ 🖉 🅿 See
Where to Stay: *p144.*

When it opened in 1927,
this 25-story hotel had 3,000
rooms, a rooftop 18-hole
miniature golf course, its own
hospital, and a 1,200-seat
theater. After the owner went
bankrupt in the mid-1930s,
the World War II Army Air
Corps purchased the Holabird
and Roche-designed redbrick
building, converting the
grand ballroom to a
mess hall.

In 1945, Conrad Hilton
acquired the building,
reopening the hotel in 1951.
Further renovations from 2000
to 2004 secured the hotel's
reputation for opulence. Its
lofty centerpiece is the
ballroom, a space decorated
in the French Renaissance style,
featuring mirrored doors and
walls, arched windows, and
huge crystal chandeliers. The
hallway is equally ornate, with
fluted columns, a marble
stairway, and a cloud mural
painted on the ceiling.

The former Dearborn Station's
high-ceilinged atrium

Marble fountain, lobby of
the Hilton Chicago

Interior of the Museum of Contemporary Photography

❻ Spertus Museum

610 S Michigan Ave. **Map** 4 D3.
Tel (312) 322-1700. Ⓜ Harrison.
Open 10am–5pm Sun–Wed (to 6pm
Thu, to 3pm Fri). **Closed** Sat, major
public and Jewish hols. 🅰 (free
10am–noon Tue, 3–7pm Thu). ♿ 📷
🎞 Concerts, lectures, films.
ⓦ **spertus.edu**

Spertus Museum, Chicago's
Jewish museum, is in the
superb Spertus Institute of
Jewish Studies building.
Designed by Chicago
architects Krueck and Sexton,
it opened in 2007. This
innovative facility features a
10-story faceted window wall
that stands out among the
masonry-faced buildings
surrounding it. The building
contains interlocking interior
spaces and offers spectacular
views of Chicago's skyline,
Grant Park, and Lake Michigan.
Highlights of the museum
include a unique visible
storage depot that showcases
its world-class collection of
art and artifacts, including
ritual objects, textiles, and
jewelry; changing special
exhibitions that explore
identity and contemporary
culture; site-specific
installations of work
commissioned from inter-
national artists; an innovative
Children's Center designed
with Redmoon Theater's
artistic director Jim Lasko;
and a resource center for
parents and teachers.
    The institute also contains
the research facilities of the
Asher Library and Chicago
Jewish archives. A green roof

and a tenth-floor sky garden
offer sweeping views. The
second-floor Wolfgang Puck
café is the only kosher café in
downtown Chicago. On the
first floor a gift- and bookshop
offers items created by some
of Israel's hottest designers.
The Feinberg Theater provides
programs of performance,
film, comedy, as well as
lectures by today's leading
thinkers, writers, and scholars.

❼ Museum of Contemporary Photography

600 S Michigan Ave. **Map** 4 D3.
Tel (312) 663-5554. Ⓜ Harrison.
🚌 1, 2, 3, 3L, 4, 6, 10, 14, 29, 127,
130, 146. **Open** 10am–5pm Mon–Sat;
10am–8pm Thu; noon–5pm Sun.
Closed major hols, Dec 25–
Jan 1. ♿ 1st, 2nd floors only.
Lectures, films. ⓦ **mocp.org**

Founded by Columbia
College Chicago in 1984
to collect, exhibit, and
promote contemporary
photography, the Museum
of Contemporary Photography
is the only museum in the
Midwest devoted exclusively
to this medium. Wide-ranging
provocative and innovative
exhibitions, housed in the
college's historic 1907
building, change regularly
as do selections from the
collection of more than 5,000
American photographs
produced since 1945.
    Temporary exhibitions
explore photography's
many roles: as artistic
expression, as documentary
chronicler, as commercial
industry, and as a powerful
scientific and technological
tool. The Midwest
Photographers Project,
which contains work by
regional photographers,
rotates annually.

❽ Grant Park

From Randolph St. to Roosevelt Rd.,
between Michigan Ave. & Lake
Michigan. **Map** 4 E2–E4. **Tel** (312) 742-
7648. Ⓜ Randolph; Madison; Adams.
🗓 See Through the Year: pp34–7.

Grant Park is the splendid
centerpiece of the 23-mile-
(37-km-) long band of green
stretching along the Lake
Michigan shoreline from the
city's south end to its northern
suburbs. Although bisected
by busy streets, the park
offers a tranquil retreat from
noisy downtown, serving
as Chicago's playground,

The main entrance to Grant Park, Ivan Mestrovic's *Bowman* to the right

View of Grant Park, looking north

garden, promenade, and sculpture park all in one, and hosting summer concerts and festivals.

The park is built on landfill and debris dumped after the 1871 Fire. Originally called Lake Park, it was renamed in 1901 for the 18th US president, Ulysses S. Grant, who lived in Galena (see p136). In 1893, the World's Columbian Exposition was held in the south end of the park.

Although the park was intended as public ground, free of buildings, various structures were erected. Not until 1890, when businessman Aaron Montgomery Ward initiated a series of lawsuits which dragged on for more than 20 years, was the preservation of Grant Park for public recreation secured.

Daniel H. Burnham and Edward H. Bennett's 1909 Plan of Chicago (see p32) envisioned the park as the "intellectual center of Chicago." The renowned landscape-architecture firm Olmsted Brothers designed the park in a French Renaissance style reminiscent of the gardens at Versailles. The symmetrical layout includes large rectangular "rooms," grand promenades, formal tree plantings, sculptures, and the central Buckingham Fountain.

A noteworthy footnote is that the park was the site of the 1968 Democratic Convention riots, when anti-Vietnam War protesters clashed with police.

❾ Buckingham Fountain

In Grant Park, east of Columbus Dr., at the foot of Congress Pkwy. **Map** 4 E3. **Tel** 742-7529. Ⓜ Harrison.

Throughout the summer one of the showiest and most impressive sights in Chicago is the water shooting from the 133 jets of Grant Park's Buckingham Fountain, culminating dramatically in a spray 150 ft (45 m) high. The fountain's one-and-a-half million gallons (5.7 million liters) of water recirculate through a computer-operated pumping system at a rate of 14,000 gallons (53,000 liters) per minute.

Hundreds of spotlights hidden within the fountain are used to create a dazzling show of colored lights. The 20-minute shows, set to music, are held from dusk to 10pm every hour on the hour, from April to October.

Financed by Kate Sturges Buckingham (1858–1937) in honor of her brother, Clarence (1854–1913), a trustee and benefactor of the Art Institute of Chicago, the fountain was designed by Marcel Francois Loyau (sculptor), Jacques Lambert (engineer), and Edward H. Bennett (architect).

The design, based on the Latona Basin in the gardens of Versailles but twice the size of that fountain, incorporates a ground-level pool 280 ft (85 m) wide, with three concentric basins rising above. In 1927, it was dedicated as the world's largest decorative fountain.

Constructed of pink marble, the Beaux-Arts fountain symbolizes Lake Michigan. The four pairs of 20-ft- (6-m-) tall seahorses diagonally across the fountain from each other represent the four US states bordering the lake: Illinois, Wisconsin, Indiana, and Michigan.

Buckingham Fountain, with sculpted seahorses in the foreground

⑩ Field Museum

The Field Museum is one of the world's great natural history museums, with a collection of over 25 million objects (just under one per cent are displayed). Following the success of the 1893 World's Columbian Exposition, a group of prominent Chicagoans decided to create a museum with objects from the fair. With funding from Marshall Field *(see p79)*, they opened, in 1894, the Columbian Museum of Chicago in Jackson Park's Palace of the Fine Arts, one of the fair's finest buildings. This lodging soon proved too small for the museum. In 1921, its current home – a white-marble Neo-Classical structure designed by Daniel H. Burnham – was built, and The Field Museum, with its celebrated collection of anthropological, botanical, zoological, and geological objects, opened to the public.

★ **Crown Family Playlab**
A miniature interactive world of art, music, science, and nature.

Egyptian Mummy Mask
This decorative linen-and-plaster burial mask encased a mummified child.

Key To Floorplan

▢ Animals, plants, and ecosystems
▢ Rocks and fossils
▢ Ancient Egypt
▢ Americas
▢ Pacific cultures
▢ Special exhibits
▢ Nonexhibition space

Ground Level

Lions of Tsavo
The two lions that, in 1898, terrorized a Kenyan outpost, consuming 35 workers before being shot, are on display in the Mammals of Africa gallery.

Museum Guide

The museum has three levels: ground, main, and upper. Most of the exhibition galleries are on the main and upper levels. Each level has east and west wings; those of the main and upper are bisected by a large central hall. The upper level features exhibitions on nature (plants and earth sciences), dinosaurs, and Pacific cultures. Exhibits on the main level focus on animals, birds, and American Indians. The highlight of the ground level is the Underground Adventure exhibition.

Hall of Jades
This impressive collection of over 500 jade artifacts includes items from Neolithic burial sites, the Chinese Dynasties, and the early 20th century.

Upper Level

★ **Pawnee Earth Lodge**
The only precise recreation of a fully furnished Pawnee earth lodge, this interactive exhibit showcases traditional artifacts used by 19th-century Great Plains Indians.

Main Level

★ **Sue**
The original bones of *Sue*, the world's largest *Tyrannosaurus rex*, are on display in the Stanley Field Hall. Other spectacular fossils can be seen in the Dino Zone on the upper level.

Field Museum Store

Egyptian Mastaba is a reconstruction incorporating two rooms from a 4,400-year-old tomb. Visitors can roam through it, as the deceased's spirit was meant to.

Main Entrance

African Elephants
These bull elephants are 1905 specimens from Kenya. One bull is poised to plunge its only tusk into the other as it rears.

Exploring the Field Museum

With its encyclopedic collection of cultural objects and biological specimens from around the globe, the Field Museum warrants many trips. More than 40 permanent exhibitions are supplemented with fascinating temporary shows. Particular strengths of the museum are dinosaur fossils – highlighted by the exhibit on Sue, the most complete *Tyrannosaurus rex* skeleton ever found – American Indian artifacts, botanical specimens, and displays relating to mammals and birds. Major crowd pleasers, especially for children, are Underground Adventure, which explores the rich diversity of life in the soil, and Inside Ancient Egypt, focusing on that civilization's funerary practices.

The monumental Neo-Classical entrance to the Field Museum

Animals, Plants, and Ecosystems

One of the museum's missions is to encourage prudent stewardship of our environment. This theme is highlighted in the animal, plant, and ecosystem exhibits, which emphasize the interconnectedness of all life on Earth. The Messages from the Wilderness gallery is a good place to start your exploration. Eighteen wilderness park settings, from the Arctic to Argentina, incorporate representative mammals and their habitats.

Also here is the Local Woodlands Four Seasons Diorama, completed in 1902 by taxidermist Carl Akeley, who transformed the way museums displayed animals. For Akeley, habitat accuracy and the authenticity of background details were equally important. Thus, each of the 17,000 wax leaves in the diorama is cast separately from a real one.

The main-level galleries in the west wing provide an overview of animal biology, behavior, and habitats, with samples from the museum's 17 million zoological specimens. Outstanding exhibits are Mammals of Asia and Mammals of Africa. Suspended from the ceiling in the World of Mammals gallery is the massive skeleton of a Right whale. The museum's collection of birds is also particularly strong, with its informative Bird Habitats, World of Birds, and North American Birds galleries.

A popular attraction is Bushman, a lowland gorilla brought from West Africa to Lincoln Park Zoo in the 1920s. So beloved by Chicagoans that the mayor gave him a voter's registration card, Bushman died in 1951. He was then moved to the museum where, preserved, he continues to delight visitors. Opened in 2011, the Field's newest permanent exhibition "Restoring Earth" uses photographs, videos and hands-on learning tools to immerse visitors in adventures with museum scientists as they promote conservation in various parts of the world.

The museum's 2.6 million botanical specimens encompass all major plant groups and every continent. Particularly rich in flowering plants and ferns of the Americas, this is the world's largest museum exhibit dedicated exclusively to plants. The tropical aerial garden has remarkably lifelike reproductions made from wax, glass and wire.

A golden eagle clutching its prey, by taxidermist Carl Akeley

Rocks and Fossils

Two of the 12 Martian meteorites on display in museums around the world are here at the Field Museum. You can touch non-Martian meteorite pieces on the upper floor, in the Earth Sciences galleries. Other fascinating and beautiful rocks in the 500-specimen display are a topaz the size of a pear, in the sparkling Grainger Hall of Gems, and a 312-lb (142-kg) block of lapis lazuli, one of the largest ever found and its origin still a puzzle.

The museum has a renowned collection of dinosaur fossils. The centerpiece, displayed in the Stanley Field Hall, is 67-million-year-old Sue, the largest, most complete *Tyrannosaurus rex* skeleton ever found. It was discovered near the Black Hills of South Dakota in 1990 by fossil-hunter Sue Hendrickson. The restored skeleton, the skull alone weighing 600 lb (270 kg), was unveiled in 2000. Interactive exhibits tell the story of its

A collection of marine skeletons, exoskeletons, and fossils

For hotels and restaurants see pp142–5 and pp148–57

A gargantuan *Apatosaurus* dinosaur skeleton

development of intricate pharaonic tombs. Here, the remains of a 5,500-year-old woman are displayed, along with items such as pottery jars thought to be needed in the afterlife. A partial reconstruction of a *mastaba*, a multiroom "mansion of eternity," features a false door at which the earth-bound and the wandering spirits meet.

Other extraordinary artifacts include the fully preserved inner coffin of Chenet-a-a, a woman who lived between 945 BC and 712 BC. It is not known what is inside the coffin since it has never been opened or X-rayed.

Ceremonial dance mask worn by Alaskan Eskimo shamans

ceremonies of this Pacific Northwest tribe. Panels on the mask are opened and closed by the dancer wearing it to show various faces.

Pacific Cultures

The highlight of the Pacific cultures exhibits, with a section on headhunting and a re-creation of a Tahitian market, is the sacred Maori meetinghouse, Ruatepupuke II. Built in 1881 in New Zealand, it was acquired by the museum in 1905. The 55-ft- (17-m-) long, beautifully carved house symbolizes the body of the Maori ancestor Ruatepupuke, credited with sharing the art of woodcarving with the world. The house's ridgepole represents his spine, the rafters his ribs, and the expansive roof-boards his arms, open in greeting. It is the only Maori meetinghouse in the western hemisphere and remains governed by Maori customs.

discovery. Scientists now know that Sue was 28 years old at the time of her death. By counting the rings in one of her rib bones, they determined Sue went through a teenage growth spurt between the ages of 14 and 18, during which she gained 4.6 lb (2.1 kg) each day.

The Hall of Jades displays jade artifacts along a chronological storyline from Neolithic burial sites through the Bronze Age, the Chinese Dynasties, and into the early 20th century. A 300 lb (136 kg) jar that once stood in the Imperial Palace of Emperor Qianlong is a highlight of the exhibit.

Ancient Egypt

The museum's Ancient Egyptian holdings consist of more than 1,400 rare artifacts, including statues, hiero-glyphics, and mummies. The predynastic burial exhibit reveals Egypt's intriguing burial practices before the

Isty's Book of the Dead, an ancient papyrus scroll

A Pacific Coast Indian carved figure, once a house entranceway

Americas

The museum's holdings of artifacts from North American Indian tribes reflect one of the Field's main missions: to encourage improved understanding among cultures. Ceremonial objects and splendid totem poles – two Haida examples rise to the ceiling of Stanley Field Hall – are just some of the treasures in this exhibit.

The Pawnee Earth Lodge, a life-size reproduction, was built in conjunction with the Pawnee, a group of American Indians based in Oklahoma.

The 19th-century cedar Kwakiutl transformation masks are colorful and vivid. Such masks are often used during the

Spirit mask from Papua New Guinea

⑪ John G. Shedd Aquarium

See pp98–9.

⑫ Adler Planetarium

See pp94–5.

⑬ Prairie Avenue Historic District

Prairie Ave., from 18th to Cullerton sts. **Map** 6 D1. Ⓜ Cermak-Chinatown then bus 21. ⚫ Jul–Sep: 2pm 2nd & 4th Sun; call (312) 326-1480. ♿

When the city of Chicago was incorporated in 1837, the area now known as the Prairie Avenue Historic District was not much more than a strip of sandy prairie bordering Lake Michigan. Its fortunes changed dramatically when the 1871 fire destroyed the city center. Chicago's wealthy, including George Pullman *(see p121)* and Marshall Field *(see p79)*, moved to the Near South Side, building their grand mansions along Prairie Avenue. It remained a mecca for the city's socialites until the late 1800s and early 1900s, when the rapidly growing Gold Coast area superseded Prairie Avenue as the address of choice. Many mansions fell to the wrecker's ball

The imposing Richardsonian Romanesque façade of Glessner House

(plaques along Prairie Avenue mark the sites of demolished houses), but those that remain offer a glimpse into its 19th-century splendor.

Along with Glessner House, highlights of the district include the Kimball House (No. 1801). This mansion, designed by Solon Spencer Beman in 1890, is one of the best remaining examples in the US of the Chateauesque style. Clarke House, the oldest house in Chicago, was moved to its current location on Indiana Avenue in 1977 to provide an additional attraction for the district.

Elbridge G. Keith House (No. 1900) is the oldest extant mansion on Prairie Avenue. Built in 1870, it was designed by John W. Roberts in the Italianate style *(see p28)*.

At 1936 South Michigan Avenue is the magnificent neo-Gothic Second Presbyterian Church, designed by James Renwick in 1874. Inside are 22 stained-glass windows by Louis C. Tiffany and 2 windows painted by British Pre-Raphaelite artist Edward Burne-Jones.

The district is reputedly close to the site of a grim event: the 1812 massacre of settlers fleeing Fort Dearborn *(see p17)*.

Elbridge G. Keith House on Prairie Avenue

⑭ Glessner House

1800 S Prairie Ave. **Map** 6 D1. **Tel** (312) 326-1480. Ⓜ Cermak-Chinatown. ⚫ mandatory: 1pm, 3pm Wed–Sun (except public hols). ♿ (free Wed). 🔊 Lectures.
Ⓦ **glessnerhouse.org**

The only extant residential design in Chicago by Boston architect Henry Hobson Richardson, whose signature style became known as Richardsonian Romanesque *(see p28)*, Glessner House helped change the face of residential architecture.

Commissioned by farm-machinery manufacturer John J. Glessner and his wife, Frances, in 1885 and completed in 1887, the two-story house represented a radical departure from traditional design and created a furor in the exclusive Prairie Avenue neighborhood. George Pullman is said to have proclaimed: "I do not know what I have ever done to have that thing staring me in the face every time I go out of my door."

A fortress-like building of rough-hewn pinkish gray granite with three modified turrets, the house dominates its corner site. The main rooms and many of the large windows face a southern courtyard. The striking simplicity of the design is perhaps best reflected in the main entrance arch, which frames a heavy oak door ornamented with grillwork.

The beautifully restored interior boasts a world-class collection of decorative art objects. Most were purchased or commissioned by the Glessners, who were keenly interested in the British Arts and Crafts movement of the late 19th and early 20th centuries. Adherents of the philosophy that everyday objects should be artistically crafted, they filled the house with tiles, draperies, and wallpaper designed by William Morris. Handcrafted pieces, from furniture to ceramics, by American designer Isaac E. Scott grace the rooms.

⑮ Willie Dixon's Blues Heaven Foundation

2120 S Michigan Ave. **Map** 6 D1. **Tel** (312) 808-1286. Ⓜ Cermak-Chinatown then bus 21. 🚌 1, 3, 4. **Open** 11am–4pm Mon–Fri, noon–2pm Sat; call ahead (mandatory). **Closed** Sun & public hols. 🎫 ♿ 🎥 (for groups). 🖥 📷

Mississippi native Willie Dixon, was one of the most prolific American blues legends alongside Muddy Waters. He set up the non-profit Blues Heaven Foundation in the 1980s to promote the musical genre, and financially support blues musicians in need.

The Blues Heaven Foundation is located in the former Chess Records Office and Studio, was declared a Chicago Landmark in 1990, and has been protected ever since. Slowly but surely the building is being restored to the glory of its mid-century heyday.

Public hours are limited so it is important to call ahead before visiting. For other than die-hard fans of the blues, there may not be much of interest apart and beyond the hour-long documentary about local blues history.

There are, however, several rooms (the former Chess offices) which have on display, framed photographs of famous

musicians/bands, from Chuck Berry to The Rolling Stones, who recorded there.

The real reason to visit the Blues Heaven Foundation is the tour guide: often Alex Dixon, the grandson of Willie Dixon, who is happy to offer story after story of his grandfather's recording streaks alongside blues greats such as Howlin' Wolf, Etta James, Muddy Wates and more.

⑯ Clarke House and Museum

1827 S Indiana Ave. **Map** 6 D1. **Tel** (312) 326-1480. Ⓜ Cermak-Chinatown then bus 21. 🎫 mandatory: noon, 2pm Wed–Sun (departs from Glessner House). **Closed** public hols. 🎫 (free Wed). ♿ 🖥 clarke housemuseum.org

Built in 1836, Clarke House is Chicago's oldest surviving building, a Greek Revival-style house constructed for merchant Henry B. Clarke and his wife Caroline. The house originally stood on what is now South Michigan Avenue but was then an old Indian path. When the house sold in 1872, the new owners moved it 28 blocks south, to 4526 South Wabash Avenue. In 1977, the City purchased the house and then, in a feat of engineering, hoisted the 120-ton structure over the 44th Street "L" tracks, moving it to its present location one block southeast of the original Clarke property.

The dining room in the Clarke House and Museum

Four Roman Doric columns mark the east entrance to the house. Solidly constructed of timber frame, with a white clapboard exterior, the two-story house was damaged in a 1977 fire. It has now been painstakingly restored, even adhering to the original color scheme, which researchers determined by delving under 27 layers of paint.

Now a museum showcasing an interior reflecting the period 1836–60, Clarke House offers a fascinating glimpse into early Chicago domestic life. It is so historically accurate that the first-floor lighting simulates gas lighting, and the upper floor has no artificial lights. A gallery in the basement documents the history of the house.

Behind the house is the Chicago Women's Park and Garden (see p190).

The Greek Revival facade of the Clarke House and Museum

⑫ Adler Planetarium

The Adler Planetarium has one of the finest astronomical collections in the world, with artifacts dating as far back as 12th-century Persia. It also has the world's first virtual-reality theater. Spectacular sky shows complement displays on navigation, the solar system, and space exploration. State-of-the-art technology enables visitors to explore exhibits hands-on.

When the Adler opened in 1930, it was the first modern planetarium in the western hemisphere. Businessman Max Adler funded the 12-sided, granite-and-marble Art Deco structure, designed by Ernest Grunsfeld. This original building, with its copper dome and a bronze depiction of a sign of the zodiac on each of the 12 corners, is now a historical landmark.

★ Definiti Space Theater
The world's first digital theater offers an unrivaled virtual-reality environment in which visitors can participate in a journey beyond the solar system.

★ Atwood Sphere
Step into North America's only walk-in planetarium, built in 1913. Light enters through the 692 holes in the surface of this huge metal ball, representing the stars in Chicago's night sky. The "stars" move across the "sky" as the sphere, powered by a motor, slowly rotates.

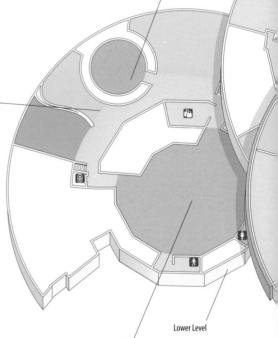

Lower Level

Key To Floor Plan

- Landmark exhibition space
- Sky Pavilion exhibition space
- Sky Pavilion special exhibits
- Grainger Sky Theater
- Definiti Space Theater
- Nonexhibition space

Universe in Your Hands
Learn about a time when people believed that Earth was the center of the universe. Astrolabes, armillary spheres, and sundials illustrate medieval conceptions of the world.

The Adler Planetarium building, the first modern planetarium in the western hemisphere, is now a historical landmark.

Our Solar System
Investigate through interactive exhibits the worlds that orbit the Sun, and program a computer-activated Rover to move across simulated Martian terrain.

The Milky Way Galaxy

★ **Milky Way Galaxy**
Immerse yourself in a 3-D, computer-animated trip through the Milky Way.

Middle Level

Upper Level

★ **Shoot for the Moon**
Stories of space exploration and future plans to return to the moon are covered in this exhibition. It includes the fully restored Gemini 12 spacecraft.

Main Entrance

Grainger Sky Theater is one of the most technologically advanced theaters in the world, with 20 different projectors making one seamless image.

Sky Pavilion
A stunning view of the city's skyline can be seen from Galileo's café, in the Sky Pavilion. This two-story addition to the east side of the landmark building also houses exhibition space and the Definiti Space Theater.

A Chinatown grocery shop

⓱ Chinatown

S Wentworth Ave., north & south of
Cermak Rd. **Map** 5 B1–C1. **Tel** (312)
326-5320. Ⓜ Cermak-Chinatown. 🚲
See Where to Eat and Drink: p146.
Ⓦ **chicagochinatown.org**

A red and green gateway
decorated with Chinese
characters inscribed by
Dr. Sun Yet-Sen,
founder of the
Republic of China,
arches over
Wentworth Avenue
just south of
Cermak Road. It
marks the entrance
to the largest
Chinatown in the
Midwest. A lively area full
of Asian grocery and herbal
shops, bakeries, and
restaurants, this densely
packed neighborhood of
approximately 10,000 residents
has been home to Chicago's
highest concentration of
Chinese people since just
before World War I.

Traditional Chinese
architecture is evident
throughout the colorful
streetscape. The temple-like
Pui Tak Center (2216 South

Detail of decorative tile on
the Chinese Cultural Center

Wentworth Avenue) was
originally the On Leong
Chinese Merchants' Association
Building; it is now a cultural
center. Sculpted lions at the
doorway guard its street-level
shops; terra-cotta ornaments
bedeck the walls. Modern
Chinatown Square Mall
(Archer, Cermak, 18th,
and Wentworth)
quarters shops
and a plaza
surrounded by
zodiac sculptures
and a mosaic mural.
Annual Chinatown
celebrations
include the Dragon
Boat Races in the
summer and the Moon Festival
in September.

⓲ Illinois Institute of Technology

31st to 35th sts, between Dan Ryan
Expy & S Michigan Ave. **Map** 5 C4–D4.
Tel (312) 567-3000. Ⓜ Sox-35th;
35-Bronzeville-IIT. 🚌 29, 35.
Ⓦ **iit.edu**

The Illinois Institute of
Technology (IIT) is a world
leader in engineering,
technology, and architecture.
The main campus is an
outstanding example of the
work of influential architect
Ludwig Mies van der Rohe
(see p32), who was hired by
architect John A. Holabird to
direct the Armour Institute's
architecture school and design
the new campus.

In the campus plan, along
with the 22 IIT buildings he
designed, Mies expressed his
modernist view that form
follow function. Geometric and
unadorned glass-sheathed
curtain-wall structures
epitomize Mies' International
style. One of Mies' masterpieces is the **S.R. Crown Hall**
(1956). This glass-walled
pavilion is an early example of
a large clear-span structure,
the four exterior columns
supporting the girders from
which the roof is hung. The
building appears to float in
space. Of it, Mies said: "This
is the clearest structure we
have done, the best to express
our philosophy."

Alumni Memorial Hall, Mies'
first classroom building on the
campus, is another notable
example of structure also
functioning as ornament. The
steel grid of the curtain wall
suggests the steel structure
within. In **Wishnick Hall**, the
curtain wall stops short of the
corner to reveal the load-
bearing column.

St. Saviour's Chapel, known
waggishly as the "God box,"
is believed to be Mies' only
church design.

The campus is also home to
the magnificent redbrick
Richardsonian Romanesque
Main Building. Designed by
Patten and Fisher (1891–3), it is
IIT's most visible landmark.

S.R. Crown Hall on the Illinois Institute of Technology campus

For hotels and restaurants see pp142–5 and pp148–57

There are two complexes of note. The McCormick Tribune Campus Center, designed by Rem Koolhaas, features a sound-buffering, concrete and steel tube that encloses the "L" tracks passing directly over the building. A residence hall complex designed by Helmut Jahn consists of terrace-topped buildings joined by glass walls that muffle train noise. A map of the campus is available from Hermann Union Hall.

🄳 Pilgrim Baptist Church

3301 S Indiana Ave. **Map** 6 D4. Office. Ⓜ 35-Bronzeville-IIT. **Closed** until further notice.

This landmark building was built in 1890–91 and designed by Adler and Sullivan for Chicago's oldest Jewish congregation, Kehilath Anshe Ma'ariv. It then became the Pilgrim Baptist Church from 1926 until January 2006 when it was destroyed by fire.

The magnificent arched doorway was the only surviving example of an ecclesiastical arch by Adler and Sullivan and reflected the strong masonry forms of the exterior. Terra-cotta panels of foliage designs provided ornament. Plans have been drawn up for its renovation but no date

has been set for its reopening to the public.

🄴 Calumet-Giles-Prairie District

Calumet to Prairie aves, from 31st to 35th sts. **Map** 6 D4. Ⓜ 35-Bronzeville-IIT.

This small enclave of restored Victorian houses was granted national landmark status in 1980. Of particular interest is Joseph Deimel House (3141 South Calumet Avenue), designed in 1887 by Adler and Sullivan and the only remaining residential commission by the firm in this area.

The Joliet limestone row houses (3144–8 South Calumet Avenue), built in 1881, are a fine example of Victorian row-house architecture.

However, only three of the original eight houses are still standing. A block to the south are the only row houses Frank Lloyd Wright designed (1894) – the Robert W. Roloson Houses (3213–19 South Calumet Avenue). Like Robie House *(see pp104–105)*, Wright used Roman bricks for the walls, here decorated with terra-cotta panels between the upper-story windows.

A trio of Richardsonian Romanesque *(see p28)* townhouses in sandstone, greenstone, and limestone are found at 3356–60 South Calumet Avenue.

Victory monument in the Calumet-Giles-Prairie District

Ida B. Wells-Barnett House

🄵 Ida B. Wells-Barnett House

3624 S King Dr. **Map** 6 E5. Ⓜ 35-Bronzeville-IIT. **Closed** to public.

Civil rights and women's suffrage advocate Ida B. Wells (1862–1931) lived in this house with her husband from 1919 to 1930. Born a slave in Mississippi, Wells became a teacher at age 14 but was dismissed for protesting segregation.

Wells' work as a columnist for *Memphis Free Speech* brought her to Chicago in 1893 to report on the lack of African-American representation at the World's Columbian Exposition. She moved to Chicago in 1895 and married Ferdinand Lee Barnett, the founder of Chicago's first Black newspaper, the *Conservator*.

Playing a key role in the 1909 founding of the National Association for the Advancement of Colored People, Wells is perhaps best known for her anti-lynching campaign, which brought national attention to the issue.

The house, designed in 1889 by Joseph A. Thain in a hybrid style of Romanesque and Victorian Gothic style, was designated a national historic landmark in 1973 in Wells' honor. An interesting feature is the corner turret made of pressed metal.

Facade of the Pilgrim Baptist Church, with its distinctive doorway

⓫ John G. Shedd Aquarium

Nearly 32,000 saltwater and freshwater animals, representing 1500 species of fish, reptiles, amphibians, invertebrates, birds, and mammals, live at the John G. Shedd Aquarium. Named after its benefactor, an influential Chicago businessman, the aquarium opened in 1930 in a Neo-Classical building designed by the firm Graham, Anderson, Probst & White. The Abbott Oceanarium and its magnificent curved wall of glass, face out to Lake Michigan. This pavilion showcases beluga whales and dolphins while Wild Reef recreates a coral reef, and houses sharks and other large predators.

Aerial view of the Shedd Aquarium, looking north toward Grant Park

★ **Abbott Oceanarium**
Beluga whales, Pacific white-sided dolphins, Alaska sea otters, tidal-pool creatures, and other marine animals live in this gigantic saltwater habitat, which seems to extend into Lake Michigan, a dramatic effect created by the stunning 475-ft- (145-m-) long glass wall. Watch dolphins and whales during daily aquatic shows, or come face to face with them in the Polar Play Zone with underwater views.

A nature trail leads visitors along winding paths through a re-created Pacific Northwest coastal forest, complete with streams and replicas of 70 species of plants.

Sea Otter Cove features informal chats about these smallest of marine mammals.

Key

- ▢ Aquarium
- ▢ Oceanarium
- ▢ Animal underwaterviewing
- ▢ Special exhibits
- ▢ Nonexhibition space

Beluga Whales
Several whales live in the Abbott Oceanarium's Secluded Bay, some of which were born at the aquarium.

For hotels and restaurants see pp142–5 and pp148–57

At Home on the Great Lakes
showcases native fish of the Great Lakes basin, including Lake Sturgeon in a touch pool.

Oceans
As part of the Waters of the World galleries, here you can see an array of animals from tide pools to the ocean floor. Particularly fascinating is the giant Pacific octopus, one of the largest species in the world.

VISITORS' CHECKLIST

Practical Information
1200 S Lake Shore Dr. **Map** 4 E4. **Tel** (312) 939-2438. **Open** Memorial Day–Labor Day: 9am–6pm daily (mid-Jun–Aug: 9am–10pm Wed). Labor Day–Memorial Day: 9am–5pm Mon–Fri; 9am–6pm Sat, Sun, public hols. **Closed** Dec 25. 🚫 (see website for various free days). ♿ 🅰 🚭 📷 🅿 Lectures.
w sheddaquarium.org

Transport
Ⓜ Roosevelt then free trolley.
🚌 146. 🚉 Roosevelt then free trolley.

Wild Reef
The blue-spot stingray is among the 500 species of reef fish on view in this underground wing. Also housed here is one of the most diverse displays of sharks in North America.

★ Amazon Rising
Experience all four seasons affecting the floodplain forest of the mighty Amazon River, and encounter stingrays, dart frogs, caimans, and many more creatures of the Amazon.

Main Entrance

Asia, Africa, and Australia
highlights fish such as the aggressive Nile knifefish that inhabit the warm freshwaters of the eastern hemisphere.

★ Caribbean Reef
More than 250 tropical animals, including a sea turtle and bonnethead sharks, live in this reef habitat, one of the aquarium's most popular exhibits. Visitors can watch as a diver feeds the creatures.

For keys to symbols *see back flap*

SOUTH SIDE

Settled in the mid-1800s as suburban estates, the South Side was soon transformed when the 1893 World's Fair, held in Jackson Park, brought tourists, money, and real-estate and transit development. Hyde Park in particular experienced dramatic change, as the City's preparation for the fair led to an influx of Chicago's elite. By the 1920s, however, pollution from nearby industry and the encroachment of poorer neighborhoods caused the wealthy to depart. By the 1950s, Kenwood and Hyde Park were in decline. That same decade, the University of Chicago led a massive urban-renewal program. Today, the area contains many classic Prairie School homes, superb museums, and two of Chicago's largest greenspaces.

Sights at a Glance

Historic Buildings
1. Rockefeller Memorial Chapel
2. Robie House
5. University of Chicago Quadrangles

Historic Districts
9. Hyde Park
10. Kenwood

Museums
3. Oriental Institute Museum
4. Smart Museum of Art
8. DuSable Museum of African American History
12. *Museum of Science and Industry pp108–111*

Parks
6. Midway Plaisance
7. Washington Park
11. Jackson Park

☐ Restaurants *pp152–3*
1. Cedars Mediterranean
2. La Petite Folie
3. Medici On 57th St.
4. Rajun Cajun
5. Salonica
6. Valois
7. Zaleski & Horvarth MarketCafé

See also Street Finder maps 7 & 8

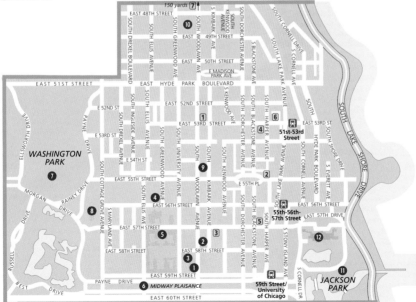

0 meters 500
0 yards 500

Street-by-Street: University of Chicago

The University of Chicago, founded in 1890 on land donated by Marshall Field, opened its doors to students – male and female, White and Black – in 1892. Today, it has the greatest number of Nobel laureates among faculty, alumni, and researchers of any US university and is particularly lauded in the fields of economics and physics. Over the years, John D. Rockefeller gave $35 million to the university. Henry Ives Cobb designed 18 of the university's limestone buildings before the Boston firm Shepley, Rutan and Coolidge took over as the main architects in 1901. Today, the campus boasts the designs of more than 70 architects. While large, it is easily explored on foot (for walking tours, *see pp184–5).*

Nuclear Energy, by sculptor Henry Moore, marks the spot where, in 1942, a team of scientists led by Enrico Fermi ushered in the atomic age with the first controlled nuclear reaction.

Bond Chapel
(1926) contains beautiful stained-glass windows by Charles Connick and elaborate wood carvings.

❺ **Main Quadrangle**
The university's tranquil central quadrangle is the largest of seven designed by Henry Ives Cobb.

❻ **Midway Plaisance**
This is the site of the 1893 World's Columbian Exposition amusement park.

Cobb Gate
was donated to the university by Henry Ives Cobb, the campus' master planner. It is ornately decorated with gargoyles.

0 meters   100
0 yards   100

❹ ★ Smart Museum of Art
This light-filled, intimate museum offers a rich, balanced survey of Western art.

Locator Map
See Street Finder maps 7 & 8

Regenstein Library
The university's main library is striking for its Brutalist architecture, which lies in stark contrast to the nearby, domed Mansueto Library.

Key

— Suggested route

❸ ★ Oriental Institute Museum
Three millennia of ancient Near East civilization are showcased at this fascinating museum.

❶ Rockefeller Memorial Chapel
Elaborate carvings and intricate stained-glass windows grace the interior of this limestone-and-brick chapel.

58TH STREET

WOODLAWN AVENUE

❷ ★ Robie House
This Frank Lloyd Wright-designed home (1908–1910) is a masterpiece of the Prairie School of architecture.

❶ Rockefeller Memorial Chapel

5850 S Woodlawn Ave. **Map** 7 C4.
Tel (773) 702-2100. Ⓜ Garfield (Red
Line) then bus 2, 6, 55. 🚆 59th.
Open 8am–5:30pm daily. ⛪ 11am
Sun, 10am daily in summer. ♿
🎵 Concerts. 🌐 **rockefeller.
uchicago.edu**

Rockefeller Memorial Chapel
is Bertram G. Goodhue's 1928
interpretation of Gothic *(see
p28)*. The chapel is topped
with a 207-ft (63-m) tower.
It is the tallest building on
campus: John D. Rockefeller,
as a condition of his bequest,
required that this structure
be the university's dominant
feature. Contributing to its
tradition of musical excellence
is one of Chicago's oldest
choral ensembles, and the
stunning E.M. Skinner organ.
The 72-bell tower, the bells
weighing from 10.5 lb (5 kg)
to 18.5 tons, is the second-
largest in the world. The
bells ring at noon and 6pm
weekdays, after service,
and during the annual
carillon festival.

Bust of a Man (c.1840 BC), at the Oriental Institute Museum

❸ Oriental Institute Museum

1155 E 58th St. **Map** 7 C4. **Tel** (773)
702-9520. Ⓜ Garfield (Red or Green
Line) then bus 2, 6, 55. 🚆 59th.
Open 10am–6pm Tue, Thu–Sat;
10am–8:30pm Wed; noon–6pm
Sun. **Closed** public hols. ♿ 🎵 📷
🌐 **oi.uchicago.edu**

The Oriental Institute Museum
is the exhibition arm of the
Oriental Institute, its scholars
having excavated in virtually
every region of the Near East
since 1919. The museum
presents the institute's
famed collection of over
100,000 artifacts from the
earliest civilizations of the
world. It is also one of only
three places in the world
where you can see a
reconstruction of an Assyrian
palace (c.721–705 BC).

Other highlights of the
museum include a monumental
sculpture (c.1334–25 BC) of King
Tutankhamen from a Luxor
temple. At 17 ft (5 m), it is the

❷ Robie House

5757 S Woodlawn Ave. **Map** 8 D4. **Tel**
(312) 994-4000. Ⓜ Garfield (Green &
Red Line) then bus 2, 6, 55. 🚆 59th.
Open Wed–Sun. **Closed** Tue, Jan 1,
Thanksgiving, Dec 24, 25 & 31. 📷
🎵 mandatory: 11am, 1pm, 3pm
Mon–Fri; 11am–3:30pm every 30
minutes at weekends; additional tours
in Jun–Aug: 4pm, 5pm, 6pm Thu. 📷
🌐 **gowright.org**

Frank Lloyd Wright's world-
famous Robie House is the
quintessential expression of
the Prairie School movement
(see p29). Designed in 1908
for Frederick Robie, a bicycle
and motorbike manufacturer,
and completed in 1910, the
home is one of Wright's last
Prairie School houses: Wright
left both his family and his Oak
Park practice during its three-
year construction.

Robie House has three
distinct parts combining to
create a balanced whole. Two,
two-story rectangular concrete

Frank Lloyd Wright-designed dining-room set from Robie House

blocks sit parallel to each other;
a smaller square third story is
positioned at their junction.
There is no basement and no
attic. The exterior design of the
house perfectly captures the
prairie landscape of flat, open
fields. The roof's sweeping
planes embody the house's
aesthetic of bold
rectilinear simplicity.
Steel beams, some 60 ft
(18 m) long, support
the over-hanging
roof. Their use was
unorthodox in residential
architecture at the time.

**Leaded stained-glass windows and
doors**, which run the length of the
living room, allow for both privacy
and natural light.

tallest ancient Egyptian statue in the western hemisphere.

The museum's Egyptian collection, which includes objects of ancient Egyptian daily life and religious and funerary practices, is one of the largest in the US.

❹ Smart Museum of Art

5550 S Greenwood Ave. **Map** 7 C4. **Tel** (773) 702-0200. Ⓜ Garfield (Red or Green Line) then bus 2, 6, 55. **Open** 10am–5pm Tue, Wed, Fri–Sun; 10am–8pm Thu. **Closed** public hols. ♿🛍️📷🎁 Ⓟ Special events. 🆆 smartmuseum.uchicago.edu

If you are feeling overwhelmed by the crowds at Chicago's major museums, this is the place to come for an intimate encounter with art. Named after David and Alfred Smart, founders of *Esquire Magazine* and the museum's benefactors, the Smart Museum was established in 1974 as the art museum of the University of Chicago. It holds more than 8,000 artworks and artifacts,

Henry Moore's *Nuclear Energy*, outside the Smart Museum

including antiquities and Old Master prints, Asian paintings, calligraphies, and ceramics. By showing its works in rotating, thematic displays, the museum ensures its collection is made available to the public. The museum also owns important post-war Chicago artwork, furniture and glass from Robie House, and early modern and contemporary painting and sculpture. A 1999 renovation has allowed for more comprehensive displays of the museum's collection of

important 20th century and Asian artworks.

The museum's café, with tall windows overlooking the tranquil sculpture garden, is a great spot for a quiet lunch.

❺ University of Chicago Quadrangles

Bounded by 57th & 59th sts., Ellis & University aves. **Map** 7 C4. Ⓜ Garfield (Red or Green Line) then bus 2, 6, 55. 🚌 59th.

The cloistered quadrangle plan for the University of Chicago – in the 1890s, one of the first in the US – was developed by architect Henry Ives Cobb. He patterned the unified campus after British universities Cambridge and Oxford. Despite years of development and modification, the six broken quadrangles surrounding a seventh still reflect Cobb's vision.

Cobb Gate, at the north entrance, is a gargoyled ceremonial gateway donated by Cobb in 1900.

A huge chimney crowns the intersection of the house's three sections, uniting the parts.

A large hearth is the focal point of the living room.

Also bold but simple, the interior is furnished with Wright-designed furniture. The innovative dining-room set is on view at the Smart Museum (*see above*). The house is a *Gesamtkunstwerk*, a total work of art. Every item in the house contributes to its beauty.

The house is an organic whole, underscored by the harmonious interplay between the exterior and interior and is admired by architects worldwide.

The building was designated a National Historic Landmark and donated to the University of Chicago in 1963.

The long Roman bricks are a Wright signature.

Main Entrance   Robie House Shop

University students playing soccer on the Midway Plaisance

❻ Midway Plaisance

Bounded by 59th & 60th sts., Cottage Grove & Stony Island aves. **Map** 7 B5–8 E5. 🚇 59th.

Midway Plaisance, a 1-mile- (1.6-km-) long greenway at the south end of the University of Chicago campus and the city's broadest boulevard, serves as the university's recreation grounds. The Midway is also an excellent vantage point from which to view the university's Gothic buildings.

Designed by Frederick Law Olmsted and Calvert Vaux as the link between Washington and Jackson parks, the Midway was the site of the 1893 Exposition's Bazaar of Nations. It was here that the Ferris wheel – 250 ft (76 m) high – made its debut.

❼ Washington Park

Bounded by 51st & 60th sts., Martin Luther King Jr. Dr. & Cottage Grove Ave. **Map** 7 A2–A5. 🚇 51st; Garfield (Green Line).

Named after the first US president, Washington Park was originally intended to be part of a grand South Park, comprising both Washington Park and Jackson Park, connected by a canal running through Midway Plaisance. Landscape architects Frederick Law Olmsted and Calvert Vaux, designers of New York's Central Park, developed the South Park plan in 1871. The park commission balked at creating a canal and so the original plan was never realized in its entirety. In 1872, Horace W.S. Cleveland was hired to oversee the completion of Washington Park.

Combining expanses of meadows with borders of trees and shrubs, Washington Park's pastoral landscape also has a pond and lagoon. At the northeast end of the park is Drexel Fountain, one of the oldest fountains in Chicago. It was designed in 1881–2 by Henry Manger.

The park's most magnificent feature is the sculpture *Fountain of Time* at the south end, where Washington Park meets Midway Plaisance. Designed in 1922 by the Chicago artist Lorado Taft (1860–1936), this haunting monument depicts the cloaked figure of Time watching the endless march of humanity. It was erected to celebrate 100 years of US-British peace.

Detail of Taft's *Fountain of Time*, Washington Park

❽ DuSable Museum of African American History

740 E 56th Pl. **Map** 7 B4. **Tel** (773) 947-0600. 🚇 Garfield (Red or Green Line) then bus 55. 🚌 4. **Open** 10am– 5pm Tue–Sat; noon–5pm Sun. **Closed** major public hols. 🎫 (children under 6 free; free Sun). ♿ 📷 book in advance. 📷 🅿 Lectures, films. 🌐 dusablemuseum.org

As part of its mission to celebrate the rich and diverse history and culture of African Americans and their contributions to the nation, the DuSable Museum highlights accomplishments of the ordinary and extraordinary alike. Founded in 1961, the museum is the oldest such institution in the US.

The museum's permanent exhibit "Songs of My People" brings together diverse images by Black photojournalists of African-American lives.

Memorabilia from the life and political career of Chicago's first Black mayor, Harold Washington, make up the "Harold Washington in Office" exhibit.

The wooden "Freedom Now" bas-relief mural illustrates centuries of Black history. Significant leaders are depicted, along with revolutionary events.

"Africa Speaks" presents art from Africa, much of which has a functional purpose. Handcrafted door panels, for example, are given to a Nigerian bride on her wedding day so she may close her boudoir while decorating it. The ritual masks from closed West African societies are particularly striking.

❾ Hyde Park

Bounded by Hyde Park Blvd., 61st St., Washington Park, & Lake Michigan. **Map** 8 D3. 🚇 53rd; 55th-56th-57th; 59th. 🎫 call (312) 922-3432. ♿ 📷

Hyde Park is one of Chicago's most pleasant neighborhoods. The University of Chicago's presence contributes a collegiate atmosphere, while the many shops, restaurants, theaters, and galleries provide a broad array of attractions.

The area was open country-side in 1853 when Chicago lawyer Paul Cornell established the community on a swath of lakeside property.

Carefully untended gardens characteristic of the Rosalie Villas, in Hyde Park

Isidore Heller House, in Hyde Park, by Frank Lloyd Wright

The quiet suburb was transformed by three events: its 1889 annexation by the City of Chicago, the 1890 founding of the University of Chicago, and the 1893 World's Columbian Exposition. Many of the houses from this 1890s spurt of development survive. Isidore Heller House (5132 South Woodlawn Avenue) is a Frank Lloyd Wright design (1897) that precedes his celebrated Robie House (see pp104–105) by a decade yet reveals his characteristic Prairie style.

Rosalie Villas (Harper Avenue, from 57th to 59th), designed by Solon S. Beman between 1884 and 1890, was Hyde Park's first planned community. It consists of about 50 Queen Anne-style residences, each unique in architectural detail.

The retail heart of Hyde Park is 53rd Street, while ethnic restaurants cluster on 55th Street. Bookstores thrive in Hyde Park; it has been called the largest center for books in the Midwest.

⑩ Kenwood

Bounded by 47th St., Hyde Park Blvd., Cottage Grove Ave. & Lake Park Ave. **Map** 7 C1. Ⓜ 47th (Green Line) then bus 28. Ⓡ 47th. Ⓒ call (312) 922-3432. ◫ ◫

Historic Kenwood was established in 1856 when dentist Jonathan A. Kennicott bought and subdivided a large plot of land near 43rd Street. Over the next three decades it became one of the most fashionable South Side communities. In the 1920s, many middle-class African

Americans moved to the area, but the late 1940s saw a period of decline. A massive urban renewal project was begun in the early 1950s, and by the 1980s, the neighborhood had undergone a revival. Kenwood's rise has further been spurred by the election of its most famous resident, Barack Obama, as President of the United States.

The neighborhood has some of the finest mansions constructed in Chicago, along with many Prairie School (see p29) homes. Two commissions Frank Lloyd Wright undertook while working for Adler and Sullivan include the George W. Blossom House (4858 Kenwood Avenue) and the Warren McArthur House (4852 Kenwood Avenue).

Noteworthy are the mansions on Greenwood Avenue between 49th and 50th, in particular the elegant Prairie style of the Ernest J. Magerstadt House (4930 South Greenwood Avenue), designed in 1908 by George W. Maher, as well as the ornate houses lining South Kimbark Avenue.

⑪ Jackson Park

Bounded by 57th & 67th sts., Stony Island Ave. & Lake Michigan. **Map** 8 E5. Ⓡ 59th; 63rd. Ⓒ call (312) 922-3432; bird walk, call (773) 493-7058.

Jackson Park was designed by Frederick Law Olmsted and Calvert Vaux in 1871 as part of the unrealized South Park plan (see p106). Even though the park was redesigned after being chosen as the main site for the 1893 World's Fair, and again in 1895, its original aquatic theme is still evident.

Osaka Garden is a re-creation of the Japanese garden built for the fair. This serene spot on Wooded Island has a pavilion, waterfall, and gorgeous cherry trees. The island is considered the best place in Chicago for bird-watching: more than 120 species of birds have been sighted here. In the center of the park, a smaller, gilded replica of the 65-ft-(20-m-) statue *The Republic* celebrates the fair's 25th anniversary.

There are also two beaches and several sports facilities.

Jackson Park's "Golden Lady," a replica of Daniel Chester French's *The Republic*

The contemplative Osaka Garden in Jackson Park

⓮ Museum of Science and Industry

The Museum of Science and Industry celebrates the scientific and technological accomplishments of humankind, with an emphasis on achievements of the 20th century. Originally called the Rosenwald Industrial Museum, after the museum's benefactor, its name was soon changed at Julius Rosenwald's urging, who said that the museum belonged not to him but to the people. While the building, a monumental Neo-Classical structure dominating Jackson Park, is a nod to history *(see p111)*, the museum within has been the North American leader in modern, interactive displays, making the exploration of science and technology an accessible experience.

Colleen Moore's Fairy Castle
This 9-sq-ft (0.8-sq-m) dollhouse is complete with miniature furniture and working electricity and plumbing.

Foucault's Pendulum
is modeled on the one invented by the French physicist in 1851 to prove that the Earth rotates.

★ U-505 Submarine
This exhibition tells the story of a World War II U-Boat that sank eight allied ships before being captured by the US Navy in 1944.

Lower Floor

Apollo 8 Command Module
This historic spacecraft played an important role in early US lunar missions, which culminated in the landing on the moon.

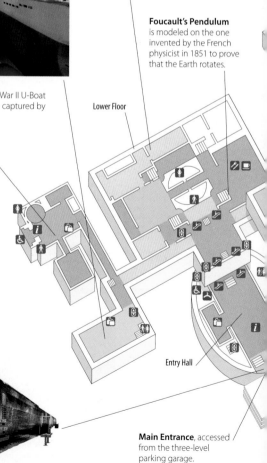

Entry Hall

★ All Aboard the Silver Streak
Climb aboard the record-breaking 1930s train that revolutionized industrial design.

Main Entrance, accessed from the three-level parking garage.

Take Flight
Learn about the technology behind modern-day flight on a Boeing 727 that is suspended above the galleries.

Coal Mine transports visitors through a reproduction of an early Illinois coal mine so realistic its walls are made of coal.

Balcony floor

Main Floor

YOU! The Experience examines the connections between the mind, body, and spirit, and demonstrates the extraordinary complexity of the human body.

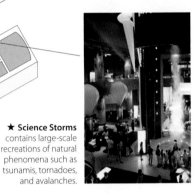

★ **Science Storms** contains large-scale recreations of natural phenomena such as tsunamis, tornadoes, and avalanches.

North Entrance

★ **Transportation Gallery**
Explore human transportation throughout the years: climb aboard the Empire State Express 999; admire the 1960s automobile, the Spirit of America; and gaze at the array of historic aircraft.

Museum Guide

The museum's Entry Hall houses the museum shop, information desk, and Silver Streak train exhibit. Permanent exhibits are displayed throughout the lower floor, main floor, and balcony. Each floor has a color-coded staircase on each corner facilitating navigation of the building. Each staircase itself features an intriguing exhibit. The Omnimax Theater is in the Henry Crown Space Center. Cafés are on the lower floor.

Key

- ▨ Space exploration
- ▨ Transportation
- ▨ The Human Body
- ▨ The Farm
- ▨ Live Science Experience
- ▨ Energy and Environment
- ▨ Permanent exhibitions
- ▨ Temporary exhibitions
- ▨ Non exhibition space

Exploring the Museum of Science and Industry

The Museum of Science and Industry has more than 35,000 artifacts, including 2,000 interactive displays, making it one of the largest science museums in the world. It encompasses everything from basic science to advanced technology. Space exploration, transportation, and human biology are particularly strong areas. With more than 350,000 sq ft (32,500 sq m) of exhibition space, there's more than enough to keep visitors of all ages engaged for a full day of investigation and discovery.

View of the Museum of Science and Industry from across Columbia Basin

Space Exploration

The Henry Crown Space Center is the epicenter of the museum's display on space exploration. Here, you can view the Apollo 8 Command Module – the first manned spacecraft to circle the moon, orbiting ten times in December 1968. Less than 13 ft (4 m) in diameter and weighing 13,100 lb (6,000 kg), the vessel still bears the scars of its epic journey on its pitted exterior.

The exhibit includes a replica of NASA's Apollo Lunar Module Trainer, used for astronaut training, and a 6.5-oz (185-g) piece of moon rock retrieved by the Apollo 17 mission.

The Space Center is also home to the Aurora 7 Mercury Space Capsule, one of the earliest manned spacecrafts to orbit the Earth – doing so four times in a row in May 1962.

Henry Crown Space Center, showcasing US space exploration

A 20-minute movie simulates for viewers the experience of blasting off in a space shuttle.

Transportation

Pick a mode of transport – from train, plane, to automobile – and you can be sure the museum has an outstanding example.

Train-nostalgia buffs will enjoy the All Aboard the Silver Streak exhibit, which showcases the first diesel-electric, streamlined passenger train in America, the Pioneer Zephyr. Built in 1934, the Zephyr was the swiftest, sleekest train in the US, initiating the conversion from steam to diesel-electric locomotion and ushering in the era of luxury passenger rail travel. The Zephyr's interior was dramatically different from the opulent Pullman cars in use at the time (see p121) yet just as elegant in its simplicity. Visitors can get behind the controls and pretend to drive this historic train.

The museum also has one of the largest train models in the world. The 3,500-sq-ft (325-sq-m) model highlights the role of the railroad in the US economy.

The history of aviation is well represented in the museum's transportation zone. Look up to the balcony to see a rare Boeing 40B-2 airplane suspended from the ceiling.

Nearby is Take Flight, an exhibit explaining the scientific principles behind the wonder of flight, such as radar, aerodynamics, and engine and wing construction. This exhibit contains one of the museum's largest attractions, a cantilevered United Airlines Boeing 727.

One of the museum's most popular exhibits is the restored U-505 Submarine, the only German U-Boat to be found in the US. This World War II boat was captured by US naval forces off the west coast of Africa in 1944. The submarine forms the centerpiece of a 35,000-sq-ft (3,250-sq-m) indoor exhibit, which gives visitors the chance to experience the interior of a vessel, learn about the psychological stresses of warfare in an enclosed space, and see over 200 original artifacts. The exhibition also tells the incredible story of how the massive U-Boat was transported to Illinois. Visitors who wish to take a guided, on-board tour must purchase an exhibit ticket.

Closer to earth is the Transportation Gallery's Spirit of America, the first car to break the 500 mph (800 kph) land speed barrier. On October 15, 1964, Craig Breedlove became the "fastest man on wheels" when he piloted this missile-like vehicle to spectacular speeds, and skidded into a pond at 200 mph (300 kph) but emerged unhurt. The stunt also earned a place in The Guinness Book of World Records for the longest set of skidmarks.

The Entry Hall, the popular Silver Streak train in the background

Fast machines in the museum's transportation zone

The Human Body

A large, interactive exhibit using sophisticated computer graphics and real-life images, YOU! The Experience showcases the connections between the human mind, body, and spirit. It examines and celebrates the experience of life, demonstrating the extraordinary complexity of the human body. Museum-goers can test their physical abilities with boxing moves and a virtual coach, for example. Human specimens include embryos and fetuses in various phases of development. You can interact with the 13 ft (4m) tall "Heart" installation by transmitting your pulse to make it beat.

Probably the most unusual display in the exhibit are the anatomical slices. In the 1940s, the corpses of a woman and man who died of natural causes were frozen and then cut in to 0.5 in (1.25 cm) sections, both vertically and horizontally, and preserved in fluid between glass. These displays allow you to look right inside the human body.

Farm Tech

This exhibit takes a look at modern technology on a 21st century farm. The Farm features a full-size tractor, a greenhouse, and replicas of a dairy barn and a cornfield.

From Plaster To Stone

Architect Charles B. Atwood (see p32) based his design of this majestic building – built as a temporary structure for the 1893 World's Fair and, today, the only surviving building from the fair – on classical Greek models. Over 270 columns and 24 caryatids, weighing 6 tons each, grace the exterior. Covered in plaster, with a roof of skylights, the building deteriorated badly after the fair. The Field Museum (see pp88–91) occupied it briefly, until 1920. The building then sat in a state of disrepair until the mid-1920s, when Julius Rosenwald, chairman of Sears, Roebuck and Co., campaigned to save it and founded the museum, donating millions of dollars to a massive reconstruction effort. Exterior plaster was replaced with 28,000 tons of limestone and marble in an 11-year renovation. The Museum of Science and Industry opened in 1933, in time for the Century of Progress World's Exposition.

Some of the original buildings during the 1893 World's Columbian Exposition

Through interactive exhibits, visitors can design their own cereal, "harvest" a field of corn or feel what it is like to milk a cow. They can also follow milk, corn and soybeans through a fascinating voyage from Midwest roots to a variety of everyday products.

Live Science Experience

Located on the balcony level, the Live Science Experience is a permanent exhibition space comprising labs and classrooms where live science demonstrations take place on a daily basis. Visitors can see a fiery chemistry show, dissect eyeballs, diagnose a real human patient simulator, and much more. Beyond hands-on lab experiments, there are several entertaining Science Theater shows inviting visitors to sit down for some science-centric entertainment. "Taste Buddies" show how taste and smell combine to make flavors

Bronze plaques on the main doors honor the sciences

while the funny science play "Poop Happens" breaks down the mystery of how food is processed in our bodies.

Shows are limited to a maximum of 70 visitors, so show up early if you want to get a seat.

Energy and Environment

One of the museum's most popular exhibits is Coal Mine. It is worth waiting for in the inevitable lineup. This re-creation of a 1933 Illinois coal mine is remarkably life-like. The 20-minute tour (exhibition ticket required) begins at the top of a mineshaft, where an elevator takes visitors down in semi-darkness to a bituminous coal seam and a fascinating demonstration of coal-mining machinery. A short ride on a mine train ends this unique, if a little claustrophobic, experience.

Nature's power is the focus of the Science Storms exhibit. The scientific principles behind tornadoes, lightning, fire, tsunamis, and avalanches are presented via large-scale recreations, including a 40 ft (12 m) tornado, an avalanche disk, and a lightning generator.

FARTHER AFIELD

Chicago's outlying areas offer a wealth of sightseeing opportunities. For lovers of architecture, Oak Park is a must-see for its Frank Lloyd Wright designs. Other Chicago neighborhoods, such as Wicker Park and Lakeview, each with its own distinct character, are ideal day-trip destinations. Pullman is one of the US's best-preserved 19th-century neighborhoods. A little farther is Brookfield Zoo, renowned for its realistic animal habitats. Walking paths lead through varied landscapes at Morton Arboretum. Visitors with more time can traverse the canal corridor, which runs alongside the 1848 historic canal and encompasses extensive recreational trails and several fine museums.

Sights at a Glance

Historic Buildings, Districts Parks, and Canals
5 Oak Park
7 Jane Addams Hull-House Museum
11 Illinois and Michigan Canal National Heritage Corridor
12 Pullman Historic District

Neighborhoods
2 Lakeview and Wrigleyville

3 Wicker Park
6 Near West Side
8 Lower West Side

Zoos and Botanic Gardens
1 Lincoln Park Zoo (pp114–15)
4 Garfield Park Conservatory
9 Brookfield Zoo
10 Morton Arboretum

Key
Urban area
Interstate highway
State highway
Major road

0 kilometers 5
0 miles 5

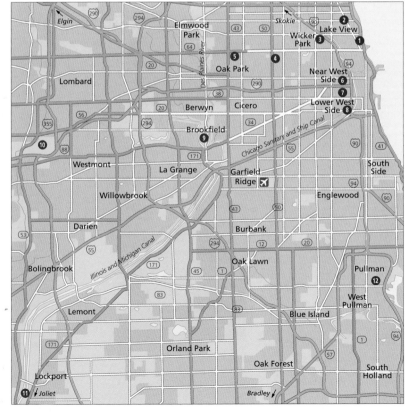

◄ Skyline of downtown Chicago, as seen from the People's Gas Education Pavilion at Lincoln Park Zoo

❶ Lincoln Park Zoo

Established in 1868 with the gift of two swans from New York's Central Park, Lincoln Park Zoo is one of the nation's only free-admission zoos. Today, more than 1,000 mammals, reptiles, and birds from around the world live here, in realistic habitats. The zoo's status as a world leader in wildlife conservation is evident in its educational exhibits, as well as in its many international efforts to save endangered species. Although it is not the Chicago area's largest zoo *(see Brookfield Zoo p119)*, Lincoln Park Zoo, in the heart of Lincoln Park, is easily accessible from the Downtown Core. The park, Chicago's largest, offers walking and biking paths, paddle-boating ponds, lagoons, and sandy beaches.

Lincoln Park Conservatory
This stunning conservatory (1890–95), designed by architect Joseph L. Silsbee, houses many exotic plants, including orchids. Thousands of flowers grown here are for park use.

West Entrance

Waterfowl Lagoon
Flamingos and other waterfowl find refuge in this peaceful lagoon, one of the zoo's earliest features.

KEY

① **Regenstein Macaque Forest** is the zoo's newest exhibition, and features the iconic Japanese snow monkeys in a lush, wooded habitat which is on view year-round.

② **Pritzker Family Children's Zoo** showcases wood-dwelling animals such as beavers, bears, and wolves.

③ **Regenstein Small Mammal-Reptile House** This exhibit showcases 40 species, including African Dwarf crocodiles.

④ **Café Brauer** was designed in 1908 by Dwight Perkins, a leading architect of the Prairie School. The building was restored in 1989. Its Great Hall has spectacular chandeliers and a skylight.

⑤ **Gateway Building**, at the zoo's main east entrance, houses the information and security desk.

STOCKTON DRIVE

★ **Farm-in-the-Zoo**
This working farm shelters cows, horses, chickens, and pigs. Children most enjoy watching the daily milking routine and horse grooming.

Regenstein African Journey
This tour is designed to immerse visitors in the African landscape by leading them through the lush habitats of giraffes, meerkats, rhinos, and other African animals.

East Entrance

Kovler Lion House
Rare cats, including Siberian tigers, inhabit this 1912 historic building.

0 meters 100
0 yards 100

★ Regenstein Center for African Apes
The zoo's collection of lowland gorillas is one of the largest in the US – testimony to the zoo's highly successful breeding program.

Antelope and Zebra Area
Various hoofed animals live in 11 outdoor habitats by the zoo's south pond, including the threatened Grevy's zebra from Africa and the endangered Bactrian camel from Mongolia, as well as rare gazelles, antelopes, deer, and alpacas.

South Entrance

For keys to symbols *see back flap*

Wrigley Field baseball stadium, home of the famous Chicago Cubs

❷ Lakeview and Wrigleyville

West of Lake Michigan to Ashland Ave., from Diversey Ave. to W Irving Park Rd. Ⓜ Belmont (Red, Brown, Purple Lines). 🚌 9, 22, 36. 🎭 See Entertainment: p159.

Lakeview and Wrigleyville are two of Chicago's most colorful neighborhoods. Now a cultural melting pot, the area was settled by German immigrants in the 1830s. Farms dotted the landscape until the mid-1800s, when the area began to develop as a residential neighborhood of working-class Swedish immigrants. After annexation by the City in 1889, a spurt of development established the area as one of the liveliest in Chicago – a distinction it continues to hold today.

Wrigleyville, the northern half of Lakeview, is named after Wrigley Field, home of the famous Chicago Cubs baseball team. This charming stadium, designed by Zachary Taylor Davis in 1914, is the oldest National League ballpark. The community resisted electric lighting of the stadium into the late 1980s.

Lakeview hosts a thriving theater scene as well as excellent restaurants, coffeehouses, bars, specialty shops, and bookshops. Vintage boutiques line Belmont Avenue between Halsted and Sheffield Streets. The Boystown region in Lakeview is also the heart of Chicago's gay community.

To sample Lakeview's architectural heritage, visit **Alta Vista Terrace**, between Grace and Byron Streets. This block of turn-of-the-century row houses was designed by Samuel Gross, who wished to replicate the row houses he had seen in London after a trip to Europe.

Hawthorne Place, north of Belmont Avenue, east of Broadway, is a rare surviving Victorian-era residential design that is typical of the area's early development.

Beautiful tombstones mark the resting places of Chicago's notables in **Graceland Cemetery** (4001 North Clark Street), just north of Lakeview. Buried here are Louis Sullivan (see p32) and George Pullman (see p121), among others. A site map is available at the cemetery's office.

Rapp House, one of Wicker Park's architectural gems

❸ Wicker Park

Bounded by North Ave., Milwaukee, Leavitt, and Division sts. Ⓜ Damen (Blue Line). 🚌 56. 🎭 Around the Coyote (Sep).

If you are looking for the trendy area of Chicago, Wicker Park, brimming with galleries, boutiques, coffeehouses, restaurants, and nightclubs is it. In the late 1800s, Scandinavian and German immigrants built mansions here and many of them remain, making this a great area for an architectural tour. Of interest are John Rapp House (1407 North Hoyne Avenue) and Holy Trinity Cathedral (1121 Leavitt Street), designed by Louis Sullivan.

❹ Garfield Park Conservatory

300 North Central Park Ave. **Tel** 746-5100. Ⓜ Conservatory-Cen￼ Park Dr. (Green Line). **Open** 9am￼ (to 8pm Wed) daily. 🅿 available￼ members. 🏠 ♿ 🅿
🅆 garfieldconservatory.org

Designed by Jens Jensen, (￼ was known as "the dean of Prairie landscapes") in 1906￼ spectacular Garfield Park Conservatory is a two-acre￼ enclosed garden which ho￼ the world's largest public horticultural collection und￼ glass. Children are well cate￼ for at the Elizabeth Morse Genius Children's Garden, w￼ exhibits showing how plan￼ grow and reproduce. Altho￼ the conservatory was great￼ damaged in a hail storm in 2011, rebuilding is nearly d￼

❺ Oak Park

Bounded by N North Ave, S Roos￼ Rd., E Austin Blvd. & W Harlem A￼ 🛈 (708) 524-7800. Ⓜ Oak Park￼ (Green Line); Harlem/Lake (Gree￼ Line). 🚆 Oak Park (Union Pacific Line). Visitors' center: 1010 Lake S￼ **Open** 10am–5pm daily. **Closed** Thanksgiving, Dec 25. 🅿 🖼 Fra￼ Lloyd Wright Information Center S LaSalle St. **Tel** (312) 994-4000. ▮ 🅆 gowright.org

In 1889, Frank Lloyd Wright moved to Oak Park, at the a￼ of 22. During the next 20 ye￼ here, he created many groundbreaking buildings a￼ legendary Prairie School sty￼ evolved. This community is home to 25 Wright building￼ the largest grouping of his ￼ anywhere. Oak Park is also

Frank Lloyd Wright's Home and Studi￼ residence for 20 years

Unity Temple, Frank Lloyd Wright's "little jewel"

architecture." It was built between 1906 and 1908 using what was then an unusual technique of poured reinforced concrete, in part because of a budget of only $45,000. Unity Temple is a masterpiece of powerful simplicity wedded with functional ornamentation.

Ernest Hemingway lived in Oak Park until the age of 20. The **Ernest Hemingway Birthplace** (339 North Oak Park Ave.) is a grand Victorian home with turn-of-the-century furnishings, and has displays on the life of this Nobel Prize winner. The **Ernest Hemingway Museum** (200 North Oak Park Ave.) features artifacts from Hemingway's early life, including a childhood diary.

known for its literary association: famed American writer Ernest Hemingway *(see p33)* was born here in 1899.

The best place to feast on Wright's achievement is the **Frank Lloyd Wright Home and Studio**. Designed by Wright in 1889, the superbly restored residence and workspace is where the architect developed his influential Prairie style.

Nearby are two private homes that reveal Wright's versatility. The **Arthur Heurtley House** (1902: 318 Forest Ave.) is typically Prairie style, with its row of windows spanning the low roofline and its simple but elegant entrance arch. The **Moore-Dugal House**

(1895: 333 Forest Ave.) is a hybrid of styles, with Tudor Revival and Gothic elements.

At the southern end of Oak Park is the masterful **Pleasant Home** (217 Home Ave.), a 30-room Prairie-style mansion designed in 1897 by George W. Maher. The house contains extraordinary art glass (designed panels of leaded glass), intricate woodwork, and decorative motifs, as well as a display on the area's history.

Wright was particularly proud of **Unity Temple** (875 Lake St.), his design for the Unitarian Universalist Congregation. He called this church, one of his most important designs, his first expression of an "entirely new

The Victorian house in which Ernest Hemingway was born

Oak Park

0 meters 300
0 yards 300

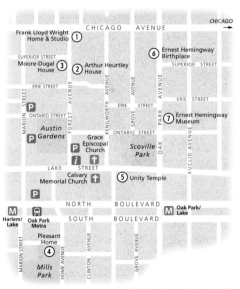

Jane Addams Hull-House Museum, seen from the courtyard

❻ Near West Side

Bounded by Chicago River, 16th & Kinzie sts., & Ogden Ave. **Map** 3 A1– A5. Ⓜ UIC-Halsted. 🚌 8, 60.

Over the years, Chicago's Near West Side has experienced waves of successive immigrant settlement. Today, it is one of the best places to experience the city's many ethnic communities.

It was settled in the 1840s and 1850s by working-class Irish immigrants. The Great Chicago Fire of 1871 began here, on DeKoven Street (No. 558), in the O'Leary barn. Appropriately (or ironically, depending on how you look at it), the **Chicago Fire Academy** is now located on the site. An arresting bronze sculpture of flames marks the spot where the devastating fire reportedly began.

Following the fire, Russian and Polish Jews settled the area in the 1890s, while to the north, a lively Greek Town developed, centered along Halsted Street, between Madison and Van Buren Streets. To the west, Little Italy, centered around Taylor Street at Halsted Street, flourished.

The **University of Illinois at Chicago** holds a prominent position in the area. Walter A. Netsch Jr. designed the university in the

1960s, in the modern style known as Brutalism. The campus is characterized by unadorned concrete buildings with rows of narrow vertical windows.

❼ Jane Addams Hull-House Museum

800 S Halsted St. **Tel** (312) 413-5353. **Map** 3 A3. Ⓜ UIC-Halsted. 🚌 7, 8, 60. **Closed** major public hols. ♿ 📷 mandatory: 10am–4pm Tue–Fri, noon–4pm Sun. 🅿
🆆 uic.edu/jaddams/hull

This museum, which is part of the University of Illinois campus, celebrates the work of Jane Addams (see p31), who won the 1931 Nobel Peace Prize for her social-justice work and advocacy and became perhaps the most famous woman in the US. In her pioneering work with the poor, Addams fought for child-labor laws, a minimum wage, and better public sanitation, among other social causes.

It was in this mansion in the then industrial center of Chicago that Addams and Ellen Gates Starr established, in 1889, a settlement house to provide social services to immigrants, the poor, and the dispossessed.

The house's interior has been restored to look as it did in its early days. There are also settlement house exhibits.

Egon Weiner's sculpture at the Chicago Fire Academy

❾ Lower West Side

Bounded by Chicago River, 16th St., & Pulaski Rd. Ⓜ 18th. 🚌 9, 18, 60.

The Lower West Side, like the Near West Side, developed as an industrial, working-class neighborhood after the 1871 fire. Immigrants from Bohemia were the first to arrive, in the 1870s, followed in the early 20th century by Germans, Poles, and Yugoslavians. In the 1950s, an influx of Mexican and Puerto Rican immigrants brought a Hispanic flavor to the community.

Today, the neighborhood of Pilsen, centered along 18th Street between South Damen Avenue and South Halsted Street, is home to many fine Mexican restaurants, bakeries, and specialty shops. The sounds of salsa are everywhere, the inviting scent of corn tortillas emanates from tortillerias, and colorful murals brighten the streetscape. Artists, lured here by low rents in the 1980s, contribute a touch of eclecticism to the area.

The best way to experience this vibrant district is to stroll along 18th Street, admire the late-19th-century buildings – one of the most interesting is the Romanesque-style Thalia Hall at the corner of Allport Street – and perhaps stop at a street vendor for a tasty cob of roasted corn or "elote".

For more substantial fare, one of the best restaurants in Pilsen is Nuevo León (No. 1515), where the food is tasty and the portions huge. Café Jumping Bean (No. 1439) exhibits work by local artists and serves up

Café Jumping Bean on Chicago's Lower West Side

For hotels and restaurants see pp142–5 and pp148–57

delicious snacks. Panaderia El Paraiso (No. 1156) is an excellent local bakery.

The cultural heart of Pilsen is the **National Museum of Mexican Art** (1852 West 19th Street; 312-738-1503; 10am–5pm Tue–Sun), the largest Mexican arts institution in the US. The museum rotates a broad range of exhibitions, covering subjects as diverse as ancient Mexico and young avant-garde artists. The more than 1,500 works in the permanent collection include Mexican masters such as Diego Rivera.

A Capuchin monkey at Tropic World watching visitors

Signs for Mexican bakeries and eateries lining the streets of Pilsen

❾ Brookfield Zoo

First Ave & 31st St., Brookfield. **Tel** (708) 608-8000. 🚊 Hollywood (Burlington Northern Santa Fe line). 🚌 304, 311. **Open** 10am–5pm Mon–Fri, 10am–6pm Sat & Sun. 🎟️ (free Jan–Feb: Tue, Thu, Sat, Sun; Oct–Dec: Tue, Thu; separate adm to some exhibits). ♿🅿️📷📖🅿️ Lectures, weekend special events.
🆆 brookfieldzoo.org

Brookfield Zoo, opened in 1934, is one of the largest zoos in the US. More than 5,900 animals representing approximately 440 species, gathered from around the world, roam realistic habitats.

Many of the animal exhibits are outdoors, along the zoo's 15 miles (24 km) of trails, but there are also a number of fascinating indoor displays, such as the Living Coast and Tropic World. The Fragile Kingdom comprises two indoor exhibits – an African desert and an Asian rainforest, with indigenous bats, squirrels, and foxes – and an outdoor display featuring large cats, including an Amur (Siberian) tiger. Nearby is the 2,000-seat Dolphinarium. Shows featuring Atlantic bottlenose dolphins are offered here daily. To the north of the Dolphinarium is Pinniped Point: outdoor pools containing sea lions, harbor seals, and walruses.

At the southeast corner of the grounds is the Children's Zoo, where kids can pet barnyard animals and watch cow and goat milking.

Another children's favorite is Tropic World, one of the largest indoor mixed-species exhibits in the world. Here, rainforest creatures and primates from South America, Asia, and Africa swing through trees and wander the forest floor while visitors watch from the observation deck. The Brazilian tapir, with a flexible snout; the giant anteater, with a 2-ft- (0.6-m-) long tongue; and Ramar, the 365-lb (165-kg) silverback gorilla, are particularly impressive. Close by is the Swamp, an indoor re-created cypress swamp with egrets, storks, and a 10-ft- (3-m-) long American alligator, which sleeps with its eyes open.

The Living Coast features three habitats of South America's western coast: open ocean, near-shore waters, and rocky shores. Jellyfish, sharks, and penguins are just a few of the creatures to be found here.

At the interactive Be a Bird exhibit, visitors can learn about bird anatomy and behavior, and test their own ability to fly.

One of the most spectacular exhibits is Habitat Africa! This re-created savanna is complete with giraffes and wild dogs. A "danger game" trail allows visitors to pretend they're thirsty animals walking to a waterhole, their steps activating taped sounds of predators.

Along the zoo's northern boundary are enclosures for large animals, including the unusual Grevy's zebras. To the south, near Roosevelt Fountain, is Pachyderm House, home to elephants, rhinos, and hippos.

A hippopotamus grazing in the Pachyderm House

⑩ Morton Arboretum

4100 Illinois Route 53, Lisle.
Tel (630) 968-0074. 🚉 Lisle
(Burlington Northern Santa Fe line).
Open 7am–sunset daily. 🎨 (discount
Wed). ♿🚻🖊🎭 **P** Workshops,
library. **W** **mortonarb.org**

Morton Arboretum is home to more than 3,400 types of trees, shrubs, and other plants from around the world. Eight lakes and ponds dot this 2.5-sq-mile (6.5-sq-km) outdoor museum, providing wonderful picnic settings.

Founded in 1922 by Joy Morton of the Morton Salt Company, the arboretum's mission is educational. It conducts scientific research as well as providing informative public displays. Collections are grouped according to plant families and habitats, allowing visitors to learn about each species' unique features and to compare related plants.

The arboretum's Daffodil Glade is particularly stunning in spring. Its Schulenberg Prairie, radiant in summer, is a pioneering landscape restoration begun in the early 1960s by Ray Schulenberg. The prairie is admired throughout the Midwest as a fine re-creation of this now-endangered prairie that covered the region before settlement. The maples are dramatic in the fall; the evergreen trees striking in winter. If you do not have time to hike along any of the

14 miles (23 km) of trails, you can drive through the arboretum in about 50 minutes via 9 miles (15 km) of one-way roads. Open-air tram tours are offered daily (weather permitting).

Begin your visit at the visitors' center, located near the entrance. The center lists daily events and seasonal bloom information. It also has an excellent bookstore and a dining area overlooking a pond. The arboretum's Thornhill Education Center (open weekdays) houses displays about Joy Morton and the Morton family. The Sterling Morton Library has a wide range of publications on plants, gardening and landscaping, and natural history. It also holds rare botanical books and prints.

⑪ Illinois and Michigan Canal National Heritage Corridor

From Chicago's south branch of Chicago River to LaSalle-Peru.
Tel (815) 220-1848. See The History of Chicago: p17. **W** **canalcor.org**

The first Europeans to explore the Chicago region – Louis Jolliet and Father Jacques Marquette – urged, in their 1673 expedition report, the building of a canal to connect Lake Michigan to the Des Plaines and Illinois rivers. They believed that such a transportation link would

St. James of the Sag, burial place of many canal laborers

be of great economic benefit to the region. It took a century and a half for their prediction to come true, and the loss of many – mostly Irish – canal laborers to diseases such as dysentery and cholera, but when the Illinois and Michigan (I&M) Canal opened in 1848, it did indeed transform the area's economy. It also established Chicago as the transportation center of the Midwest.

As the use of rail to transport freight became increasingly popular, however, canal traffic declined. Carrying waste away from Chicago became the canal's primary purpose, until the Sanitary and Ship Canal took over this function in 1914. The I&M Canal, with its 15 locks, was abandoned entirely in 1933 when the Illinois Waterway replaced it as a connection between the Great Lakes and Mississippi River.

Fifty years later, in 1984, the canal was designated a national heritage corridor. Today, with almost 100 miles (160 km) of multiuse trails running alongside the canal, the canal route offers abundant recreational opportunities, from bird-watching to biking, hiking, and canoeing. The route passes through more than 40 towns and cities, sites of historic buildings and fascinating museums.

A good place to begin your exploration is the town of Lockport, 30 miles (48 km) southwest of Chicago. During the canal's heyday, this town

Lush trees reflected in one of Morton Arboretum's several lakes

thrived as the center of the boat-building and -repair trades. The visitors' center (200 West 8th Street) in Lockport's historic Gaylord Building, the oldest industrial structure along the waterway, offers maps and information. Adjacent to the center is a restored pioneer settlement, its buildings characteristic of those built during the development of the canal.

Will County Historical Society Museum is located in Lockport's scenic 1837 canal headquarters building. Tour guides tell stories of the canal and explain historic artifacts.

⑫ Pullman Historic District

Bounded by 111th & 115th sts., Ellis & Cottage Grove aves. **M** 95/Dan Ryan then bus 111. **R** 111th St. (Electric District line). **i** 11141 S Cottage Grove Ave. **Tel** (773) 785-8901. **Open** 11am–3pm Tue–Sun. **📷** May–Oct: 12:30pm, 1:30pm 1st month; call (773) 785-8901. **P** **W** pullmanil.org

Pullman Historic District, one of Chicago's best-preserved 19th-century communities, is the site of a fascinating – if ultimately unsuccessful – experiment. The town, the first of its kind in the US, was built by George M. Pullman, founder of the luxury rail-carriage manufacturer Pullman Palace Car Company, to house his employees. In 1879, Pullman purchased 6.25 sq miles (16 sq km) of

Interior of Hotel Florence, typical of the town's Queen Anne-style elegance

marshland in Chicago's far south side, 12 miles (19 km) south of downtown Chicago. He hired architect Solon S. Beman and landscape architect Nathan F. Barrett to plan the company town. Most of the more than 1,700 row houses and apartment units were constructed between 1880 and 1885.

Workers rented the living quarters from Pullman, who expected to realize a 6 per cent profit by collecting rent on all the buildings, including the church and library. This was the first development to offer the working class indoor plumbing, gas, and recreational facilities.

The experiment ended in acrimony when Pullman laid off workers and cut wages without lowering rents during the 1894 depression. A huge strike, which eventually spread across the

Ornate west window of Greenstone Church

entire nation, ensued. The US government intervened, sending in federal troops. The workers lost the seven-week strike, but Pullman's experiment was tainted with failure. He died three years later, in 1897, still resentful. By 1907, all the houses in Pullman had been sold to private buyers.

Plans in 1960 to demolish the area's buildings and create an industrial park were defeated by residents. The district of Pullman was designated a national landmark in 1971. Today, many of the row houses have been restored and are individually owned. The town is easily explored in an afternoon; maps are available at the visitor center.

Hotel Florence (11111 S Forestville Ave), named for Pullman's favorite daughter, is a superb 1881 example of Queen Anne style. The hotel is now a small museum, and is gradually undergoing an extensive renovation.

The mansions lining 111th and 112th streets were built for Pullman executives; the Pullman colors of maroon and green frame the windows and doors. The Greenstone Church (1882) and the curved Beman-designed Colonnade Apartments and Town Houses by Market Hall are also worth a look. The Market Circle apartments (1892) were bachelor units.

A building that once housed several Pullman Palace Car Company workers

THREE GUIDED WALKS

With a rich architectural history that demands to be examined up close, Chicago is particularly rewarding to visitors exploring on foot. Three guided walks, two of which are on the city's North Side, and one in the Downtown Core, are described here.

The first, farther north in Lakeview, is a short urban stroll that takes in the eclectic shops of Belmont Avenue, the lively gay scene of Boystown, with its rainbow-colored pylons lining Halsted Street, and the American baseball shrine that is Wrigley Field. Also here you'll find the intriguing Alta Vista Terrace, a narrow street of 1904 row houses modeled after London's Mayfair, and the fascinating Graceland Cemetery, where such

Chicago luminaries as Marshall Field and Mies van der Rohe are laid to rest. The second walk, just to the north of the city's Downtown Core, explores Lincoln Park itself and the neighborhood to the park's west. This three-hour walk can include visits to the new Chicago History Museum and to several gems within the park, such as Lincoln Park Zoo with its child-friendly working farm, the beautiful Lincoln Park Conservatory, as well as the scenic path along Lake Michigan.

The third walk is a visual feast of outdoor art and architecture with the skyline of the Loop readily displaying its treasures in the background.

CHOOSING A WALK

The Three Walks
This map shows the location of the three guided walks in relation to the main sightseeing areas of Chicago.

0 kilometers 2

0 miles 2

Key

• • • Walk route

Lakeview Walk
(p 123)

A Walk in
Lincoln Park
(pp 124–5)

*Lake
Michigan*

*North
Side*

A Walk in
Downtown Core
(pp 126–7)

*South Loop
& Near
South Side*

Curious sea lion at Lincoln Park Zoo *(see p124)*

A 90-Minute Walk in Lakeview

From gray concrete streets to the gentle green slopes of Graceland Cemetery, this stroll through the north side of Lakeview is an urban adventure that reveals the charms – both historic and present-day – of one of Chicago's liveliest nooks. After taking in the sports-fanatic atmosphere of baseball's famous Wrigley Field and the colorful epicenter of Chicago's gay scene, meander your way past restaurants, eclectic boutiques, and cultural landmarks, joining the motley crowd of young and old.

⑤ Lifesize statue of 6-year-old Inez Clark, Graceland Cemetery

0 meters	400
0 yards	400

Wrigleyville

Back on Halsted Street, take a left at Addison Street, and you'll see the legendary Wrigley Field ③ (see p116) in the distance. Built in 1914, it's one of the oldest ballparks in the US, and home of the Chicago Cubs who, dubbed "lovable losers," haven't won a World Series in over 100 years. Go north on Sheffield Avenue, then a left turn on Grace Street. Here you will find an architectural gem, the Alta Vista Terrace District ④ (see p116).

Graceland Cemetery

Head northwest up W. Irving Park Road, to see the lush Victorian-style Graceland Cemetery ⑤ (see p116), the final resting place of some of Chicago's finest.

Southport Avenue

From here, stroll west on Irving Park Road to charming Southport Avenue, with its pubs, boutiques, and restaurants. At 3745 N. Southport Avenue is the former silent movie house, the Mercury Theater ⑥, a 300-seat space hosting local and touring productions. Just south of this, you'll spot the old-time marquee ⑦ of the Music Box Theatre ⑦, built in 1929 and still drawing crowds for obscure arthouse films.

Clark and Belmont/Boystown

Turn right out of the Belmont station and you soon hit Ann Sather's ①, a historic Swedish

③ Wrigley Field, one of the oldest ballparks in the US

Key

••• Walk Route

café at 909 W. Belmont Avenue famous for its cinnamon rolls. A few doors down is the lively intersection of N. Clark Street and Belmont Avenue – a great spot for people-watching. Continue across N. Clark Street, once an Indian trail that ran 200 miles (322 km) north to Green Bay, Wisconsin, and you're in Boystown, the gay pocket of Lakeview. At the next corner is Halsted Street ②, officially the country's first designated gay neighborhood, with its pairs of tall, rainbow-ringed pylons erected in 1999.

Tips for Walkers

Starting point: Belmont El station.
Length: 3.5 miles (5.5 km).
Getting there: Take the Purple (rush hours only), Brown or Red Line train to Belmont, or the No. 22 bus to Clark and Belmont.

For keys to symbols *see back flap*

A Three-Hour Walk in Lincoln Park

One of Chicago's greatest treasures is its park system, and this leisurely walk is a lovely way to explore one of the quiet open spaces that lie within minutes of the skyscrapers of Downtown. Lincoln Park covers more than 1,200 acres (486 hectares) along Lake Michigan north of the Magnificent Mile, and offers diversions for strollers of all ages, including the nation's oldest free public zoo. Visitors can also visit the Chicago History Museum and an infamous site in gangster lore.

④ South Pond, with paddleboats for rental on fine days

① Front of the renovated Chicago History Museum

Chicago History Museum

After expensive renovations, the once-modest Chicago Historical Society reopened in late 2006 as the sleek, airy, family-friendly Chicago History Museum ① *(see p76)*, bringing the city's past to life with two floors of interactive exhibits. In the lobby a colorfully painted 1978 Chevy lowrider greets visitors; in the galleries beyond are permanent exhibits such as historical dioramas, one of the city's first El cars, and family-friendly displays. From the museum, take the path behind the building to admire

an example of one of Chicago's many works of public art, Augustus Saint-Gaudens' 1887 bronze of President Abraham Lincoln ②, depicted deep in thought.

Lincoln Park Zoo and Beyond

Returning toward the museum, take the sidewalk path to the right and under the LaSalle Drive overpass, following the signs for the zoo. On a stretch of green to the west, on Wednesday and Saturday mornings from May to October, the organic Green City Market ③ has tempting displays of fresh cheeses, breads, and produce. A few minutes' walk farther up the path brings you to South Pond ④, a small haven for frogs, turtles, ducks, and geese. At the north end is the Café Brauer ⑤, a handsome red-brick, Prairie Style structure that bustles in summer. Stop for a beer or just to take in the fine views of the city skyline. Weather permitting, paddleboats can also be hired from here. Just north of the café is the southern entrance to the Lincoln Park Zoo ⑥ *(see pp114–15)*, one of the city's top attractions. Established

in 1868, the zoo is free and open daily, and despite its modest size of 35 acres (14 hectares) boasts more than 1,000 animals. Take the zoo's north exit and you're steps away from the lush, green Lincoln Park Conservatory ⑦, where a path leads through four glass display houses of towering

⑦ Lincoln Park Conservatory, four glasshouses of tropical greenery

palms, cycads, ferns, mosses, and fragrant orchids. North and just west of the Conservatory on Fullerton Parkway is another Chicago landmark, the lesser-known Alfred Caldwell Lily Pool ⑧, an intimate, serene garden designed in the Prairie School style with layered stone ledges and a waterfall.

⑨ Peggy Notebaert Nature Museum , with child-friendly exhibits

praying mantises feed at the Istock Family Look-In Lab; and observe 1,000 butterflies in the Judy Istock Butterfly Haven. This eco-friendly museum is "green" from its solar rooftop panels to rooftop gardens to the native prairie grasses that surround it.

The St. Valentine's Day Massacre

Just a few blocks away – but a world apart from the serenity of the park – is the site of one of the grisliest events in Chicago's history. Walk west on West Fullerton Parkway to North Clark Avenue Turning left here, make your way to 2122 North Clark Avenue ⑩, where stands a vacant, fenced-in lawn with a few trees. You'll find no marker here, but this is one of the most infamous spots in the city. In a warehouse here on the morning of Valentine's Day 1929, seven of George "Bugs" Moran's men were

gunned down by thugs dressed as cops hired by Al Capone. The warehouse was torn down in 1967 but a central tree marks the spot where the men were killed.

Second City and St. Michael's Church

Continuing south on Clark Avenue, bear right onto North Wells Street (past Lincoln Ave.); on the northwest corner is the Piper's Alley center ⑪, home to one of the nation's legendary comedy theaters, Second City (see p169). Top comics such as John Belushi, Tina Fey, Bill Murray, Gilda Radner, and Mike Myers got their start here, and newcomers still perform the company's signature blend of sketches, music, and improvisational comedy six nights a week.

Now head west on North Avenue four blocks to Cleveland Street; on your right you will see the majestic 1873 St. Michael's Church ⑫ (see p72), one of the city's oldest and grandest. The towering, airy interior features stained glass windows and five altars – one of which is Romanesque and made of silver, gold, and onyx.

⑫ Interior of St Michael's Church, with fine stained glass windows

Tips for Walkers

Starting point: Chicago History Museum.
Length: 3 miles (4.8 km).
Getting there: Take bus No. 22 or 36 to North Ave., or the Brown Line El to Sedgwick and walk east 5 mins to Clark Street.
Stopping off points: Café Brauer, 2021 N. Stockton Dr., has fast fare – burgers, salads, ice-cream, beer – at an outdoor café. North Pond Café, 2610 N Cannon Dr., is a good place for brunch or lunch.

Map labels:
⑨
⑧
⑦
Lincoln Park Zoo ⑥
NORTH CANNON DRIVE
LAKE SHORE DRIVE
⑤
④ South Pond
③
NORTH CLARK AVENUE
NORTH WELLS STREET
N LA SALLE DRIVE
②
①
W NORTH AVE

Stroll across Fullerton Parkway to the Peggy Notebaert Nature Museum ⑨, a contemporary glass and stone structure housing child-friendly exhibits on regional plant and animal life. Visitors can build a dam at the River Works display; watch

0 meters   300
0 yards   300

Key

••• Walk Route

A Three-Hour Walk in the Downtown Core

Dozens of works by world-renowned artists are on public display throughout Chicago's Downtown Core. This walk explores a selection from this huge outdoor art gallery and the buildings in the area, many of which are themselves works of art. The spectacular backdrop that the Loop's commanding architecture provides ensures excellent sights along the way.

Continue to walk north, passing the Marquette Building *(see p45)* on your left, to *The Four Seasons* (1974) ⑥ by Marc Chagall (1887–1985), at First National Plaza. This huge, four-sided mosaic consists of thousands of tiles in more than 250 colors that illustrate various Chicago scenes. Across the street is the ground-breaking Inland Steel Building ⑦. Steel pilings were driven 85 feet (26 m) down to the bedrock to support the building. Follow

State. Continue north, bearing left at Jackson, to the Ralph Metcalfe Federal Building and the stainless steel and aluminium sculpture *The Town-Ho's Story* (1993) ④ by Frank Stella (b.1936).

⑧ Miró's Chicago

③ View of buildings in the Loop looking west from Grant Park

South Michigan Avenue to South Dearborn Street

Start at the Adams CTA Station ① and walk east on Adams Street, turning right onto South Michigan Avenue and past the stately Art Institute of Chicago *(see p48–51)*. Lorado Taft's (1860–1936) *Fountain of the Great Lakes* (1913) ②, with its five female figures, is at the south end of the main building. One block farther south is the main entrance to Grant Park ③, from where there is a good view of the buildings along Michigan Avenue, including the Santa Fe Building *(see p47)*. Walk west along Van Buren Street, turning right at

Dearborn Street to West Randolph Street

Cross Dearborn Street and enter the courtyard of the Federal Center *(see p45)* to see American sculptor Alexander Calder's (1898–1976) dramatic *Flamingo* (1974) ⑤. Retrace your steps to Dearborn Street.

Dearborn Street to Washington, bearing left. On the left is Catalan artist Joan Miró's (1893–1983) *Chicago* (1981) ⑧, a surreal feminine figure made of plaster and bronze and studded with colorful ceramic tiles. Just north across the street in the Richard J. Daley Plaza is an untitled sculpture by Pablo Picasso (1881–1973) ⑨. The piece created a stir when first erected, as Chicagoans debated its

⑥ *The Four Seasons* by Marc Chagall

merits. Daley Plaza is considered to be the political center of Chicago. City Hall ⑩, with its 75-foot (23-m) Corinthian columns, can be seen at the corner of Washington and Clark. Continue along Washington Street, turning right onto LaSalle. On the northwest corner of Lasalle and Randolph is the Illinois State Office Building. Step inside to experience its "Story

Atrium". On its exterior is *Freeform* (1993) ⑪, which Chicago sculptor Richard Hunt (b.1935) created to symbolize "a government supporting individual freedoms." Walk east on Randolph Street to the James R. Thompson Center *(see p58)* and French Art Brut artist Jean Dubuffet's (1901–1985) fiberglass sculpture *Monument with Standing Beast* (1984) ⑫.

⑭ **Lantern on No. 35 East Wacker Drive**

Tips for Walkers

Starting point: Adams CTA station, at the corner of Wabash Avenue and East Adams Street.
Time: Three hours.
Getting there: Take the Brown, Green, Orange, or Purple Line CTA train to Adams Station.
Stopping-off point: Numerous cafés and restaurants can be found along the route, though many may be open only during weekday business hours. Soprafina Marketcaffe, at 10 North Dearborn Street, serves Italian fare, from biscotti to pizza. West Egg Cafe, at 66 East Washington Street, offers breakfast and lunch at modest prices.

Wacker Drive. At No. 35 ⑭ *(see p57)* is the former Jewelers Building, designed in 1926 and one of the last skyscrapers built in Chicago in the Beaux Arts style. Follow Wacker Drive east, turning right at Michigan Avenue, then left at Randolph Street to Prudential Plaza ⑮, consisting of two buildings. The Prudential Building, a towering limestone and aluminum structure built in 1952, was the first skyscraper to be built in the Loop since the 1930s. "Pru Two," with its chevron top, suggests New York's Chrysler Building.

State Street to East Randolph Street

One block east, on State Street, is the elegant Chicago Theatre ⑬ *(see p56)*. It was dubbed "the wonder theater of the world" when it opened in 1921. Its grand exterior features a miniature replica of Paris' Arc de Triomphe. Turn right at

Key

••• Suggested route

0 meters 250
0 yards 250

⑬ **Facade of the Chicago Theatre**

⑮ The two Prudential buildings, left; the AON Center, right

For keys to symbols *see back flap*

BEYOND CHICAGO

Exploring Beyond Chicago

Visitors eager to discover more of Illinois won't be disappointed by the rich mix of historical sights, recreational activities, and picturesque countryside Chicago's environs have to offer. Excursions to the attractive North Shore towns of Evanston, Wilmette, Glencoe, and Lake Forest will take you along the shoreline of Lake Michigan, affording stunning views.

For those wishing to venture farther, the resort area of Lake Geneva awaits just across the Wisconsin state line. The delightful, historic town of Galena lies near the Iowa border, a three-and-half hour drive west of Chicago. The drive to both leads through rural farmland dotted with small towns and state parks. The typically flat Midwestern terrain gives way to rolling hills just outside Galena.

Galena's Belvedere Mansion
(see p136)

Key

▬▬ Highway
— Major road
═══ Minor road
▬▬ Major railroad
— Minor railroad
▬▬ State boundary

A picturesque circular barn near Highway 20, West Galena

◀ Baha'i House of Worship, Wilmette, Illinois

For keys to symbols see back flap

Rustic Road No. 29, on the outskirts of Lake Geneva

0 kilometers   40
0 miles   20

Getting Around

Chicago has excellent Metra commuter rail links to the northern suburbs. The Union Pacific/North line, departing from the Ogilvie Transportation Center, services Evanston, Wilmette, Glencoe, and Lake Forest, with frequent trains during rush hour and every one to three hours at other times. The CTA purple line also services Evanston. You will need a car to reach Lake Geneva and Galena. Highway I-94 leads north from Chicago; I-90 is the western route.

Francis Stupey Log Cabin in Highland Park, on Chicago's North Shore

For hotels and restaurants see pp142–5 and pp148–57

❶ Evanston

Evanston, on the shores of Lake Michigan, 14 miles (22 km) north of Chicago, offers stunning beaches, charming boutiques and restaurants, and exciting museums, art galleries, and theater. Originally known as Ridgeville, it began as a community of farmers from New England, and Irish and German immigrants. In 1850, a group of Chicago Methodists bought a large tract of lakefront land, opening Northwestern University five years later. Ridgeville changed its name to Evanston in 1857 to honor John Evans, one of the university's founders. By the 1870s, wealthy Chicagoans, in search of cleaner neighborhoods, were moving to Evanston. Many of their mansions still stand.

Charles Gates Dawes House, overlooking Lake Michigan

Exploring Evanston

Many of Evanston's attractions are concentrated in the historic downtown around Grove Street and Sherman Avenue, an area easily explored on foot. Other interesting districts include those at Central Street, and at Chicago Avenue and Dempster Street. The large lakefront university campus, the buildings of which reflect widely varied architectural styles, provides greenspace ideal for strolling. Or you can saunter along Forest Avenue to see the historic mansions built for Chicago's wealthy.

🏛 Charles Gates Dawes House and Evanston History Center

225 Greenwood St. **Tel** (847) 475-3410. **Open** 1–4pm Thu–Sun. **Closed** major public hols. 🎟 (children under 6 free). 📷 mandatory. ♿

This massive Chateauesque mansion was designed in 1894 by Henry Edwards-Ficken for Robert Sheppard, treasurer of Northwestern University.

Sheppard sold the mansion in 1909 to Charles Gates Dawes, who went on to become US vice-president under Calvin Coolidge. The restored 25-room house, home to the Evanston Historical Society, showcases the period 1925–9.

🏛 Frances Willard House

1730 Chicago Ave. **Tel** (847) 328-7500. **Open** 1–4pm 1st & 3rd Sun of month or by appt. **Closed** major hols. 🎟 📷 mandatory. 🏠 🖥 **franceswillard house.org**

Pioneering suffragist and Woman's Christian Temperance Union (WCTU) activist Frances Willard lived here from 1865 until her death in 1898.

This quaint, Gothic Revival style *(see p28)* house, built by Willard's father in 1865, is now a museum devoted to Willard's life and the history of the WCTU. The world's oldest voluntary, non-sectarian women's organization, the WCTU is best known for its campaign against alcohol.

🏛 Block Sculpture Garden

40 Arts Circle. **Tel** (847) 491-4000. **Open** 10am–5pm Tue, Sat & Sun; 10am–8pm Wed–Fri.

The Block Museum's sculpture garden showcases 20th-century sculpture. Among the garden's treasures are two large, bronze abstract sculptures by British artist Barbara Hepworth (1903–1975) and an intriguing movable bronze sculpture by Spanish artist Joan Miró (1893–1983).

🏛 Mary and Leigh Block Museum of Art

40 Arts Circle. **Tel** (847) 491-4000. **Open** 10am–5pm Tue–Sun, 10am–8pm Wed & Fri. ♿ 📷 call for details. Lectures, films, concerts. 🖥 **blockmuseum. northwestern.edu**

Artwork from the 14th century onward and thematic historical displays are featured at this art museum of Northwestern University, one of the US's top university museums. Major exhibits also often stop here.

🏛 Grosse Point Light Station

2601 Sheridan Rd. **Tel** (847) 328-6961. **Closed** hol weekends. 🎟 📷 mandatory: Jun–Sep: 2, 3, 4pm Sat, Sun. 🖥 **grossepointlighthouse.net**

This lighthouse was built in 1873 in response to one of the worst maritime disasters on the Great Lakes – the 1860 sinking of the paddle wheeler *Lady Elgin*, in which nearly 300 people died.

During the summer, visitors can climb to the top of the lighthouse for wonderful views of the town and lake.

A maritime museum is on the lower floor. Plants native to Illinois are grown in the

Grosse Point Light Station, guiding ships since 1873

Interior of the Mitchell Museum of the American Indian

Wildflower Trail Garden, on the grounds of the station.

Evanston Art Center
2603 Sheridan Rd. **Tel** (847) 475- 5300. **Open** 10am–9pm Mon–Thu; 9am–4pm Fri & Sat; 1–4pm Sun. **Closed** major public hols. by donation. 1st-floor gallery. Lectures, workshops.
W evanstonartcenter.org
Housed in a 1926 mansion, the gallery of this community art center exhibits regional contemporary artwork by both established and emerging artists. Gallery talks by exhibiting artists

are offered regularly. The center's annual spring art auction is a great opportunity to acquire work by Midwest artists.

The lovely grounds of the center were designed by the Prairie School-influenced landscape architect Jens Jensen, who designed several parks in Chicago, including Columbus Park and the conservatory in Garfield Park, which is on Chicago's west side.

Mitchell Museum of the American Indian
3001 Central St. **Tel** (847) 475-1030. **Open** 10am–5pm Tue–Sat; 10am–8pm Thu; noon–4pm Sun. **Closed** major public hols, last two weeks Aug. by donation. Lectures, concerts, films.
W mitchellmuseum.org

The Mitchell Museum showcases North American Indian cultures from prehistoric to contemporary times. More than 6,000 domestic objects, including pottery, baskets, clothing, and textiles, are on display. The Mitchell is particularly rich in artifacts of Indians of the Midwest. Temporary exhibitions at the museum highlight ancient and present-day Native crafts.

Evanston

1. Charles Gates Dawes House
2. Frances Willard House
3. Block Sculpture Garden
4. Mary and Leigh Block Museum of Art
5. Evanston Art Center
6. Grosse Pointe Light Station
7. Mitchell Museum of the American Indian

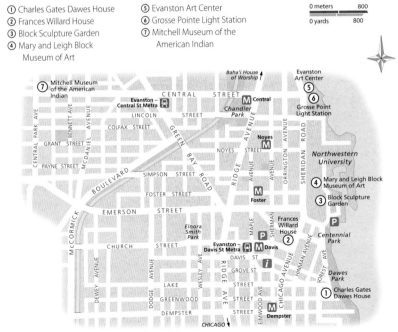

For keys to symbols see back flap

❷ National Vietnam Veterans Art Museum

4041 N Milwaukee Ave. **Map** 6 D1.
Tel (312) 326-0270. Ⓜ Irving Park
(Blue Line) then bus 80. **Open**
10am–5pm Tue–Sat. **Closed** major
hols. 🅿 ♿ ⬚ (for groups). ▢ 🖼

The National Vietnam Veterans
Art Museum is the only
museum in the world with a
permanent collection that
focuses on the subject of war
from a personal point of view.
Bringing together more than
700 works of art in diverse
media created by 140 artists
who participated in one of
America's most divisive wars,
this collection presents a
humanist statement on behalf
of veterans of all wars.

This adamantly apolitical
museum began when two
Chicago veterans, Ned
Broderick and Joe Fornelli,
began collecting artworks
created by fellow veterans.
The City of Chicago donated
an abandoned warehouse
and the museum opened
in its new home in 1996.

The belongings of prisoner-
of-war Major General John L.
Borling, who lived in captivity in
North Vietnam for seven years, is
documented in the display *My
Cup Runneth Over*. In 2001, the
museum dedicated a permanent
memorial called "Above and
Beyond" honoring all Americans
killed in the Vietnam War.

❸ Baha'i House of Worship

100 Linden Ave., Wilmette. **Tel** (847)
853-2300. Ⓜ Linden. **Open** Gardens
6am–10pm daily; Visitors' Center Jun–
Sep: 10am–8pm, Oct–May:
10am–5pm. Devotions: 9:15am &
12:30pm. ♿ 🅿 🅦 **us.bahai.org**

The Baha'i House of Worship,
gleaming like a white beacon, is
the North Shore's most striking
building. There are seven major
Baha'i houses of worship in the
world; this is the only major one
in North America.

Construction of the house, which
began in 1920, wasn't completed
until 1953. There are nine sides to
this building designed by French-

Fountains and pools dot the serene grounds of the Chicago Botanic Gardens

Canadian architect Louis Bourgeois.
An entrance door is on each side.
Quotations from Baha'u'llah are
carved into the stone, one above
each entrance and each of the nine
alcoves. Elaborate filigree-like
carvings adorn the exterior. A
dome of quartz and white cement
rises 135 ft (41 m) above the central
auditorium, which can seat almost
2,000 people. It is lovely to take a
stroll in the gardens.

❹ Chicago Botanic Garden

1000 Lake Cook Rd., Glencoe.
Tel (847) 835-5440. 🚆 Braeside;
Glencoe (Union Pacific/North line)
then bus 213 or trolley. **Open** Jun–
Sep: 7am–9pm daily, Oct–May: 8am–
sunset daily. **Closed** Dec 25. ♿ ⬚
▢ 🖼 🅿 Lectures, exhibits.
🅦 **chicagobotanic.org**

The Chicago Botanic Garden, 25
miles (40 km) north of downtown
Chicago, is dazzling with its 20
themed gardens and three native

The Baha'i House of Worship, with its
beautifully filigreed dome

habitats of flowers, vines, shrubs,
and trees. Opened in 1972, the
Garden contains 2 million
specimens representing 8,000 plant
families from around the world.

The Gateway Visitor Center,
near the entrance, leads to
the main island, the site of the
majority of the themed gardens.

The English Walled Garden
consists of a secluded enclosure
with six garden "rooms," each. The
Heritage Garden is modeled after
Europe's first botanical garden.
Intoxicating scents of the Rose
Garden's 5,000 rose bushes
accompany the colorful blooms.
Unsurprisingly, the jewel of
the Waterfall Garden is a 45-ft
(14 m) waterfall. Sansho-En, or
"garden of three islands," reflects
the tranquil minimalism of
Japanese garden design.

The Gardens of the Great
Basin include Lakeside
Gardens, Evening Island,
and Water Gardens.

The Garden's three natural
habitat areas (an oak woodland,
a prairie, and a riverscape) offer
wonderful walking trails
through secluded sections of
the grounds.

❺ Lake Forest

🚆 Lake Forest (Union Pacific/North
line). 🚌 472. Deer Path Golf Course:
500 W Deerpath Rd. **Tel** (847) 234-
4282. 🅦 **lakeforestchamber.com**

Lake Forest is one of Chicago's
most affluent suburbs, about
30 miles (48 km) north of
Chicago's Downtown Core.

For hotels and restaurants see pp142–5 and pp148–57

The town was established in the 1850s by a group of Presbyterians who planned to build a college. The St. Louis landscape architect hired to plan the town took advantage of the area's beautiful prairie lands, ravines, and hills, designing streets to follow the natural curves of the landscape.

Presbyterian Lake Forest College, established in 1857, has many grand, late-1800 buildings. The Romanesque-style Hotchkiss Hall was designed by Henry Ives Cobb (see p28) in 1890 and named after the town's planner.

The First Presbyterian Church (700 N Sheridan Rd) was designed by Charles Frost in 1887. The church's unusual design is an adaptation of the New England cottage style, known as Shingle style.

Market Square, in downtown Lake Forest, is one of the first planned suburban shopping centers in the US. Designed in 1916 by Howard Van Doren Shaw, this pleasant town square has a quaint English character.

The best way to experience Lake Forest is to drive on meandering Sheridan Road. Along the route are many beautiful homes on spacious, landscaped grounds.

Golfers can take advantage of Deer Path Golf Course, while at Forest Park Beach, beachgoers can enjoy the cooling waters of Lake Michigan during the summer heat.

Lady of the Lake, a reproduction of a Mississippi paddle wheeler

❻ Lake Geneva

🛈 201 Wrigley Dr, WI. **Tel** (262) 248-4416, 800-345-1020. **Open** 9am–5pm Mon–Fri; 10am–4pm Sat & Sun. 🛝 🏠 🅆 **lakegenevawi.com**

Lake Geneva, 70 miles (113 km) north of Chicago in the state of Wisconsin, nestles on the shores of a spring-fed lake of the same name. There is much to keep you occupied for a weekend in this picturesque resort town and its surrounding rural communities. Boating on the wide lake, hiking, and ballooning are just a few of the possibilities.

Lake Geneva is also a shopper's and diner's paradise. Many of the charming boutiques and antique stores are in turn-of-the-century buildings. Several of the town's restaurants, particularly those along Wrigley Drive, provide spectacular views of the lake.

In autumn, the countryside is ablaze with fall foliage. It is an ideal backdrop to the 21-mile (34-km) trail encircling the lake, a trail that once connected Indian camps. On the western edge of town is a state-designated "Rustic Road," an ideal route for a leisurely drive through the country. In winter, skiing and snowmobiling are popular activities. However, accommodations fill up quickly in summer and traffic is heavy.

Lake Geneva has a rich history. The Oneota tribes of the now-extinct Hopewell Culture Indians, an agricultural people, lived in the area as long ago as 1000 BC. In 1836, the local Potawatomi tribe was evicted from the area, and pioneer Christopher Payne built the first log cabin in town. The site is marked with a plaque on Center Street, north of White River.

The town, laid out in 1837, was originally a sawmill town. Following the Civil War, it became a resort for wealthy Chicagoans, who built their homes on the lakefront.

One of the best ways to see these mansions is by boat. Geneva Lake Cruise Line's fleet of ships includes replicas of a Southern paddle wheeler and a turn-of-the-century lake steamer. The *Walworth II* operates as a US mail boat, one of the last in service. A mail carrier delivers mail during the tour.

Geneva Lake Area Museum of History (255 Mill Street) displays interesting historical photographs and artifacts.

Riviera Docks, departure point for Lake Geneva boat cruises

❼ Galena

A visit to Galena, "the town that time forgot," is like stepping into a bygone era. More than 85 percent of this town, in Jo Daviess County, is on the National Register of Historic Places. Its architectural gems, museums, and unique landscape make Galena a great weekend destination. As early as the 1600s, Indians were mining the area's rich deposits of lead and ore. In the 1820s, as prospectors flocked to Galena, the town became one of the US's most important mining centers. By the mid-1800s, it was a major Mississippi River port. But as rail displaced shipping as the mode of freight transportation, the town went into decline. The expense of tearing down the old buildings ensured that its historic core remained intact.

The old town hall, built in 1872, in historic East Galena

A trolley tour is a great way to explore Galena

Exploring Galena

The best way to explore Galena is on foot or by trolley tour. Downtown parking is limited; it is best to park at the lot by the visitors' center at the old railroad depot.

Galena has a number of noteworthy historic churches. The **Union Baptist Church** (1854) features a Romanesque Revival doorway, and the enchanting **First Presbyterian Church** (1838) has a Georgian spire. The 1838 Erban organ is still played at the Gothic Revival-style *(see p28)* **Grace Episcopal Church**.

The **Galena post office** (1857–9) was originally the Galena Customs House and is the second-oldest continuously operating post office in the US.

❶ Old Train Depot

101 Bouthillier St. **Tel** (847) 464-2536. **Open** Memorial Day weekend–Oct: 9am–5pm Mon–Thu; 9am–7pm Fri, Sat; 10am–5pm Sun. Nov–Memorial Day weekend: 9am–5pm Mon–Sat; 10am–4pm Sun. 🚻

Originally Galena's station for passenger rail service, it was from here that former US president Ulysses S. Grant set off for war. The 1857 Italianate *(see p28)* building is now the Visitor Information Center.

🏛 Belvedere Mansion

1008 Park Ave. **Tel** (815) 777-0747. **Open** 11am–3:30pm daily; 11am–5pm Sat. **Closed** Nov–Memorial Day. 🚻 📷 🅆 **galena belvederemansion.com**

Built in 1857 for J. Russell Jones, a steamship owner and US ambassador to Belgium, the Italianate-style Belvedere Mansion is the largest house in Galena.

Completely restored to its original condition, the 22 rooms contain Victorian furnishings. Pieces include furniture belonging to former US president Theodore Roosevelt, a gold-painted cabinet once owned by entertainer Liberace, and green drapes from the film set of *Gone with the Wind*.

🏛 Washburne House

908 Third St. **Tel** (815) 777-3310. **Open** 10am–4pm Fri. 🚻 📷 mandatory: on the hour and half-hour. 🅃 🅆 **granthome.com**

A stunning example of Greek Revival architecture, this house was built in 1843 for prominent Galena attorney and later US congressman Elihu Washburne (1816–87). Washburne was a comrade of Abraham Lincoln and a strong supporter of the career of Ulysses S. Grant. It was in the library of Washburne's home that Grant first heard the news that he had won the 1868 US presidential election.

The restored interior of the house reflects Victorian middle-class elegance.

🏛 Ulysses S. Grant Home

500 Bouthillier St. **Tel** (815) 777-3310. **Open** Apr–Oct: 9am–4:45pm Wed–Sun. Nov–Mar: 9am–4pm, Wed–Sun. **Closed** public hols. 🚻 📷 mandatory. 🅃 🅆 **granthome.com**

This two-story, brick Italianate *(see p28)* house designed by William Dennison was constructed in 1860. It was given to returning Civil War hero General Ulysses S. Grant by a group of prominent Galena citizens in 1865.

Even though Grant spent little time in the house after being elected US president in 1868, it has been restored to its 1870s appearance and contains furnishings used by the Grant family. Costumed guides lead visitors through the house while telling Grant's story.

The Old Illinois Central Railroad Depot now housing Galena's visitors' center

View of Galena looking northeast from the pedestrian bridge

Dowling House

220 Diagonal St. **Tel** (815) 777-1250. **Open** 11am–4pm daily. 🅿️ 🕐 mandatory.

This 1826 example of vernacular architecture is Galena's oldest house. Built of limestone, it originally served as a miner's trading post and rather crude residence. Informative tour guides recount the history of the house. It has been restored to reflect the era of Galena's early pioneers.

DeSoto House Hotel

230 S Main St. **Tel** (815) 777-0090, (800) 343-6562. 🅿️ 🕐 🅿️ 🆆 desotohouse.com

This hotel was considered the largest, most luxurious hotel west of New York City when it opened its doors in 1855. It was built by Galena merchants in preparation for the boom that accompanied the 1854 arrival of Illinois Central Railroad service in Galena. Many famous Americans, including writer Mark Twain, have stayed here. Abraham Lincoln made a speech from its balcony in 1856, and it was from the DeSoto House Hotel that Ulysses S. Grant ran his 1868 presidential campaign.

Old Market House

123 N Commerce St. **Tel** (815) 777-2570. **Open** 9am–5pm daily. **Closed** Thanksgiving, mid-Dec–mid-Mar. 🅿️ 🕐 mandatory. 🅿️

The handsome Greek Revival-style Market House was built by the City of Galena in 1846. One of the Midwest's oldest extant market houses, it was a hive of activity until the early 1900s. Farmers sold produce, city offices were on the second floor, and the basement was a city jail. Today, an exhibition space has displays of historical interest.

Galena History Museum

211 S Bench St. **Tel** (815) 777-9129. **Open** 9am–4:30pm daily. **Closed** Jan 1,

Easter, Thanksgiving, Dec 24, 25, 31. 🅿️ (children under 10 free). 🅿️ 🆆 galenahistorymuseum.org

This 1858 Italianate mansion, designed by William Dennison, was built for merchant Daniel Barrows. It is now occupied by a museum specializing in the area's history and houses over 10,000 artifacts, including Civil War memorabilia.

The creation of the stunning geology of Jo Daviess County – rugged hills, rocky bluffs, and riveting vistas – is depicted in a large landform model, which shows how Ice Age glaciers detoured around the land, sparing this hilly part of Illinois.

A display on the Galena River tells the story of the Army Corps of Engineers' building of the town's flood dike and massive gate.

Galena City Center

① Old Train Depot
② Belvedere Mansion
③ Washburne House
④ Ulysses S. Grant Home
⑤ DeSoto House Hotel
⑥ Galena History Museum
⑦ Dowling House
⑧ Old Market House

0 meters   300
0 yards   300

For keys to symbols *see back flap*

TRAVELERS' NEEDS

WHERE TO STAY

Chicago has a room for every taste and budget. The top hotels are good value by international standards. For those traveling on a budget, there are many inexpensive, comfortable hotels and youth hostels in the city. Two-room suites are suitable for families, and some come with kitchenettes for guests who want to do their own cooking. Bed-and-breakfasts, often located in charming Victorian houses in residential areas, are also a good option for visitors to Chicago. The listings that follow on pages 142–5, will help you narrow down the numerous choices. We have selected places that represent the best of their kind, in all price categories.

Hotel Burnham's lobby, modeled on the 1891 original *(see p144)*

Where to Look

Most of Chicago's hotels are clustered in two areas – the Downtown Core and the North Side. Downtown hotels are particularly convenient for visitors interested in Chicago's cultural sights such as the Art Institute of Chicago, Museum Campus, and the theater district, as well as those attending conventions at McCormick Place. However, this area can become quiet at night. By contrast, hotels on the North Side, just north of the Loop, are in one of the liveliest areas of the city.

Contact the **Illinois Bureau of Tourism**, the **Visitor Information Center** or the **Chicago Convention and Tourism Bureau** for information.

Facilities

Air-conditioning and cable TV are both standard in Chicago hotels. Fax and photocopy service, Wi-Fi, in-room speaker-phones, exercise facilities, and a swimming pool are amenities to inquire about. Be sure you understand the charges; some hotels offer these facilities for free, other hotels will charge handsomely for them.

The many conventions and trade shows held in the city provide Chicago's hotels with a major part of their business, so most hotels offer an array of business meeting rooms.

Hotel Rates and Discounts

Hotel prices in Chicago are competitive, but keep in mind when booking that they charge a steep 16.4 per cent room tax.

Some establishments offer discounts to visitors attending a convention or major exhibition. They may also offer corporate rates and discounts to persons in the military, senior citizens, teachers, automobile-club members, and frequent flyers. Business travelers often leave the city on weekends, and hotels will offer special weekend rates, so be sure to ask.

With the exception of B&Bs, hotels in Chicago do not usually include meals in the room rate.

Agencies such as **Hotels.com** and **Priceline.com** offer a price comparison service, and have good rates. Both charge a fee if you cancel for any reason.

Hidden Costs

Room rates are usually quoted assuming double occupancy; but always check in advance because some hotels quote single-occupancy rates and charge as much as $35 per night for a second person.

Keep in mind, too, that a room with a view will likely come at a premium.

Convenience costs money. Parking at the hotel can lead to an increase of as much as $50 a day in the bill. There is also a steep premium charge for any drinks and snacks consumed from the room's mini-bar. A telephone call made from the room will cost substantially more than one made from the pay phone in the hotel lobby.

Federal law states that hotels must inform guests of any extra charges, but check the small print yourself while making a reservation.

Guests relaxing in their suite at Palmer House Hilton *(see p143)*

◀ The Palmer House Hilton, one of the oldest and grandest hotels of Chicago

Lobby of Hotel Allegro *(see p142)*, inspired by the building's 1920s design

How to Reserve

If there is one secret to finding a good room, it is planning. Reserve as far in advance as possible. Hotels can fill up quickly when a convention is in town. Alternately, sites like Hotels.com and Priceline.com offer great last-minute deals on unbooked rooms.

Reservations usually require a deposit by credit card. You will be given a confirmation or reservation number when a room is booked. Always confirm the reservation before arriving at the hotel.

Those who have special requirements, such as elevators, ice machines, and a quiet room away from busy streets, should make these known when booking a room.

Notify the hotel if you expect to arrive later than 5pm, or you may lose your reservation. To cancel the reservation, it is advisable to record the cancelation number to avoid being charged for the room later. Most hotels do not charge a cancelation fee if they are given up to 24 or 48 hours' prior notice. Without sufficient notice, the room may be chargeable.

Travelers with Disabilities

Hotels in the United States are by law required to provide facilities for wheelchair-bound persons (some older properties are exempted from this rule). Most establishments are happy to provide rooms and assistance to travelers with disabilities. Persons with visual impairments are allowed to bring guide dogs into hotels.

Traveling with Children

Children are welcome in all Chicago hotels, and few charge extra when one or two children aged under 12 stay in their parent's room. Ask about family rates when making reservations, and make sure the room is suitable. The hotel may offer a room with two beds or a sofa that easily converts to a bed to accommodate children. Many hotels will provide a cot for an additional $15 to $35 a night. Suite hotel rooms are also a good option for familiies.

Bed-and-Breakfasts

A B&B can be a charming alternative to a standard hotel. Primarily found in residential neighborhoods, such accommodations range from rooms in Victorian homes to high-rise buildings. Some have private bathrooms. In general, B&Bs are reasonably priced. For more information, get in touch with the **Illinois Bed and Breakfast Association.**

Recommended Hotels

The hotels listed in this guide have been chosen to represent a wide variety of the type of accommodations available, suitable to the needs of any traveler. These include quaint inns, trendy boutique hotels, budget chains, and hotels that are listed among the top five-star options in the world. For an inexpensive stay in the city, one can head to the **Hostelling International Chicago** website, to choose from a host of budget accommodations. Another option is the **Chicago Getaway**

Hostel, a youthful spot located in the Lincoln Park neighborhood.

Accommodations outside of the central downtown area also often offer better value than downtown hotels, so we've included a section of recommended accommodations from throughout the city and surrounding area.

For the best of the best, look out for hotels featuring the DK Choice symbol. These establishments have been highlighted in recognition of an exceptional feature – a stunning location, notable architecture, ambience, or exceptional facilities, etc. The majority of these are very popular, so be sure to reserve ahead of time.

Where to Stay

Boutique
Downtown Core

Hotel Allegro $$
171 W Randolph St., 60601
Tel *312-236-0123* **Map** 3 C1
W allegrochicago.com
Comfort and upscale amenities
in the heart of the theatre district.

Hotel Monaco $$
225 N Wabash Ave., 60601
Tel *312-960-8500* **Map** 4 D1
W monaco-chicago.com
Bright, cheerful hotel, with a free
evening wine hour in the lobby.

W Hotel City Center $$
172 W Adams St., 60603
Tel *312-332-1200* **Map** 3 C2
W wchicagocitycenter.com
Hip hotel with a clubby feel,
popular with young people.

Hard Rock Hotel $$$
230 N Michigan Ave., 60601
Tel *312-345-1000* **Map** 4 D1
W hardrockhotelchicago.com
Music-themed hotel in a 1929 Art
Deco building, with unique rooms.

The Wit $$$
201 N State St., 60601
Tel *312-467-0200* **Map** 3 C1
W thewithotel.com
Funky, well-located Downtown
hotel, of the Doubletree chain.

North Side

DK Choice

Flemish House B&B $
68 E Cedar St., 60611
Tel *312-664-9981* **Map** 2 D3
W chicagobandb.com
This B&B offers seven comfort-
able, well-appointed apartments
in the heart of Chicago's Gold
Coast. Self-catering breakfasts are
included, and the fridges are
stocked nightly for the next day.

Tremont Hotel $
100 E Chestnut St., 60611
Tel *312-751-1900* **Map** 2 D4
W tremontchicago.com
European-style hotel, with Mike
Ditka's steak house on site. Good
location for sightseeing.

Hotel Palomar $$
505 N State St., 60654
Tel *312-755-9703* **Map** 1 C5
W hotelpalomar-chicago.com
A pet-friendly Kimpton Group
hotel, with swanky

accommodations, a sophisticated
lounge, a pool on the 17th floor
and an adjacent sun deck.

**Sofitel Chicago Water Tower
Place** $$
20 E Chestnut St., 60611
Tel *312-324-4000* **Map** 2 D4
W sofitel-chicaco.com
Airy rooms with huge bathrooms
and great views. The restaurant,
Café des Architects, serves hot
croissants in the morning.

Hotel Chicago $$$
333 N Dearborn St., 60654
Tel *312-245-0333* **Map** 1 C5
W thehotelchicago.com
Hotel Sax was rebranded in early
2014 as Hotel Chicago, a stylish,
sleek member of the Marriott's
Autograph Collection of
boutique hotels.

Old Town Chicago B&B $$$
1442 N North Park Ave., 60610
Tel *312-440-9268* **Map** 1 B1
W oldtownchicago.com
This self-catering B&B has
splendid common spaces. Can
be rented by individual rooms or
as a whole, for groups.

Talbott Hotel $$$
20 E Delaware Pl., 60611
Tel *800-825-2688* **Map** 2 D3
W talbotthotel.com
An elegant hotel with modern
amenities. Guests get free access
to the nearby Equinox fitness club.

The James $$$
55 E Ontario, 60611
Tel *312-337-1000* **Map** 2 D4
W jameshotels.com/chicago
Sophisticated hotel, with an in-
house spa, plus 24-hour room
service from an acclaimed
Chicago steak house.

Whitehall Hotel $$$
105 E Delaware Pl., 60611
Tel *312-944-6300* **Map** 2 D3
W hotelwhitehallchicago.com
A classic boutique hotel, with tiny
elevators, and Continental decor.
Located near the northern end
of Magnificent Mile.

South Loop and Near
South Side

Wyndham Blake Hotel $$
500 S Dearborn St., 60605
Tel *312-986-1234* **Map** 3 C3
W hotelblake.com
Stylish, modern rooms with
upscale amenities, located in the
historic Printer's Row.

Price Guide
Prices are based on one night's stay in
high season for a standard double room,
inclusive of service charges and taxes.

$	up to $125
$$	$125 to $200
$$$	over $200

South Side

DK Choice

Benedictine B&B $$
3111 S Aberdeen St., 60608
Tel *773-927-7424* **Map** 5 A4
W chicagomonk.org
This Bridgeport monastery
offers two fully equipped, self-
catering apartments that can
accommodate up to five guests
each. Price includes free
breakfast and off-street parking.

Welcome Inn Manor $$
4563 S Michigan Ave., 60653
Tel *312-493-2963*
W welcomeinnmanor.com
A luxuriously appointed B&B in
an 1893 mansion near Hyde Park.

Farther Afield

Magnolia Studios Guest House $
*5705 N Magnolia St., Andersonville,
60660*
Tel *773-319-2331*
W 5705Magnolia.com
Colonial home with two spacious
self-catering studios and one
apartment. Situated near a beach.

City Scene Bed and Breakfast $$
*2101 N Clifton Ave., Lincoln
Park, 60614*
Tel *773-549-1743*
W cityscenebb.com
A garden-level brownstone
apartment with a full kitchen,
parlor, and a serene garden.

Hotel Monaco's bright and cheerful lounge
has a crackling fire

City Suites Hotel $$
933 W Belmont Ave., Lakeview, 60657
Tel *773-404-3400*
w chicagocitysuites.com
The decor here is a mix of vintage and modern styles. Free breakfast.

House of Two Urns B&B $$
1239 N Greenview Ave., Wicker Park, 60622
Tel *773-235-1408*
w twourns.com
A charming B&B with a lovely garden. Hot breakfasts.

Majestic Hotel $$
528 W Brompton Ave., Lakeview, 60657
Tel *773-404-3499*
w majestic-chicago.com
Vintage hotel with a welcoming lobby fireplace. Free breakfast.

Wicker Park Inn B&B $$
1329 N Wicker Park Ave., Wicker Park, 60614
Tel *773-486-2743*
w wickerparkinn.com
Three apartments and four rooms in a trendy neighborhood.

Willows Hotel $$
555 W Surf St., Lakeview, 60657
Tel *773-528-8400*
w willowshotelchicago.com
European-style decor in a stunning Art Nouveau-style building.

Beyond Chicago

Homestead Hotel $$
1625 Hinman Ave., Evanston, 60201
Tel *847-475-3300*
w thehomestead.net
Quaint hotel with the decor and spirit of a European country inn.

Budget
Downtown Core

Congress Hotel $
520 S Michigan Ave., 60605
Tel *312-427-3800*   **Map** 4 D3
w congressplazahotel.com
Historic hotel located across Grant Park, with signs of wear.

Hostelling International $
24 E Congress Pkwy, 60605
Tel *312-360-0300*   **Map** 4 D3
w hichicago.org
Bright, clean hostel with 24-hour access, in a student-filled area.

Travelodge Downtown Chicago $
65 E Harrison St., 60605
Tel *312-427-8000*   **Map** 4 D3
w travelodgechicago.com
No-frills family-friendly lodging near the Museum Campus.

Well-appointed rooms at the House of Two Urns B&B

North Side

Howard Johnson Inn $
720 N LaSalle St., 60610
Tel *312-664-8100*   **Map** 1 C4
w hojo.com/chicago-hotel
Cheap, no-frills option located off the beaten path. Free parking.

Best Western River North $$
125 W Ohio St., 60654
Tel *312-467-0800*   **Map** 2 D5
w rivernorthhotel.com
Offers free parking and Wi-Fi, and an indoor pool. Suits families.

South Loop and Near South Side

DK Choice

Essex Inn Chicago $$
800 S Michigan Ave., 60605
Tel *312-939-2800*   **Map** 4 D3
w essexinn.com
This family-friendly inn feels more upscale than most hotels in the same price range. The fourth-floor pool offers sweeping views of Grant Park. The rooms include small fridges and free Wi-Fi. There is a nice French restaurant on the premises, as well as a fitness center.

South Side

The Abode $
5412 S Blackstone Ave., 60615
Tel *312-576-4299*   **Map** 8 D3
w theabodechicago.com
Victorian house with self-catering rooms and apartments, for nightly or monthly rental.

The Amber Inn $
3901 S Michigan Ave., 60653
Tel *773-285-1000*
w amberinn2u.com
Comfortable, safe rooms at a fraction of the downtown price. An added bonus is their soul food restaurant, Pearl's Place.

Farther Afield

DK Choice

Chicago Getaway Hostel $
616 W Arlington Pl., Lincoln Park, 60614
Tel *773-929-5380*
w getawayhostel.com
This bright, youthful hostel is located in a posh area close to nightlife and Lake Michigan. Free netbooks, printing, breakfast, and even guitars are available to guests. Outings, such as pub crawls, are regularly scheduled.

Heart O' Chicago Motel $
5990 N Ridge Ave., Lake Michigan, 60660
Tel *773-271-9181*
w heartochicago.com
Neat but dated rooms, with breakfast and free parking.

Inn at Lincoln Park $
601 W Diversey Pkwy, Lincoln Park, 60614
Tel *773-348-2810*
w innlp.com
Modest, well-located option that includes two suites with kitchens.

Beyond Chicago

Budget Host Diplomat Hotel $
1060 Wells St., Lake Geneva, WI, 53147
Tel *262-248-1809*
w budgethost-lakegeneva.com
Clean rooms plus an outdoor pool. Good for families.

Historic
Downtown Core

Palmer House Hilton $$
17 E Monroe St., 60603
Tel *312-726-7500*   **Map** 3 C2
w palmerhousehiltonhotel.com
An 1871 showcase hotel, with the lobby restored to its former glory.

For more information on types of hotels *see page 141*

DK Choice

Hotel Burnham $$$
1 W Washington St., 60602
Tel *312-782-1111* **Map** 3 C1
W burnhamhotel.com
Luxe comfort and top-notch
amenities characterize this
stand-out Kimpton hotel, set
in the historic, renovated
Reliance building in the heart
of the Chicago Loop.

Silversmith Hotel & Suites $$$
10 S Wabash, 60603
Tel *312-372-7696* **Map** 4 D1
W silversmithchicago.com
Stylish accommodations designed
by Burnham & Co, set in a historic
building on Jeweler's Row.

North Side

The Allerton Hotel $$
701 N Michigan Ave., 60611
Tel *312-440-1500* **Map** 2 D4
W theallertonhotel.com
Renovated vintage hotel on the
Mag Mile, with smallish rooms.

The InterContinental $$
505 N Michigan Ave., 60611
Tel *312-944-4100* **Map** 2 D5
W icchicagohotel.com
A 1929 Art Deco hotel featuring an
ornate pool once used by Johnny
Weissmuller of *Tarzan* fame.

The Millennium Knickerbocker Hotel $$
163 E Walton Pl., 60611
Tel *312-751-8100* **Map** 2 D3
W millenniumhotels.com/chicago
Jazz-age gem that offers good
value for a premium location.

DK Choice

The Drake $$$
140 E Walton Pl., 60611
Tel *312-787-2200* **Map** 2 D4
W thedrakehotel.com
The most iconic of the classic
Chicago hotels, the elegant
Drake is the go-to hotel for
special occasions, with a grand
lobby that always inspires awe.
High tea is served every day in
the Palm Room.

South Loop and Near South Side

Chicago Hilton and Towers $$$
720 S Michigan Ave., 60605
Tel *312-922-4400* **Map** 4 D3
W hiltonchicagohotel.com
Enormous 1920s hotel with top-
notch fitness facilities. Good
location across Grant Park.

Lobby of The Drake, grand and
awe-inspiring

Renaissance Blackstone Chicago Hotel $$$
636 S Michigan Ave., 60605
Tel *312-447-0955* **Map** 4 D3
W blackstonerenaissance.com
Classic 1910 hotel featuring stylish,
modern decor and an excellent
on-site tapas restaurant.

Beyond Chicago

Carleton of Oak Park Hotel $$
1110 Pleasant St., Oak Park, 60302
Tel *708-848-5000*
W carletonhotel.com
Boutique amenities and brightly
patterned rooms in this 19th-
century hotel. The on-site bar
and restaurant are popular.

Hilton Orrington Hotel $$
1710 Orrington Ave., Evanston, 60201
Tel *847-866-8700*
W hotelorrington.com
Handsome rooms in a renovated
vintage building, near the
Northwestern University campus.

Luxury
Downtown Core

Fairmont $$$
200 N Columbus Dr., 60601
Tel *312-565-8000* **Map** 4 D1
W themillenniumparkhotel.com
Contemporary, upscale
accommodations in close
proximity to Millennium Park
and Michigan Avenue.

North Side

Four Seasons Hotel Chicago $$$
120 E Delaware Pl., 60611
Tel *312-280-8800* **Map** 2 D3
W fourseasons.com/chicagoFS
Posh, family-friendly hotel with
ice-cream sundae delivery and
pizza-making classes for teens.

The Conrad $$$
521 N Rush St., 60611
Tel *312-645-1500* **Map** 2 D5
W conradchicagohotel.com
An upscale Hilton brand, with
luxurious accommodations and
a great rooftop lounge.

The Peninsula $$$
108 E Superior St., 60611
Tel *312-337-2888* **Map** 2 D4
W chicago.peninsula.com
Classic decor and opulent rooms
at what is one of the country's
top-rated hotels.

The Ritz-Carlton Chicago $$$
160 E Pearson St., 60611
Tel *312-266-1000* **Map** 2 D4
W fourseasons.com/chicagoRC
Classic elegance located on the
Magnificent Mile.

Trump International Hotel and Tower $$$
401 N Wabash Ave., 60611
Tel *312-588-8000* **Map** 2 D5
W trumpchicagohotel.com
A notable addition to Chicago's
skyline, this hotel offers stellar
views and over-the-top luxury.

South Loop and Near South Side

DK Choice

Wheeler Mansion $$$
2020 S Calumet Ave., 60605
Tel *312-945-2020* **Map** 6 D1
W wheelermansion.com
Gorgeously restored mansion
offering luxurious B&B accommodations close to McCormick
Place Convention Center. Rich,
over-sized rooms are tastefully
decorated with antiques and
European imports. Compli-
mentary Wi-Fi and parking.

Beyond Chicago

Chestnut Mountain Resort $$
8700 W Chestnut Rd., Galena, 61036
Tel *815-777-1320*
W chestnutmtn.com
Offers serviceable lodge-type
accommodations, with water-
slides for summer and 19 ski
runs for winter.

Renaissance Chicago North Shore $$
933 Skokie Blvd., Northbrook, 60062
Tel *847-498-6500*
W marriot.com/CHINB
Bright, stylish hotel offering
posh rooms. There is a cocktail
lounge, and a steak house for the
adults. Kids enjoy the pool and
table tennis.

Eagle Ridge Resort and Spa $$$
444 Eagle Ridge Dr., Galena, 61036
Tel *815-777-5000*
W eagleridge.com
Choose a room at the inn, or rent an entire villa. Guests have a choice of four golf courses and great spa services.

Grand Geneva Resort and Spa $$$
7036 Grand Geneva Way, Lake Geneva, WI, 53147
Tel *800-558-3417*
W grandgeneva.com
Rooms and suites feature classic lodge-style decor, but with modern comforts. Golf, water parks, tennis, horse riding, and a variety of other activities.

Hilton Chicago O'Hare $$$
O'Hare International Airport, Rosemont, 60666
Tel *773-686-8000*
W hilton.com/chicago_ohare
The only hotel located within O'Hare International Airport, with sound-proof windows and blackout curtains.

Hyatt Lodge at McDonald's Office Campus $$$
2815 Jorie Blvd., Oak Brook, 60523
Tel *630-568-1234*
W thelodge.hyatt.com
Family-friendly accommodations amid a peaceful landscape connected to the McDonalds' Hamburger University campus.

Hyatt Regency O'Hare $$$
9300 Bryn Mawr Ave., Rosemont, 60018
Tel *847-696-1234*
W ohare.hyatt.com
An upscale business travel and conference hotel, this Hyatt is located near the O'Hare airport.

Modern

Downtown Core

Hyatt Regency Chicago $$
151 E Wacker Dr., 60601
Tel *312-565-1234*   **Map** 4 D1
W chicagoregency.hyatt.com
Renovated recently, this enormous hotel caters to conference, convention, as well as tour groups.

North Side

Doubletree Hotel Magnificent Mile $$
300 E Ohio Dr., 60611
Tel *312-787-6100*   **Map** 2 E5
W doubletreemagmile.com
Reliable services and amenities, as expected from the Hilton family of hotels; and good value for the location.

Holiday Inn Chicago Mart Plaza $$
350 W Mart Dr., 60654
Tel *312-836-5000*   **Map** 1 B5
W martplaza.com
Located a little off the beaten path, this family chain offers premium downtown views.

Sheraton Hotel and Towers $$
301 E North Water St., 60611
Tel *312-464-1000*   **Map** 2 E5
W sheratonchicago.com
A good choice for those on a budget, with stellar views and a great workout area.

Embassy Suites $$$
600 N State St., 60610
Tel *312-943-3800*   **Map** 2 D4
W embassysuiteschicago.com
Standard chain-hotel decor, but all suite rooms with small kitchens, plus free daily breakfast.

Hilton Chicago/Magnificent Mile Suites $$$
198 E Delaware Pl., 60611
Tel *312-664-1100*   **Map** 2 D3
W hilton.com
Suites at this hotel are equipped with a microwave and refrigerator.

South Loop and Near South Side

Best Western Grant Park $$
1100 S Michigan Ave., 60605
Tel *312-922-2900*   **Map** 4 D4
W bwgrantparkhotel.com
The outdoor pool, easy access to the Museum Campus, and free parking make this hotel particularly good for families.

South Side

Chicago Lake Shore Hotel $
4900 S Lake Shore Dr., 60615
Tel *773-288-5800*   **Map** 8 E1
W chicagolakeshorehotel.com
Basic but serviceable hotel, popular mainly due to the dearth of accommodations nearby.

Farther Afield

Days Inn Lincoln Park North $$
644 W Diversey Pkwy, Lincoln Park, 60614
Tel *773-525-7010*
W daysinnchicago.net
Clean, comfortable, reliable, and good-value hotel in Lincoln Park.

Beyond Chicago

Courtyard Chicago Highland Park $$
1505 Lake Cook Rd., Highland Park, 60035
Tel *847-831-3388*
W marriot.com
Free parking and shuttle service make this bright, well-appointed hotel appealing to visitors.

French Country Inn on the Lake $$
W4190 West End Rd., Lake Geneva, WI, 53147
Tel *262-245-5220*
W frenchcountryinn.com
This waterfront inn has rooms with fireplaces and lakeside balconies.

Stoney Creek Inn $$
940 Galena Square Dr., 61036
Tel *815-777-2223*
W stoneycreekinn.com
Charming decor with stone fireplaces and timbered walls. Rooms with bunk beds available.

Inside one of the well-furnished rooms of the Best Western Hawthorne Terrace

For more information on types of hotels *see page 141*

WHERE TO EAT AND DRINK

Chicago is a big city and many establishments, from coffee shops to four-star restaurants, ask big-city prices. However, with thousands of places to eat and drink in the city, competition between restaurants is fierce, and visitors can find great food at reasonable prices. The city's immigrant roots mean that tourists can sample dishes from around the world, from Greek and Italian dishes to Vietnamese and Korean specialties. For those visiting Chicago during the annual Taste of Chicago festival *(see p35)*, there will be the opportunity to sample cuisine from dozens of Chicago's restaurants. Those in our listings that follow *(pages 148–57)*, have been selected as among the best Chicago offers.

Chicago's Restaurants

The plethora of places to eat in Chicago represent the many cultures that make up the city. Some ethnic restaurants are clustered together, such as those in Chinatown *(see p96)* or on Greek Town's Halsted Street. Italian eateries abound on Taylor Street between Halsted and Western Avenues, and many authentic Mexican spots line 18th Street in Pilsen.

However, restaurants on the city's major streets offer a broad range of cuisines. Those in the Loop tend to cater to office workers, though many stay open till much later due to the area's theater district, while River North and Lincoln Park are home to many of the city's premier restaurants.

Generally speaking, most establishments in Chicago are wheelchair accessible *(see p173)*. However, it is best to check beforehand.

Restaurant Menus

Most menus offer three courses: appetizer (starter), entrée (main course), and dessert. When restaurants serve bread and butter it is always at no charge. Water glasses are filled with (free) tap water, but bottled water is also usually available.

Most Italian menus list pasta as a first course before a main course of meat or fish, but many restaurants also treat pasta as an entrée.

Coffee and dessert conclude the meal. It is common to have your coffee mug refilled until the servers are asked otherwise.

Other Places to Eat

Delicatessens offering soups, salads, and sandwiches are mostly found in the Downtown area. Hot-dog stands and lunch counters are an inexpensive alternative to restaurants.

Most malls have food courts selling a variety of dishes. Some don't rise above fast-food fare, but a few are excellent, notably Foodlife at Water Tower Place, and Frontera Fresca at Macy's.

Brewpubs are popular in Chicago. They serve beer brewed on site, as well as pub grub such as hamburgers or fish 'n' chips.

Alcohol

The legal drinking age in Chicago is 21 and is strictly enforced. Alcohol is served until 2am on most days of the week. Some bars have late-night licenses and are open until 4am or 5am on Saturdays. On Sunday, alcohol is not served before 11am.

Hours and Prices

The city opens early: coffee shops and diners as early as 6am. Coffee and a roll costs about $3.50. A breakfast of bacon and eggs costs about $5 in neighborhood diners and twice that much in hotel restaurants.

Lunch is offered between 11am and 2pm. Most restaurants open for dinner at 5.30pm. Kitchens close once business tapers, around 10pm on weekdays, later on weekends. The most difficult time to secure a table is from 7.30pm to 9.30pm.

Salads and appetizers generally cost between $5 and $9 each, entrées between $12 and $30. Many restaurants offer superb wines by the glass for between $6 and $10.

Ethnic restaurants offer good value for the money. Mexican and Thai restaurants are always a good bet, as are the pizzerias and fast food joints across the city. Indian and Greek eateries are also a good bargain.

Some restaurants let you bring your own bottle (BYOB) of wine, but may charge a corkage fee to serve it.

Valet parking, a facility offered by many restaurants these days, costs between $6 and $12.

Handsomely furnished bar at North Pond *(see p156)*

Gorge on top-notch Italian fare at Café Spiaggia *(see p150)*

Paying and Tipping

Nearly all restaurants accept major credit cards. Traveler's checks are accepted with appropriate identification. Personal checks are not welcome *(see p168)*.

A sales tax of 9.25 per cent will be added to meal checks in downtown Chicago; 8.25 per cent in surrounding areas. Diners are expected to tip servers 15 per cent for average service, 18 to 20 per cent for excellent service. Calculate the tip before tax. The gratuity is usually added to the check for parties of six or more.

An especially helpful wine steward may be tipped $2 or $3. There is no need to tip the host or hostess, nor will slipping him or her money help you get a better table or position on the waiting list.

Dress Codes

Only the most upscale, high-end restaurants expect men to wear jackets and ties, or women to be dressed-up. At trendier spots, diners may be expected to be fashionably attired. Inquire when making reservations.

Reservations

Try to make a reservation at any restaurant unless it's a fast-food joint. If booking more than a day in advance, confirm the booking on the day of the reservation. Some restaurants will not accept reservations for parties of fewer than six.

Children

Most restaurants in the city are happy to serve well-behaved children. Many are particularly kid-friendly, supplying high chairs and offering children's portions or menus. However, you may feel uncomfortable bringing children to some of the more romantic or high-price spots. In general, Greek, Mexican, and chain restaurants are more family-oriented. Children may accompany adults to taverns and pubs if food is ordered.

Recommended Restaurants

The restaurants featured in the pages that follow represent the diversity of Chicago's culinary offerings: from favored neighborhood diners, to iconic Chicago institutions, to Michelin-starred fine dining, these choices showcase the best places the city has to offer.

Most visitors to Chicago spend the bulk of their time in the Downtown core and River North areas, where many sights and attractions are located. The majority of these listings focus on those areas. However, many fine restaurants are located farther off the beaten path. These include local favorites as well as renowned culinary destinations. Whether your travels bring you farther afield or you are seeking out a culinary adventure, there are enough options here for everyone.

The listings are organized by price and location and divided into different categories to help users make an informed decision. Categories such as Mexican, Sushi, and Pizzeria are self-explanatory. Fine Dining indicates upscale restaurants that use the highest-quality ingredients and preparations. The Mediterranean category encompasses Greece and the Middle East. Brunch restaurants specialize in breakfast and lunch, and often close in the early afternoon. Family restaurants offer child-friendly environments and a menu most likely to appeal to diners of all ages. The Fast Food category indicates a place to get a quick, no-frills meal for cheap, often "to go."

Restaurants marked DK Choice are extra special. We consider them to have historical charm, especially high standards, or an above average location. These are usually very popular, so reserve a table ahead of time.

Goose Island Brewery, brewing beer on the premises *(see p153)*

Where to Eat and Drink

Downtown Core

Artist's Café $
Diner **Map** 4 D2
412 S Michigan Ave., 60605
Tel *312-939-7855*
Serves standard comfort food
in a vintage space across the
street from the Art Institute.
In the summer, the outdoor
patio is an ideal perch for
people-watching.

Cafecito $
Fast Food **Map** 4 D2
26 E Congress Pkwy, 60602
Tel *312-922-2233*
The extensive menu of Cuban-
style pressed sandwiches is
popular with South Loop locals.
Expect slow service and long
lines during lunch.

Frontera Fresco $
Mexican **Map** 3 C1
111 N State St., 60602
Tel *312-781-2955* **Closed** *Sun*
Mexican street food is the
focus of this fast-food chain by
Frontera Grill's Rick Bayless. On
the seventh floor of Macy's, it is
a good choice for a quick lunch
while shopping.

Heaven on Seven $
Southern **Map** 4 D1
111 N Wabash Ave., 60602
Tel *312-263-6443* **Closed** *Sun*
Jimmy Bannos' original New
Orleans restaurant, featuring
po'boys, jambalaya, and the like.

Miller's Pub $
Pub **Map** 3 C2
134 S Wabash Ave., 60603
Tel *312-263-4988*
Hearty fare such as burgers and
steaks in a classic pub ambience.
Especially popular with the after-
work crowd.

Native Foods Café $
Vegetarian **Map** 3 C2
218 S Clark St., 60604
Tel *312-332-6332*
The all-vegan wraps, salads,
and bowls at this California-
based chain offer health-
minded diners a welcome
reprieve from the fast-food
chains in the Loop.

Park Grill $
Family **Map** 4 D1
11 N Michigan Ave., 60602
Tel *312-521-7275*
Lots of outdoor seating with
great views to while away a
summer day. The menu lists a
number of American favorites.

DK Choice

Pastoral $
Deli **Map** 4 D1
53 E Lake St., 60601
Tel *312-658-1250*
A cheese and wine shop turned
deli turned wine bar, Pastoral is
a great place to pick up upscale
picnic fare for Millennium Park
concerts. Prepared baskets
include a baguette and an
assortment of olives, cheese,
and salami. They also offer
sandwiches to go and a limited
dine-in menu.

Pizano's Pizza $
Pizzeria **Map** 4 D1
61 E Madison St., 60603
Tel *312-236-1777*
Good-quality thin-crust and
Chicago-style pizzas in a sports-
themed venue, with a number
of televisions on which to catch
the game.

Plymouth Pub $
Pub **Map** 3 C2
327 S Plymouth Ct, 60604
Tel *312-362-1212* **Closed** *Sun*
Located near the financial district,
the Plymouth is most notable for
its rooftop open-air sports bar.
The food – mostly pub fare – is
good value, considering the
Downtown location.

Aria $$
International **Map** 4 D1
200 N Columbus Dr., 60601
Tel *312-444-9494*
Sleek, upscale restaurant that
offers a creative menu featuring
local produce. The bar menu
includes sushi and sliders.

Sample a variety of fine wines and cheeses
at Pastoral

Price Guide

Prices categories include a three-course
meal for one, a glass of house wine, tax,
and a 15-20% tip:

$	up to $40
$$	$40 to $75
$$$	over $75

Atwood Café $$
Café **Map** 3 C1
1 W Washington St., 60602
Tel *312-368-1900*
Stylish Atwood is ideally
situated for lunch or dinner
while shopping on State Street.
Their delicious chicken pot pies
are the ultimate cold-weather
comfort food.

Henri $$
French **Map** 4 D2
18 S Michigan Ave., 60603
Tel *312-578-0763*
The more elegant sister of the
boisterous brewpub The Gage,
located next door. Offers
updated takes on classic
French fare.

Italian Village $$
Italian **Map** 3 C2
71 W Monroe St., 60603
Tel *312-332-7005*
This Loop mainstay consists
of three Italian restaurants
on three floors. The Village,
on the top floor, is charming,
with kitschy decor and
a menu of comforting
Italian standards.

Lockwood $$
American **Map** 3 C2
17 E Monroe St., 60603
Tel *312-917-3404*
Located in the historic Palmer
House hotel, Lockwood
offers eclectic American fare,
made with fresh, locally
sourced produce.

Petterino's $$
Italian **Map** 3 C1
150 N Dearborn St., 60601
Tel *312-422-0150*
Popular with the pre-theater
crowd for its location in the
theater district, and an excellent
prix fixe menu.

Russian Tea Time $$
Eastern European **Map** 4 D2
77 E Adams St., 60603
Tel *312-360-0000*
Enjoy hearty East European
fare and vodka flights in this
banquet hall-style restaurant.
Full tea service is available in
the afternoon. Family platters
are good value.

Quartino is the best choice for delicious Italian fare

DK Choice

The Gage $$
Pub **Map** 4 D2
24 S Michigan Ave., 60603
Tel *312-372-4243*
The menu at this upscale tavern offers creative, well-executed versions of classic comfort food, such as an award-winning house *poutine* that marries smoked pork confit, pickled onions, cheese curds, and French fries into a scrumptious goop. Great location near Millennium Park.

Trattoria No.10 $$
Italian **Map** 3 C1
10 N Dearborn St., 60602
Tel *312-984-1718* **Closed** *Sun*
A pre-theater favorite that offers delicious Italian cooking in a romantic lower-level space.

Catch 35 $$$
Seafood **Map** 3 C1
35 W Wacker Dr., 60601
Tel *312-346-3500*
Crab cakes, lobster, and oysters are among the options offered at this seafood restaurant. The tenderloin sliders and bone in rib-eye are good choices for carnivores.

Morton's The Steakhouse $$$
Steak House **Map** 4 D1
65 E Wacker Pl., 60601
Tel *312-201-0410*
Come with a big appetite to Morton's. The menu features jumbo crab cakes, jumbo shrimp cocktail, jumbo baked potatoes, and jumbo steaks.

Rosebud Prime $$$
Steak House **Map** 4 C2
1 S Dearborn St., 60603
Tel *312-384-1900*
Steaks, chops, and seafood plus seven different preparations for the humble potato equals a classic Chicago steak house experience.

North Side

Billy Goat Tavern $
Fast Food **Map** 2 D5
430 N Michigan Ave., 60611
Tel *312-222-1525*
The original location for the Chicago chain. The classic cheeseburger remains the most popular option on their menu.

Café Iberico $
Tapas **Map** 1 C4
737 N La Salle St., 60654
Tel *312-573-1510*
Cavernous, lively tapas restaurant that is a good choice for well-prepared classic tapas (tuna cannelli, *croquetas*, garlic shrimp) and paellas. Fun for groups.

Cyrano's Farm Kitchen $
French **Map** 1 C4
546 N Wells St., 60654
Tel *312-467-0546* **Closed** *Sun*
Warm and welcoming Gallic spot with classic bistro fare such as home-made sausages with potato salad, rabbit rillettes, and excellent steak frites.

Foodlife $
Fast food **Map** 2 D3
835 N Michigan Ave., 60611
Tel *312-335-3663*
More like a Las Vegas buffet than a food court; Foodlife has an extensive array of high-quality fast-food options with a simple one-stop card payment system.

Gino's East $
Pizzeria **Map** 1 C4
500 N La Salle St., 60654
Tel *312-988-4200*
Kids love the graffiti-walled ambience of this classic Chicago pizza place. The menu includes standard American bar fare, but the real draw is the deep-dish pizza.

Lou Malnati's Pizzeria $
Pizzeria **Map** 1 C5
439 N Wells St., 60610
Tel *312-828-9800*
This favorite venue for classic Chicago-style deep-dish pizza also ships its pizzas to anywhere in the country.

Mity Nice Bar and Grill $
Family **Map** 2 D4
835 N Michigan Ave., 60611
Tel *312-335-4745*
Retro-styled diner in Water Tower Place; serves creative updates of classic American comfort food such as turkey and stuffing, and meatloaf.

Mr. Beef $
Fast Food **Map** 1 B3
666 N Orleans St., 60654
Tel *312-337-8500* **Closed** *Sun*
The city's best Italian beef sandwich is created at this unassuming River North shack. A bag of fries alongside makes it perfect. Place your order at the counter.

Pizzeria Uno $
Pizza **Map** 2 D5
29 E Ohio St., 60611
Tel *312-321-1000*
Expect a wait at this popular tourist destination, which claims to be where the Chicago-style deep-dish pizza originated.

Portillo's Hot Dogs $
Fast Food **Map** 1 C4
100 W Ontario St., 60654
Tel *312-587-8910*
Family-friendly Portillo's is ground zero for classic Chicago grub including Italian beefs, charburgers, and, of course, hot dogs, served Chicago-style with mustard, tomato, and pickle spear.

Quartino $
Italian **Map** 1 C4
626 N State St., 60654
Tel *312-698-5000*
A bustling, spacious restaurant that offers tapas-style Italian plates. They also have a comprehensive selection of Neapolitan pizzas, including one with onion, duck prosciutto, and wild arugula.

RA Sushi Bar $
Sushi **Map** 2 D3
1139 N State St., 60611
Tel *312-274-0011*
The clubby atmosphere at this youthful sushi bar is well-suited to its proximity to Rush Street nightlife. Signature sushi rolls on the menu include the predictable "RA"ckin Roll, featuring tempura-battered crab and cream cheese, plus guacamole and shrimp.

For more information on types of restaurants *see page 147*

As the decor suggests, Hugo's Frog Bar and Fish House serves amazing seafood

XOCO $
Mexican Map 1 C5
449 N Clark St., 60654
Tel *312-334-3688* **Closed** *Sun & Mon*
Has counter-service only. Visit for fresh and well-prepared Mexican street food that is served without the pomp and splendor of her popular sibling restaurants, Frontera Grill and Topolobampo.

Café Spiaggia $$
Italian Map 2 D3
980 N Michigan, 60611
Tel *312-280-2750*
The more affordable neighbor of the four-star Spiaggia, Café Spiaggia offers top-notch Italian with a lovely view of the Magnificent Mile.

DK Choice

Frontera Grill $$
Mexican Map 1 C5
445 N Clark St., 60610
Tel *312-661-1434* **Closed** *Sun & Mon*
Outstanding Mexican fare at Rick Bayless's flagship restaurant sets the standard for high-quality Mexican food. From the excellent guacamole and *ceviches*, to the grilled meats, to the inventive selection of margaritas, this eatery is worthy of a culinary pilgrimage. One way to avoid the long lines is by arriving late and taking a table at the bar.

Hugo's Frog Bar and Fish House $$
Seafood Map 2 D3
1024 N Rush St., 60611
Tel *312-640-0999*
Seafood and fish reign supreme at this popular Rush

Street bistro. Steaks and chops are provided by Gibson's – a popular steak house.

Le Colonial $$
Asian Fusion Map 2 D3
937 N Rush St., 60611
Tel *312-255-0088*
Serves elegant Franco-Vietnamese cuisine in an airy, palm-filled venue. Try the wok-seared monkfish and ginger-marinated roast duck.

Mike Ditka's Restaurant $$
Family Map 2 D4
100 E Chestnut St., 60611
Tel *312-587-8989*
Former Chicago Bears coach Mike Ditka's predictably sports-themed steak house. The menu includes Coach's Pot Roast Nachos, and Da Pork Chop.

Osterio Via Stato $$
Italian Map 1 C4
620 N State St., 60654
Tel *312-642-8450*
Upbeat, casual restaurant with the option to order à la carte individually or from the family-style Italian Dinner Party menu for groups.

P.F. Chang's $$
Chinese Map 2 D5
530 N Wabash Ave., 60611
Tel *312-828-9977*
Casual Asian chain that is a good option for Chinese-food fans who can't make it to Chinatown. Delivery and curbside pick-up add to the convenience.

Rosebud Steakhouse $$
Steak House Map 2 D3
192 E Walton St., 60611
Tel *312-397-1000*
The success of the legendary Rosebud restaurant on the Loop,

sparked a series of satellites throughout the Chicago area, including this steak house. Fettucine alfredo with king crab, and 16-ounce bone-in filet feature on the menu. There is also a raw bar.

The Purple Pig $$
International Map 2 D5
500 N Michigan Ave., 60611
Tel *312-464-1744*
Featured on *Bon Appetit*'s best new restaurants list, the Purple Pig specializes in all things porcine, but also whips up a killer bone marrow.

Wildfire $$
Mediterranean Fusion Map 1 C4
159 W Erie St., 60654
Tel *312-787-9000*
From pizza to prime rib, to a kids' menu and a wide range of gluten-free options, there is a wide range of options at this family-friendly burger and steak joint.

Capital Grille $$$
Steak House Map 2 D4
633 N St. Clair St., 60611
Tel *312-337-9400*
The Chicago branch of this upscale chain offers classic steak house fare in a warm, handsome room. The signature dish is a porcini-rubbed Delmonico steak with aged balsamic.

Coco Pazzo $$$
Italian Map 1 C5
300 W Hubbard St., 60610
Tel *312-836-0900*
This loft-like contemporary Tuscan restaurant in the River North gallery district has an excellent selection of antipasti, along with excellent pastas, steaks, and seafood.

David Burke's Primehouse $$$
Steak House Map 2 D4
616 N Rush St., 60611
Tel *312-660-6000*
Steaks are dry-aged on the premises at this popular steak house attached to the James Hotel. One of the few upscale restaurants in Chicago to offer a kids' menu.

Gibson's Steakhouse $$$
Steak House Map 2 D3
1028 N Rush St., 60611
Tel *312-266-8999*
Nirvana for the hungry carnivore, Gibson's is the only steak house in the country to have its own USDA designation. Prime steaks range from 10-ounce filet sirloins to the 48-ounce Porterhouse.

Joe's Seafood, Prime Steak & Stone Crab $$$
Seafood Map 2 D5
60 E Grand Ave., 60611
Tel *312-379-5637*
Gets bone-in prime steaks, an extensive seafood selection, and stone crab claws delivered daily from the gulf of Mexico. A gluten-free menu is also available.

Kiki's Bistro $$$
French Map 1 B3
900 N Franklin Ave., 60610
Tel *312-335-5454* **Closed** *Sun*
Serves the classic french fare expected from a top-notch Paris bistro, including dishes such as *magret du canard, steak au poivre,* and *poulet roti.*

Lawry's The Prime Rib $$$
Steak House Map 2 D4
100 E Ontario St., 60611
Tel *312-787-5000*
Prime rib in a choice of thicknesses, along with classic sides like creamed corn, spinach, and Yorkshire pudding.

Les Nomades $$$
French Map 2 D4
222 E Ontario St., 60611
Tel *312-649-9010* **Closed** *Sun & Mon*
Globally renowned chef Roland Liccioni presents exquisitely prepared French cuisine with an Asian twist, in a warmly decorated century-old brownstone. Jackets required.

MK Restaurant $$$
American Fusion Map 1 B3
868 N Franklin St., 60610
Tel *312-482-9179*
American fusion cuisine in a romantic, special-occasion venue. There's an abundance of fish, as well as a chef's tasting menu with wine pairings for the indecisive.

NoMI Kitchen $$$
Fusion Map 2 D4
800 N Michigan Ave., 60611
Tel *312-239-4030*
Located on the seventh floor of the Park Hyatt, the inventive cuisine at NoMI includes fresh seafood, and sushi *maki* alongside rack of lamb, and braised short rib, all made with locally sourced ingredients.

Roy's $$$
Asian Fusion Map 1 C4
720 N State St., 60654
Tel *312-787-7599*
Fresh flavors that range from an upscale take on Thai green papaya salad to Hawaiian-style short ribs. Offers a good-value *prix fixe* menu, which comes with a choice of appetizers, entrées, and desserts.

Signature Room at the 95th $$$
American Map 2 D3
875 N Michigan Ave., 60611
Tel *312-787-9596*
The location, on top of the Hancock, is as popular as the menu here, which features contemporary American fare. Order of an entrée is required to be seated.

DK Choice

Spiaggia $$$
Italian Map 2 D3
980 N Michigan Ave., 60611
Tel *312-280-2750*
One of the most renowned restaurants in the country and a local date favorite for President and Michelle Obama. Both the room, which overlooks the Magnificent Mile and the Lake, and the menu, featuring gorgeous presentations of Italian cuisine made with top-of-the-line ingredients, are the very definition of elegance.

The Pump Room $$$
Continental Map 2 D2
1301 N State Pkwy, 60610
Tel *312-229-6740*
Supper club and lounge whose classic Continental menu has been given a fresh spin by James Beard award-winner Jean-Georges Vongerichten.

Topolobampo $$$
Mexican Map 1 C5
445 N Clark St., 60654
Tel *312-661-1434* **Closed** *Sun & Mon*
Frontera Grill's sister restaurant presents an upscale take on south-of-the-border fare. Unlike Frontera, Topolambompo accepts reservations.

Tru $$$
Fine Dining Map 2 D4
676 N St. Clair St., 60611
Tel *312-202-0001* **Closed** *Sun*
Warm service, a gallery-quality art collection, immaculate presentations, and the choice of a seven-

to 13-course tasting menu equals a superb dining experience.

South Loop and Near South Side

Bongo Room $
Brunch Map 4 D4
1152 S Wabash Ave., 60616
Tel *312-291-0100*
Popular brunch spot, offering breakfast standards such as sandwiches and omelets alongside decadent pancakes.

Buddy Guy's Legends $
Southern Map 3 C3
700 S Wabash Ave., 60605
Tel *312-427-1190*
Popular South Loop blues venue; serves a robust menu of classic Southern and New Orleans-style fare.

Chicago's Home of Chicken & Waffles $
Southern
3947 S King Dr., 60653
Tel *773-536-3300*
In addition to chicken and waffles, this soul-food destination also serves eggs, fried catfish, and a number of sides in an inviting space. Friendly service.

DK Choice

Eleven City Diner $
Deli Map 4 D4
1112 S Wabash Ave., 60605
Tel *312-212-1112*
Modeled after a classic Jewish deli, with a soda fountain, this family-friendly, upbeat restaurant serves corned-beef sandwiches piled six-inches thick and chicken soup with baseball-sized matzo balls. The booths and banquettes are roomy, and the counter seating offers have a diner vibe. In addition to freshly made milk shakes and malts, pies and cakes are made daily.

One of restaurant Spiaggia's beautifully plated dishes

For more information on types of restaurants *see page 147*

Emperor's Choice $
Chinese   **Map** 5 B2
2238 S Wentworth Ave., 60616
Tel *312-225-8800*
A Chinatown standby for good Chinese fare, this small, non-descript storefront has attracted a loyal following for its large portions and reasonable prices.

Epic Burger $
Fast Food   **Map** 3 C3
517 S State St., 60605
Tel *312-913-1373*
Sustainably marketed Epic Burger's tagline is "A more mindful burger." They use only grass-fed, pastured beef and nitrate-free bacon. Turkey and portabello burgers also available.

Hackney's Printer's Row $
Pub   **Map** 3 C3
733 S Dearborn St., 60605
Tel *312-461-1116*
The main claim to fame here are burgers, for which the meat is ground in-house. Lively bar with a good selection of draft beers.

Harold's Chicken Shack $
Fast Food   **Map** 3 C3
636 S Wabash Ave., 60605
Tel *312-362-0442*
Local chain with an uninspiring fast-food ambience, but its fried chicken and fish dishes have a loyal fan following.

Kroll's $
Family   **Map** 4 D5
1736 S Michigan Ave., 60616
Tel *312-235-1400*
Chicago outpost of the Green Bay-based sports bar and grill that is trying hard to win the locals over. Beloved by Wisconsin expats for their cheese curds and bratwurst.

Little Branch Café $
Brunch   **Map** 4 D4
1251 S Prairie Ave., 60605
Tel *312-360-0101*
Order the quiche of the day or mascarpone-stuffed French toast at the counter of this delightful brunch spot. There is also a full bar to complement brunch.

Ming Hin $
Chinese   **Map** 5 B1
2168 S Archer Ave., 60616
Tel *312-808-1999*
Dim sum is served late into the night at this spacious, tastefully decorated Chinatown favorite. Adventurous diners can dig into dishes like the beef tripe with ginger and onion as well as siz-zling pork liver and kidney hot pot.

Dine on juicy steak at the handsome Chicago Firehouse

Phoenix Restaurant $
Chinese   **Map** 5 B1
2131 S Archer Ave., 60616
Tel *312-328-0848*
Bustling favorite in Chinatown, particularly for dim sum brunch. The general menu is extensive enough to please all but the pickiest eaters. Visit on a weekday to avoid a wait.

Yolk $
Brunch   **Map** 4 D4
1120 S Michigan Ave., 60605
Tel *312-789-9655*
The menu at this cheerful breakfast and lunch spot includes generous portions of eggs, skillets, and a variety of pancakes and French toast. Expect a long wait during peak brunch hours.

Gioco $$
Italian   **Map** 4D4
1312 S Wabash Ave., 60605
Tel *312-939-3870*   **Closed** *Sun*
One of the pioneers of upscale dining in the South Loop, Gioco serves rustic Italian comfort food in a suitably shabby-chic venue reputed to be a former Al Capone-era speakeasy.

Lao Sze Chuan $$
Chinese   **Map** 5 B1
2172 S Archer Ave., 60616
Tel *312-326-5040*
Chef Tony Hu's flagship restaurant is a favorite with the local Chinese community and Chicago's foodies. The staff aren't always fluent in English but do try to help.

SouthCoast Sushi $$
Sushi   **Map** 4 D5
1700 S Michigan Ave., 60616
Tel *312-662-1700*
This sleek eatery offers fresh sushi, including a solid representation of vegetarian *maki*, and signature rolls such as the *ceviche* roll.

Zapatista $$
Mexican   **Map** 4 D4
1307 S Wabash Ave., 60605
Tel *312-435-1307*
Fans of Mexican food will find much to like at this upbeat place. The guacamole is made fresh, and the tacos and burritos upgraded with premium ingredients. Excellent tequila selection.

Acadia $$$
Nouvelle   **Map** 4 D5
1639 S Wabash Ave., 60616
Tel *312-360-9500*   **Closed** *Mon*
Michelin-starred restaurant serving beautifully presented nouvelle cuisine. The tongue and cheek, for example, consists of halibut cheek and corned beef tongue with truffle emulsion.

Chicago Firehouse $$$
Steak House   **Map** 4 D5
1401 S Michigan Ave., 60605
Tel *312-786-1401*
Set in a handsome, out-of-commission Chicago firehouse, this steak house serves favorites like chateaubriand and iceberg wedge salad.

Everest $$$
French   **Map** 3 C2
440 S LaSalle St., 60605
Tel *312-663-8920*   **Closed** *Sun & Mon*
On the 40th floor of the Chicago Stock Exchange, popular for, of all things, wedding proposals. Awarded a Michelin star for its classic Alsatian cuisine.

DK Choice

Mercat a la Planxa $$$
Tapas   **Map** 4 D3
638 S Michigan Ave., 60605
Tel *312-765-0524*
Bold, dramatic dining room on the second floor of the historic Renaissance Blackstone hotel with sweeping views of Grant Park. Iron Chef winner Jose Garces serves delicious Catalan-styled tapas and a variety of grilled meats and planks. A full suckling pig can be arranged with two days' notice. Well-chosen wine list.

South Side

Cedars Mediterranean $
Mediterranean   **Map** 7 C3
1206 E 53rd St., 60615
Tel *773-324-6227*
Popular restaurant that features all the Middle Eastern standards on the menu, as well as a small handful of Indian options.

Medici On 57th St. $
Italian   Map 8 D4
1327 E 57th St., 60637
Tel *773-667-7394*
Familiar Italian-American fare
at this Hyde Park institution is
augmented by an on-site bakery
and deli carry-out.

Rajun Cajun $
Fusion   Map 8 D2
1459 E 53rd St., 60615
Tel *773-955-1145*
Standard Indian fare combines
with classic Southern dishes
at this unlikely, but rather
long-standing Hyde Park
cafeteria. Lots of fruit juices
to choose from.

Salonica $
Diner   Map 8 D4
1440 E 57th St., 60637
Tel *773-752-3899*
A classic diner in the best
sense, Salonica serves favorites
such as ham and eggs, plus
a variety of club sandwiches,
rounded out with Greek
specialties such as souvlaki
and mousaka.

Valois $
Diner   Map 8 D2
1518 E 53rd St., 60615
Tel *773-667-0647*
Popular for its classic diner
breakfasts, this Hyde Park
mainstay features daily specials
for lunch and dinner, all offered
cafeteria-style.

Zaleski & Horvarth MarketCafé $
Café   Map 7 C1
1126 E 47th St., 60653
Tel *773-538-7372*
Competent café and deli
with gourmet aspirations;
caters to the Hyde Park crowd.
Sandwiches and other popular
items are available for carry-out
or dine-in.

La Petite Folie $$
French   Map 8 D3
1504 E 55th St., 60615
Tel *773-493-1394*   **Closed** *Mon*
Distinguished as the special
occasion restaurant in Hyde Park,
La Petite Folie offers French
standards in a quiet setting.
All-French wine list.

Farther Afield

Ann Sather $
Brunch
909 W Belmont Ave., Lakeview, 60657
Tel *773-348-2378*
Swedish-American breakfast
and lunch institution, with
legendary warm cinnamon

rolls with every meal. Try
the Swedish pancakes with
lingonberries.

Birchwood Kitchen $
Brunch
*2211 W North Ave., Wicker Park,
IL, 60647*
Tel *773-276-2100*   **Closed** *Mon*
Although they do offer a
limited dinner menu on
weeknights, this Wicker
Park spot is best known for
high quality brunch items
including daily quiches
and an ever-changing
sandwich board.

Birreria Reyes de Ocatlan $
Mexican
1322 W 18th St., Pilsen, 60608
Tel *312-733-2613*
Goat stew and gracious
service are the specialties
at this no-frills Mexican fast-
food storefront favored by
Frontera's Rick Bayless. Portions
are generous and the simple
menu also includes goat and
beef tacos. Cash only.

Chicago Diner $
Vegetarian   Map 1 A1
3411 N Halsted, 60657
Tel *773-935-6696*
American comfort food
goes vegetarian in a classic
diner setting. Try the vegan
Salisbury steak with mashed
potatoes and gravy, or the
Radical Reuben, washed
down with craft beers or a
vegan milk shake.

Goose Island Brewery $
Pub
1800 N Clybourn, 60614
Tel *312-915-0071*
A pilgrimage site for beer
aficionados, the original Goose
Island brewpub has a variety
of small batch brews, along
with a selection of pub grub
such as sausages and goulash.

DK Choice

Hot Doug's $
Fast Food
3324 N California Ave., 60618
Tel *773-279-9550*   **Closed** *Sun*
At lunchtime, a line forms down
the block at this encased meat
emporium, where freshly made
sausages include daily specials
like *foie gras* and sauternes duck
or bacon, smoked buffalo, or
regular menu favorites like the
"mighty, mighty, might hot"
Brigitte Bardot (formerly the
Salma Hayek) andouille
sausage. The classic Chicago-
style dog, and mini-bagel dogs
for kids, are also hits, as are the
duck-fat french fries. Credit
cards are not accepted.

Kuma's Corner $
Pub
2900 W Belmont Ave., 60618
Tel *773-604-8769*
Freshly ground, handpressed,
heavy metal-themed burgers (the
Metallica features bacon, blue-
cheese dressing, and buffalo
sauce) delivered by heavily
tattooed servers to an
appropriately raucous soundtrack.

Lou Mitchell's $
Family   Map 3 B2
565 W Jackson Blvd., 60661
Tel *312-939-3111*
A Chicago institution, this classic
family restaurant serves up diner
fare and hearty breakfasts. All
baked goods are made in-house.

Manny's Coffee Shop and Deli $
Deli   Map 3 A4
1141 S Jefferson St., 60607
Tel *312-939-2855*   **Closed** *Sun*
A true Chicago institution
operated by Ken Raskin, the late
Manny's son, this cafeteria-style
deli is hallowed ground to local
politicians who make deals over
their pastrami and knishes.

Hot Doug's, a crowded fast food joint, has a plethora of hot dog options to choose from

For more information on types of restaurants *see page 147*

m. henry $
Brunch
5707 N Clark St., 60660
Tel *773-561-1600* **Closed** *Mon*
Baked goods are made in-house at this popular brunch spot that also offers a number of vegetarian options in addition to the usual breakfast and lunch fare.

Nuevo Leon $
Mexican
1515 W 18th St., Pilsen, 60608
Tel *312-421-1517*
This Pilsen institution attracts long queues at mealtimes for its extensive menu of tasty, fresh Mexican meals that includes classics like *carne asada* and *pollo ranchera*, along with tacos, and enchiladas. Bring your own bottle (BYOB) and cash only.

Pegasus $
Mediterranean **Map** 3 A2
130 S Halsted St., 60661
Tel *312-226-3377*
Well-prepared classic Greek fare. In the summer, they serve a meze-only (small plates) menu on their rooftop deck – which features a full bar, occasional live music, and a terrific view of the Chicago skyline.

Raw $
Vegetarian **Map** 3 B1
131 N Clinton St., 60661
Tel *312-831-2729* **Closed** *Sun*
Located in the French Market, across the street from the Ogilvie transportation center, this raw-food restaurant and health-food store serves the likes of kale burritos and raw-apple pie.

R.J. Grunt's $
American
2056 N Lincoln Park W, 60614
Tel *773-929-5363*
Being across the street from Lincoln Park Zoo is one of the biggest advantages of this casual, no-frills spot. Burgers, milk shakes, and a soup-and-salad bar make for a family-friendly fill-up spot.

Sweet Maple Café $
Brunch
1339 W Taylor St., University Village, 60607
Tel *312-243-8908*
Guests enjoy the Southern hospitality at this classic American diner. Lines form for breakfast and lunch, which include various egg scrambles, large fresh biscuits, pancakes, and club sandwiches.

The Wiener's Circle $
Fast Food
2622 N Clark St., Lincoln Park, 60614
Tel *773-477-7444*
Although this notorious late-night fast-food eating place is popular with the after-bar crowd, the atmosphere is tamer and more family-friendly during the day. The signature Maxwell Street Char-dogs, the cheese fries, and hamburgers are delicious and major crowd pullers.

Anteprima $$
Italian
5316 N Clark St., Andersonville, 60650
Tel *773-506-9990*
Making the best of local, organic and seasonal ingredients, Anteprima offers an ever-changing menu of creative, home-style Italian cuisine. Delicious breadsticks come free with the meal. The peaceful back deck is a good place to sit when the weather is pleasant.

Au Cheval $$
Pub
800 W Randolph St., West Loop, 60607
Tel *312-929-4580*
Primarily a cocktail lounge with an ambitious brunch and bar menu. In addition to the renowned burgers, the menu offers crispy french fries topped with a farm egg and aioli on the side, griddled bratwurst with mashed potatoes, and a fried sandwich of delicious house-made bologne.

Au Cheval, a cocktail bar, also serves fantastic burgers

Avec $$
French/Mediterranean **Map** 3 A1
615 W Randolph St., West Loop 60606
Tel *312-377-2002*
Expect to share a table with strangers while enjoying well-executed Franco-Mediterranean small plates such as whipped *brandade* with garlic bread and chives, and cured charcuterie.

Blackbird $$
American **Map** 3 A1
619 W Randolph St., West Loop 60661
Tel *312-715-0708* **Closed** *Sun*
James Beard award-winning American cuisine served in a modern, minimalist space. Good-value lunch *prix fixe*. At dinner, an eight-course chef's tasting menu is available.

Café Ba-Ba-Reeba! $$
Tapas
2024 N Halsted St., Lincoln Park, 60614
Tel *773-935-5000*
This convivial Lincoln Park tapas spot is a fun place for groups. Look for well-made tapas standards like *queso de cabra*, garlic shrimp, and meatballs, which wash down well with the house red sangria.

Davanti Enoteca $$
Italian
1359 W Taylor St., University Village, 60607
Tel *312-226-5550*
Many of the dishes at this intimate rustic-styled *enoteca* are meant to be shared tapas-style. They also offer a few options for family-style menus that are suitable for groups. An impressive collection of Italian wines is available by the glass or bottle.

Greek Islands $$
Mediterranean
200 S Halsted St., Near West Side, 60661
Tel *312-782-9855*
Cavernous space with decor reminiscent of a Greek fishing village. A great place to go with a group to sample from the family-style menu of traditional Greek dishes such as flaming cheese, spit-roasted leg of lamb, and spinach pie.

Hopleaf $$
Belgian
5148 N Clark St., Andersonville, 60640
Tel *773-334-9851*
Specializing in Belgian beer and food (think *moules frites*), Hopleaf has an extensive beer

selection and serves wine on tap. The food menu is unpretentious. The dining area on the third floor is quieter and less boisterous, and also has its own bar.

Japonais by Morimoto $$
Asian Fusion Map 1 A4
600 W Chicago Ave., 60610
Tel *312-822-9600*
The interior of this Japanese restaurant is sleek and clubby. The riverfront patio is a lovely venue to appreciate the high-quality sushi and elegant Asian fusion cuisine on the menu.

La Scarola $$
Italian Map 1 A5
721 W Grand Ave., 60654
Tel *312-243-1740*
A textbook Italian-American restaurant, with a classic menu. Expect stuffed clams, chicken vesuvio, and generous portions of pasta.

Longman & Eagle $$
Pub
2657 N Kedzie Blvd., Logan Square, 60647
Tel *773-276-7110*
Gastropub grub in a trendy, bustling atmosphere. The ambitious upscale menu ranges from bar snacks like venison pâté and buffalo frog legs to small plates (roasted marrow bones, octopus confit). The wild boar sloppy joes with beef-fat fries are worth a try. There is also a small inn located on the premises.

Lula Café $$
Café
2537 N Kedzie Blvd., Logan Square, 60647
Tel *773-489-9554* **Closed** *Tue*
Airy cafe, popular with young, arty types, serving creative café fare, with an emphasis on locally sourced ingredients. On Mondays, the popular farm dinner special offers three original courses for good value. Reservations not accepted.

Mon Ami Gabi $$
French
2300 N Lincoln Park W, 60614
Tel *773-348-8886*
Mon Ami Gabi is a classic Paris-style bistro that offers a menu of comforting French standards such as onion soup and steak frites. The location, across the street from Lincoln Park, makes for pleasant alfresco dining in warm weather.

Enjoy your meal on one of the communal-style tables at the Publican

DK Choice

Publican $$
Pub
837 W Fulton Market, West Loop, 60607
Tel *312-733-9555*
With this gastropub, Paul Kahan, the chef and owner of Blackbird and Avec, presents brasserie fare like fresh oysters and house-made charcuterie in a handsome space dominated by enormous communal-style tables reminiscent of a European beer hall. Heartier meals include beef short ribs and suckling pig. An extensive local and international beer list rounds out the menu.

The Rosebud $$
Italian
1500 W Taylor St., Near West Side, 60607
Tel *312-942-1117*
A Chicago institution known for its well-done Italian-American classics, from minestrone and baked clams to eggplant parmesan and veal marsala. The expansive portions are reasonably priced.

Vinci $$
Italian
1732 N Halsted St., Lincoln Park, 60614
Tel *312-266-1199* **Closed** *Mon*
Located close to the Lincoln Park theater district, this casually upscale Italian resturant is a neighborhood standby for generous portions of unpretentious trattoria fare and delicious, home-made pastas that can be ordered in family-sized portions.

Alinea $$$
Fine Dining
1723 N Halsted St., Lincoln Park, 60614
Tel *312-867-0110* **Closed** *Mon & Tue*
With three Michelin stars, Grant Achatz's Alinea is widely recognized as one of the top culinary destinations in the country. A theatrical ambience combines with fanciful presentations and sophisticated flavor combinations, to create a scrumptious experience from start to finish.

Arun's $$$
Thai
4156 N Kedzie Ave., Northwest Side, 60618
Tel *773-539-1909* **Closed** *Mon*
This Michelin-starred foodie destination offers 12 courses of beautifully presented and flavorful Thai cuisine in a dining space filled with Thai silks and exquisite paintings.

DK Choice

Bistro Campagne $$$
French
4518 N Lincoln Ave., Lincoln Square, 60625
Tel *773-271-6100*
Expect warm service and well-executed classic French bistro fare such as steak frites, roasted chicken, and *crème brûlée* at this charming bungalow restaurant in the quaint Lincoln Square neighborhood. Filled nightly with loyal regulars and special-occasion diners, the space expands to a pretty, private patio for alfresco dining when the weather permits.

For more information on types of restaurants *see page 147*

Classy and sophisticated, North Pond serves great seasonal cuisine

Boka $$$
Fine Dining
1729 N Halsted, Lincoln Park, 60614
Tel *312-337-6070*
More accessible and easier to get a reservation at than the neighboring Alinea, this is a good choice for a special night out. Upscale American fare served in an intimate space. The tasting menu is accompanied by a wine flight.

Goosefoot $$$
Fine Dining
2656 W Lawrence Ave., Lincoln Square, 60625
Tel *773-942-7547* **Closed** *Sun, Mon & Tue*
Book well in advance to sample the visually stunning nouvelle American tasting menu at Chris Nugent's Michelin-starred establishment, located in an Albany Park storefront. BYOB.

L20 $$$
Seafood
2300 N Lincoln Park W, Lincoln Park, 60614
Tel *773-868-0002* **Closed** *Tues*
Exquisitely presented New American fish and seafood preparations served in an intimate, elegant, Michelin-starred restaurant. Diners can choose between a five-course *prix fixe* or a more elaborate chef's tasting menu.

Moto $$$
Fine Dining
945 W Fulton Market, Near West Side, IL, 60607
Tel *312-491-0058* **Closed** *Mon*
Much more an experience destination than a place to refuel, this is one of the pioneers in the field of molecular gastronomy. It serves a 12-course tasting menu of playful, albeit sometimes gimmicky, haute cuisine, complete with edible menus.

Next $$$
Fine Dining
953 W Fulton Market, Near West Side, 60607
Tel *312-226-0858* **Closed** *Mon & Tue*
Reservations for Alinea's sister restaurant are presold as all-inclusive tickets; no money changes hands at the restaurant. What diners can expect is an extraordinary chef's tasting experience based on a theme, which changes three times a year. Past themes include The Hunt, Vegan, and Kyoto.

North Pond $$$
Fine Dining
2610 N Cannon Dr., 60614
Tel *773-477-5845* **Closed** *Mon*
The bucolic setting within Lincoln Park sets a romantic stage for North Pond's seasonal upscale American cuisine. Expect *foie gras*, sweetbreads, seared duck breast and grass-fed New York striploin.

Michelin-starred Takashi offers an interesting mix of French and Japanese cusine

Schwa $$$
Fine Dining
1466 N Ashland Ave., Wicker Park, 60622
Tel *773-252-1466* **Closed** *Sun & Mon*
A favorite with local chefs, Schwa offers an elevated, multicourse dining experience amid an upbeat ambience with a complete lack of pretense or formality. Reserve well ahead of time. BYOB.

Takashi $$$
Asian Fusion
1952 N Damen, Bucktown, 60647
Tel *773-772-6170* **Closed** *Mon*
Michelin-starred namesake restaurant of former Iron Chef Masters contestant Takashi Yagihashi. Serves flavorful and innovative Franco-Japanese fusion cuisine in an airy and modern environment.

Girl and the Goat $$$
New American
809 W Randolph, Near West Side, 60607
Tel *312-492-6262*
Goat, pig, and seafood feature prominently in Top Chef winner Stephanie Izard's boisterous New American-style brasserie favored by local foodies. A popular dish on the frequently changing menu is the oven-roasted pig face.

Beyond Chicago

Blind Faith Café $
Vegetarian
525 Dempster St., Evanston, 60201
Tel *847-328-6875* **Closed** *Mon*
Local option for family-friendly vegetarian fare. Internationally inspired entrées include the teriyaki-fried rice bowl and seitan marsala. The menu indicates which items are vegan and/or gluten-free.

Edzo's Burger Shop $
Fast Food
1571 Sherman Ave., Evanston, 60201
Tel *847-864-3396* **Closed** *Mon*
The beef at this popular local burger joint is ground fresh and hand-pressed daily on site. Fresh milk shakes and tasty fries and dogs round out the menu.

Little Tokyo $
Sushi
300 N Main St., Galena, 61036
Tel *815-777-8883*
Locals and tourists alike are crazy about this small sushi restaurant. The menu includes popular favorites, like *edamame* and *gyoza*.

Next Door Pub $
Pizzeria
411 Interchange N, Lake Geneva, WI, 53147
Tel *262-248-9551*
A Lake Geneva pizza spot that has been serving savory stone-hearth pies for more than 40 years to happy crowds. Local brews are served on tap.

DK Choice

Pita Inn $
Mediterranean
3910 Dempster St., Skokie, 60076
Tel *847-677-0211*
Order fresh and flavorful Mediterranean favorites at the counter, which are then served at the tables. The 11am-3pm business lunch special – a combination plate of shish kebab, *kifta* kebab, *shawerma*, and falafel served with rice pilaf, salad, and home-made pita bread – is an outrageously good deal.

Poor Phil's Bar & Grill $
Seafood
139 S Marion St., Oak Park, 60302
Tel *708-848-0871*
Casual bar and grill, where Cajun fare meets bar grub, serves unpretentious shellfish dishes. Catch the game while slurping oysters.

Procento's Pizzeria $
Pizzeria
105 Franklin St., Galena, 61036
Tel *815-777-1640*   **Closed** *Tues*
Appealing family-owned pizza place that serves up reasonably priced, tasty hand-tossed pies for dine-in, carry-out, or delivery. Beer and wine available.

Simple Café $
Brunch
525 Broad St., Lake Geneva, WI, 53147
Tel *262-248-3556*
Cheerful café that serves creative breakfast and lunch, using products from local farms and producers when possible. Try the delicious smoked trout, baby spinach, and beet salad.

Sprecher's Restaurant and Pub $
Pub
111 Center St., Lake Geneva, WI, 53147
Tel *262-248-7047*
From nachos and burgers to German specialties, the food menu at this brewpub originates from an affinity with beer. They also brew terrific root beer and cream soda, so there is no need to leave the kids at home.

Find plenty of fresh fish dishes at Davis Street Fishmarket

Taste of Brasil Café $
Brazilian
906 S Oak Park Ave., Oak Park, 60304
Tel *708-383-3550*
Tiny storefront BYOB serves authentically flavored Brazillian comfort food, from lentil soup to traditional meatloaf stuffed with ham and cheese to *feijoada*, a meat-laden black bean stew.

Victory Café $
Brunch
200 N Main St., Galena, 61036
Tel *815-777-4407*
Classic American diner set in Galena's first post office. From Hobo Hash to free refills on coffee, everything here meets good café standards.

Campagnola $$
Italian
815 Chicago Ave., Evanston, 60202
Tel *847-475-6100*   **Closed** *Mon*
Contemporary Italian comfort food, including braised octopus, beef carpaccio, and rack of lamb, is served at this friendly eating place.

Davis Street Fishmarket $$
Seafood
501 Davis St., Evanston, 60201
Tel *847-869-3474*
With a hearty nod to New Orleans, the Davis Street Fishmarket features a raw bar and several varieties of fresh fish, along with sides like jambalaya and red beans and rice.

Marion Street Cheese Market $$
American
100 S Marion St., Oak Park, 60302
Tel *708-725-7200*
This cheese shop doubles as a wine bar with a bistro menu of contemporary American dishes such as bison carpaccio and upscale mac 'n' cheese.

New Rebozo $$
Mexican
1116 Madison St., Oak Park, 60302
Tel *708-445-0370*   **Closed** *Sun*
Neuvo Mexican spot that offers a fresh take on classic comfort food, with creative presentations and equally upscale prices.

One Eleven Main $$
American
111 N Main St., Galena, 61036
Tel *815-777-8020*
Fried cheese curds and beef pot roast are characteristic of the comforting Midwestern fare at this warm, family-friendly American bistro.

Quince $$
American
1625 Hinman Ave., Evanston, 60201
Tel *847-570-8400*   **Closed** *Mon*
Located in the Homestead hotel, Quince delivers contemporary American cuisine in a subdued, romantic wood-paneled room. They also have a warm cocktail lounge for social gatherings.

Sen Sushi Bar $$
Sushi
814 S Oak Park Ave, Oak Park, 60304
Tel *708-848-4400*   **Closed** *Mon*
A small, Zen-like space serving fresh sashimi and creative *maki* dishes such as the extravagant Sen *maki*, made with shrimp tempura, octopus, scallion, fire-torched scallop, squid, lime juice, cilantro, and lemongrass reduction. Vegetarian options are also available.

Geneva Chophouse $$$
Steak House
7036 Grand Geneva Way, Lake Geneva, WI, 53147
Tel *262-249-4788*
Standard steak house fare like steaks, chops, seafood, and enormous sides. One of the five restaurants in the Grand Geneva Resort and Spa.

Perry Street Brasserie $$$
Fine Dining
124 N Commerce St., Galena, 61036
Tel *815-777-3773*   **Closed** *Mon & Tue*
One of Galena's favorite restaurants for special occasions, the intimate, rustic-decored Perry Street Brasserie may be more expensive than most local options but makes up for it in the quality of food served and the service. Extensive wine list.

For more information on types of restaurants *see page 147*

SHOPS AND MARKETS

Shopping, rather than sports, may well be the major pastime of Chicagoans. The sheer number of shops in the small area around Michigan Avenue alone makes Chicago a world-class shopping destination. Everything from basic necessities to outrageous luxuries can be found at Chicago's boutiques, specialty shops, and legendary department stores. No matter what your passion, you will find a merchant in Chicago who shares it. Many of the shops listed on pages 160–63 will take you off the beaten track into the city's many distinct and charming neighborhoods.

Ghirardelli Chocolate Shop and Soda Fountain

When to Shop

Most chain stores are open seven days a week, from 10am to 6pm. Some shops open an hour later and close an hour earlier on Sundays. Malls and shopping centers usually stay open evenings as well as on Sundays.

Neighborhood shops, antique dealers, vintage-clothing stores, and galleries keep more relaxed hours. Many are closed on Mondays and Tuesdays and may not open until noon on other days. Shops are blissfully empty on weekday mornings, gradually becoming crowded as the evening approaches. On the weekends, downtown shops and malls are packed.

Sales

Pre-season sales, end-of-season sales, 13-hour sales, Mother's Day sales – it is easy to find some kind of sale each day of the year.

Many sales, especially when shops want to clear their racks to make way for the next season's merchandise, offer great bargains.

Be wary of "going out of business" sales – some have been going on for years. However, some are legitimate sales; ask at nearby stores.

Taxes

Sales tax in Chicago is 9.25 per cent and is added to everything except newspapers, magazines, and groceries. Sales tax is not refundable to visitors from overseas. However, if the shop ships your purchase to an address outside Chicago or Illinois, you can avoid city and/or state sales tax. Foreign visitors may be required to pay duty on the purchase once they arrive home.

Payment

Major credit cards are accepted in most Chicago stores, as are bank debit cards, though small businesses may have a minimum-price policy (usually a $10 minimum) for purchases paid for this way. Traveler's checks must be accompanied by identification. Personal checks are discouraged; foreign currency is never accepted. A few smaller shops are still run on a cash-only basis.

Returns

Be sure you understand the shop's return policy before you make an important purchase. Keep your receipt as a proof of purchase.

Each store sets its own return-and-exchange policies; they are generally posted at the cash register. Some shops will give a full refund with no questions asked, whereas other shops

Vibrant window signs brightening a storefront in Chinatown

Sunday morning in the busy Maxwell Street Market *(see p161)*

Water Tower Place, with eight levels of boutiques and stores

maintain an all-sales-are-final policy. Some places offer an in-shop credit rather than a refund. Sale items are often not returnable.

Malls and Shopping Centers

Chicago's malls come in two varieties. Suburban malls resemble small cities surrounded by vast parking lots. City malls tend to rise upward from the ground. The most notable of these vertical malls are on the Magnificent Mile *(see pp62–3)*.

Water Tower Place contains major department stores, eight levels with more than 100 boutiques and specialty shops, and a movie theater.

Across the street is **900 North Michigan Shops**, an elegant mall on seven levels with over 70 luxury shops and boutiques, including Gucci, MaxMara,

Montblanc, and Bloomingdale's, as well as numerous restaurants and cafés.

The Shops at North Bridge has world-class specialty shops, more than twenty restaurants and five hotels.

Block 37 is located in a four-storey structure in the Loop. Designers such as Anthropologie and Eileen Fisher, as well as chocolatier Ghiradelli's few local boutiques, are spread over three floors.

Department Stores

Many department stores have a prominent street location. **Macy's** (formerly Marshall Field's; *see pp52–3)* is the benchmark for luxurious department stores across the country. Don't leave Chicago without a box of its Frango mints.

Seattle-based **Nordstrom**, which is known for its quality clothing and shoes for men, women, and children, has its flagship Midwest store on the Magnificent Mile.

Posh **Neiman Marcus** bills itself as a world-famous specialty store and prides itself on its personal service and exclusivity. The store specializes in clothing and accessories by many top fashion

designers. Its epicurean shop offers delectable items, including caviar and wine.

Saks Fifth Avenue attracts a ritzy clientele with its selection of designer and private-label clothing.

Bloomingdale's is also stylish but less pricey. It has a great selection of fashionable clothing and shoes, and a floor devoted to housewares. Watch for its sales, which are legendary.

Parking

Downtown parking lots are expensive, and street parking is almost nonexistent *(see p185)*. Many department stores offer discounted parking in their lots, but the few dollars saved are rarely worth the time spent in the parking maze. The CTA (Chicago Transit Authority) offers convenient public transit *(see p186)*.

An interior-furnishings shop on the street level of the historic Santa Fe Building *(see p47)*

DIRECTORY

Malls and Shopping Centers

Block 37
108 N State St.
Map 1 C4.
Tel (312) 261-4700.
Ⓦ block37.com

900 North Michigan Shops
900 N Michigan Ave.
Map 2 D4.
Tel (312) 915-3916.
Ⓦ shop900.com

The Shops at North Bridge
520 N Michigan Ave.
Map 2 D5.
Tel (312) 327-2300.
Ⓦ theshopsatnorth
bridge.com

Water Tower Place
835 N Michigan Ave.
Map 2 D4.
Tel (312) 440-3166.
Ⓦ shopwatertower.
com

Department Stores

Bloomingdale's
900 North Michigan Shops,
900 N Michigan Ave. **Map**
2 D4. **Tel**(312) 440-4460.
Ⓦ bloomingdales.com

Macy's
(formerly Marshall Field's)
111 N State St. **Map** 4 D1.
Tel (312) 781-1000.
Water Tower Place
835 N Michigan Ave.
Map 2 D4. **Tel** (312) 335-
7700. Ⓦ macys.com

Neiman Marcus
737 N Michigan Ave.
Map 2 D4.
Tel (312) 642-5900.
Ⓦ neimanmarcus.com

Nordstrom
55 E Grand Ave.
Map 2 D5. **Tel** (312) 464-
1515. Ⓦ nordstrom.com

Saks Fifth Avenue
700 N Michigan Ave.
Map 2 D4. **Tel** (312) 944-
6500. Ⓦ sacksfifth
avenue.com

Where to Shop

Chicago is a shopper's paradise. The city's many neighborhoods attract locals and tourists alike with ethnic and one-of-a-kind shops. Visitors looking for fine and unusual artwork are sure to find a treasure in the River North Gallery District. Furnishing shops are clustered at Clybourn Corridor, while Oak Street is home to top fashion boutiques. Myriad shops, including chain and department stores, line the Magnificent Mile.

Art

River North Gallery District has Chicago's highest concentration of art galleries, though there are several good galleries outside its traditional boundaries. **Stephen Daiter Gallery** offers vintage 20th-century and experimental photography. **Carl Hammer Gallery** is known for its collection of "outsider art". **Alan Koppel Gallery** is a contemporary gallery with sculpture and paintings from both local and international artists. **Zolla/Lieberman Gallery** specializes in contemporary painting, sculpture, drawings, and photographs. **Mongerson Galleries** showcases Western art: paintings, sculpture, and photographs from the 18th to 20th centuries.

The collection of original European advertising posters dating from the late 1800s on display at **Spencer Weisz Galleries** is really marvelous. **Posters Plus** specializes in aviation, circus, food, and wine posters.

Antiques

Most of the antique shops in the former antique district at West Belmont and North Lincoln Avenues have dispersed to other areas. Some of the shops remaining are still worth visiting, but many resemble thrift shops rather than authentic antique shops. For genuine antiques, go to **Robert's Antiques** or visit **Salvage One** if you are looking for the likes of an antique doorknob or leaded stained glass. **Architectural Artifacts** has a great selection of

salvaged pieces, and stocks everything from wooden desks to original church pews.

Art and Craft Supplies

Dick Blick stocks drafting, etching, and silk-screening supplies, in addition to paints, papers, and brushes. **Paper Source** sells specialized papers and the city's largest assortment of rubber stamps.

EnBeadia is known for having the best selection of beads, semi-precious stones, and necklace chains in the city.

Tom Thumb Hobby & Crafts offers a great selection of beads and craft materials.

Books

Local bookshops abound in Chicago. **Barbara's Bookstore** specializes in small- and alternative-press titles. The **Chicago Architecture Foundation Shop** has an excellent selection of books dedicated to the city's architecture.

Powell's Bookstore has two stores (one in north and one in south Chicago), selling quality rare, used, and discount books. It buys and sells used books, specializing in rare, out-of-print, and scholarly titles.

The top bookshop for gay and lesbian literature in Chicago is **Unabridged Books**. **57th Street Books** has a wonderful general selection of books but specializes in cookbooks, mysteries, and film, computer, and especially in children's books.

Women & Children First is one of the largest feminist bookstores in the country,

stocking more than 30,000 books by and about women.

Buttons and Fabrics

Everything from reams of fabric to craft materials and seasonal holiday supplies line the generous aisles at **JoAnn Fabric**.

From decorator fabrics to bridal finery, try the dizzying selection at **Vogue Fabrics**. **Fishman's Fabrics** carries a range of theatrical fabrics, laces, and decorative trims as well as silks, woolens, and cottons.

Cameras and Electronics

Camera buffs will want to visit **Central Camera**, an old-world shop crammed with cameras of every make and model. **Helix Camera & Video** carries underwater equipment and used cameras.

Visit **Bang & Olufsen** for high-quality Danish entertainment centers. **The Apple Store** is a wonderland of high-tech gadgets and electronics, while **Best Buy** has superb home and car stereo systems and knowledgeable staff.

Coins

The full-service coin dealer **Harlan J. Berk** buys and sells all currencies of coins. It also deals in paper money and rare and ancient coins. Another respected dealer is **Chicago Coin Company**, located near Midway Airport.

Discount Clothing

Discount clothing stores are plentiful in Chicago. **Marshall's, TJ Maxx**, and **Filene's Basement** all have great selections.

Many department stores *(see p159)* also have discount outlets scattered throughout the suburbs.

Designer Clothing

For cutting edge and women's fashions by designers such as Givenchy and Rodarte, **Ikram** is a must-visit. **Giorgio Armani** stocks the designer's entire collection, including eyewear and fragrances. Italian design house **Prada** sells its fashions from a sleek and ultra-hip Oak Street shop. **Barneys New York** has an excellent selection of designer clothing.

For the more adventurous, there's **Sugar Magnolia**, for fashions from European and US designers.

Shoes

Stocking stylish women's shoes, purses, and accessories, **Lori's Designer Shoes** is a treasure. The somewhat hectic store is self-serve. **Altman's Men's Shoes**, a Chicago mainstay since 1932, offers current men's styles and specialty sizes.

Furs and Leathers

The midwest's largest fur importer and wholesaler is **Chicago Fur Mart**. A large selection of furs at reasonable prices is also available at **Chicago Fur Outlet**. Chic furs and leathers by top designers are sold at **Elán Furs**. **Glove Me Tender** has a vast array of gloves for men, women, and children.

Jewelry

The gems of the jewelry district are clustered along Wabash Avenue between Madison and Washington Streets. Some are open only to the trade, but several open to the public. **Harold Burland & Son** sells diamonds and other precious stones. **Tiffany & Co.** sells designer jewelry, crystal, and clocks. **Lester Lampert** sells high-end custom jewelry from a historic location on Oak Street.

Food and Wine Shops

Visiting **The Spice House** is an aromatic adventure. Its proprietors will gladly discuss the differences between the several varieties of cinnamon or basil they sell. **Treasure Island** carries hard-to-find imports and the city's best selection of gourmet foodstuffs. The organic food at **Whole Foods** is delicious.

For a rare Bordeaux or obscure Puerto Rican rum, visit **Binny's Beverage Depot**. **House of Glunz** carries wines in vintages as early as 1804. It also has a tasting room and wine museum.

Markets

From June to October, Midwest farmers come to sell their produce at Chicago's 30 or so markets. Some markets are on weekdays, but Saturday is the main market day. Hours are usually from 7am to 1pm. **Near North Market** is held Saturdays, as is **Lincoln Park Market**. **Evanston Farmers' Market**, on Saturday mornings, has wonderful organic produce. The fabulous **Daley Plaza Market** is alternate Thursdays.

Chicago's famous **New Mawell Street Market** (now on Roosevelt Rd) has been around since 1871. Up to 400 vendors sell new and used items, from power tools to fresh delicacies. The market runs Sundays, April to October. Be prepared to pay with cash at the markets. Prices are generally not negotiable. Call the **Farmers' Market Information Line** for details and to confirm locations.

Gifts and Souvenirs

The **Chicago Architecture Foundation Shop** has a good selection of souvenir books, posters, and Chicago memorabilia.

Purchase hats, shirts, mugs, and other items at the **Navy Pier Store**. The **Illinois Artisans Shop** is an excellent source of affordable crafts by local artisans, while the **After School Matters Retail** sells a wide range of artwork by teenagers enrolled in its nonprofit art program.

Home and Garden Furnishings

Upscale reproductions of vintage furniture and fixtures are the specialties of **Restoration Hardware**. **Jayson Home & Garden** carries unusual furnishings and garden pots. **Williams-Sonoma** sells all kinds of homewares and gifts, including garden gadgets.

Memorabilia

You will find a fascinating, and broad, collection of political, sports, and movie memorabilia at **Yesterday**.

Music

A vast classical-music collection, as well as folk, jazz, rock, pop, and show tunes, is to be found at **Best Buy**.

What is arguably the world's best collection of jazz recordings is found at **Jazz Record Mart**. Staff here are extremely knowledgeable. **Reckless Records** is a fun place to browse through secondhand CDs.

Sporting Goods

Everything the company manufactures can be found at **Nike Town**, while **Vertel's Authentic Running & Fitness** is serious about athletic shoes. If outdoor equipment is an interest, an expedition to **The North Face** is worthwhile.

Toys, Gadgets, and Specialty Shops

Chicago Kite/Kite Harbor entices with an astonishing selection of kites and radio-controlled toys. Everything from chemistry kits to telescopes is sold at **American Science and Surplus**.

For children, a firm favorite is **The Disney Store**, which is filled with trinkets, costumes, and stuffed toys. The popular **American Girl Place** sells historic and contemporary dolls and doll accessories. Clothing, accessories, and furniture are also available.

DIRECTORY

Art

Alan Koppel Gallery
806 N Dearborn St.
Map 1 C4.
Tel 312-640-0730.

Carl Hammer Gallery
740 N Wells St. **Map** 1 C4.
Tel 312-266-8512.

Mongerson Galleries
740 N Wells St. **Map** 1 C4.
Tel 312-943-2354.

Posters Plus
30 E Adams St., Suite 1150
Map 4 D2. **Tel** 312-461-9277.

Spencer Weisz Galleries
843 W Chicago Ave. (near West Side). **Map** 1 A4.
Tel 312-527-9420.

Stephen Daiter Gallery
230 W Superior St.
Map 2 D4. **Tel** 312-787-3350.

Zolla/Lieberman Gallery
325 W Huron St.
Map 1 B4. **Tel** 312-944-1990.

Antiques

Architectural Artifacts
4325 N Ravenswood Ave.,
Ravenswood. **Tel** 773-348-0622.

J Roberts Antiques
149 W Kinzie St.
Map 1 C5. **Tel** 312-222-0167.

Salvage One
1840 W Hubbard St.
Grand Avenue Corridor.
Tel 312-733-0098.

Art and Craft Supplies

Dick Blick
42 S State St.
Map 4 D3.
Tel 312-920-0300.

EnBeadia
653 W Armitage Ave.
(Lincoln Park north of near North Side). **Tel** 312-280-2323.

Paper Source
232 W Chicago Ave.
Map 1 C4.
Tel 312-337-0798.

Tom Thumb Hobby & Crafts
1026 Davis St., Evanston.
Tel 847-869-9575.

Books

Barbara's Bookstore
233 S Wacker Dr., Willis Tower.
Map 3 B2.
Tel 312-466-0223. One of several locations.

Chicago Architecture Foundation Shop
224 S Michigan Ave.
Map 4 D2.
Tel 312-922-3432.

57th Street Books
1301 E 57th St.
Map 8 D4.
Tel 773-684-1300.

Powell's Bookstore
1801 S Halsted St.
Tel 312-243-9070.
1501 E 57th St. **Map** 8 D4.
Tel 773-955-7780.

Unabridged Books
3251 N Broadway,
Lakeview.
Tel 773-883-9119.

Women & Children First

5233 N Clark St.
Map 3 B2.
Tel 773-769-9299.

Buttons and Fabrics

Fishman's Fabrics
1101 S Des Plaines St.
Map 3 A4.
Tel 312-922-7250.

JoAnn Fabric
2639 N Elston Ave., Logan Sq. **Tel** 773-227-7874.

Vogue Fabrics
718 Main St., Evanston.
Tel 847-864-9600. One of three locations.

Cameras and Electronics

Bang & Olufsen
609 N State St.
Map 2 D3. **Tel** 312-787-6006.

Best Buy
See Music, *p163*.

Central Camera
230 S Wabash Ave.
Map 4 D3. **Tel** 312-427-5580.

Helix Camera & Video
310 S Racine Ave.,
Near West Side. **Tel** 312-421-6000.

The Apple Store
679 N Michigan Ave.
Map 2 D4. **Tel** 312-529-9500.

Coins

Chicago Coin Company
6455 W Archer Ave.,
Garfield Ridge.
Tel 773-586-7666.

Harlan J. Berk
31 N Clark St.
Map 3 C1.
Tel 312-609-0016.

Discount Clothing

Filene's Basement
830 N Michigan Ave.
Map 2 D4.
Tel 312-482-8918.
One of two locations.

Marshall's
600 N Michigan Ave.
Map 2 D4.
Tel 312-280-7506.
One of several locations.

TJ Maxx
11 N State St.
Map 3 C1.
Tel 312-553-0515.
One of three locations.

Designer Clothing

Barneys New York
15 E Oak St.
Map 2 D3.
Tel 312-587-1700.

Giorgio Armani
800 N Michigan Ave.
Map 2 D4.
Tel 312-327-3120.

Ikram
15 E Huron St.
Map 2 D4.
Tel 312-587-1000.

Prada
30 E Oak St.
Map 2 D3.
Tel 312-951-1113.

Sugar Magnolia
34 E Oak St.
Map 2 D3.
Tel 312-944-0885.

Shoes

Altman's Shoes For Men
120 W Monroe St.
Map 3 C2.
Tel 312-332-0667.

Lori's Designer Shoes
824 W Armitage Ave.,
Lincoln Park.
Tel 773-281-5655.

DIRECTORY

Furs and Leathers

Chicago Fur Mart
645 N Michigan Ave.
Map 2 D4.
Tel 312-951-5000.

Chicago Fur Outlet
777 W Diversey Pkwy.
Tel 773-348-3877.

Elán Furs
675 N Michigan Ave.
Map 2 D4. Tel 312-640-0707.

Glove Me Tender
900 N Michigan Ave.
Map 2 D3. Tel 312-664-4022.

Jewelry

Harold Burland & Son
5 S Wabash Ave. suite 712.
Map 4 D2.
Tel 312-332-5176.

Lester Lampert
57 E Oak St (North Side).
Map 2 D3.
Tel 312-944-6888.

Tiffany & Co.
730 N Michigan Ave.
Map 2 D4.
Tel 312-944-7500.

Food and Wine Shops

Binny's Beverage Depot
1720 N Marcey St.,
DePaul.
Tel 312-664-4394.

House of Glunz
1206 N Wells St.
Map 1 C2.
Tel 312-642-3000.

The Spice House
1512 N Wells St.
Map 1C1.
Tel 312-274-0378.

Treasure Island
1639 N Wells St.
Map 1 C1.
Tel 312-642-1105. One
of several locations.

Whole Foods
30 W Huron St.
Map 1 A4.
Tel 312-932-9600.
One of several locations.

Markets

Daley Plaza Market
Richard J. Daley Center
Plaza, Washington &
Dearborn sts.
Map 3 C1.

**Evanston Farmers'
Market**
Tel 847-866-2936 for
market times, location,
and further details.

**Farmers' Market
Information Line**
Tel 312-744-3315 for
market times, locations,
and further details.

Lincoln Park Market
Armitage Ave. & Orchard
St. Lincoln Park.
Near North Market
Division & Dearborn sts.
Map 1 C3.

**Maxwell Street
Market**
548 W Roosevelt.
Map 3 B4–B5.
Tel 312-745-4676.

Gifts and Souvenirs

**After School Matters
Retail**
66 E Randolph St.
Map 4 D2.
Tel 312-744-7274

**Chicago Architecture
Foundation Shop**
See Books, p152.

Illinois Artisans Shop
100 W Randolph St.
Map 3 C2.
Tel 312-814-5321.

Navy Pier Store
700 E Grand Ave., Navy
Pier. Map 2 F5.
Tel 312-595-5400.

Home and Garden Furnishings

**Jayson Home &
Garden**
1885 N Clybourn Ave.,
Clybourn Corridor.
Tel 773-248-8180.

**Restoration
Hardware**
938 W North Ave.,
Lincoln Park.
Tel 312-475-9116. One
of two locations.

Williams-Sonoma
1550 N Fremont St.,
Clybourn Corridor.
Map 2 D3.
Tel 312-255-0643.

Memorabilia

Yesterday
1143 W Addison St.,
Lakeview.
Tel 773-248-8087.

Music

Best Buy
875 N Michigan Ave.
Map 2 D3.
Tel 312-397-2146.

Jazz Record Mart
27 E Illinois St.
Map 2 D5.
Tel 312-222-1467.

Reckless Records
26 E Madison St.
Map 8 D2.
Tel 312-795-0878.
One of three locations.

Sporting Goods

Nike Town
669 N Michigan Ave.
Map 2 D4.
Tel 312-642-6363. One of
two locations.

The North Face
875 N Michigan Ave.
Map 2 D3.
Tel 312-337-7200.

**Vertel's Authentic
Running & Fitness**
24 S Michigan Ave.
Map 4 D2.
Tel 312-683-9600.

Toys, Gadgets, and Specialty Shops

American Girl Place
835 N Michigan Ave.
Map 2 D4.
Tel 312-247-5223.

**American Science
and Surplus**
5316 N Milwaukee Ave.,
Jefferson Park.
Tel 773-763-0313.

**Chicago Kite/Kite
Harbor**
5445 N Harlem Ave.,
Harwood Heights.
Tel 773-467-1428.

The Disney Store
717 N Michigan Ave.
Map 2 D2.
Tel 312-654-9208.

ENTERTAINMENT IN CHICAGO

Tens of millions of dollars have been spent in recent years by the City of Chicago to rejuvenate old theaters and build cultural attractions. Today, a portion of the money raised through the hotel tax *(see p140)* is channeled directly to the department of culture. And it shows. Chicago's world-class orchestras and opera, intimate jazz ensembles, high-profile musicals, and alternative theater help to attract more than 5 million tourists to Chicago each year. Festivals of all kinds, from music to dance to ethnic, are held in the city's many parks and more than 75 diverse communities *(see pp34–7)*. There are also numerous sports events throughout the year for visitors to Chicago to watch or participate in *(see pp166–7)*.

Chicago's listings magazine, *The Reader*, published weekly

Information

The city's most complete entertainment listings are in *The Reader*, a free newspaper distributed on Thursdays. *Chicago Magazine*, available at newsstands, is a glossy monthly with listings of the city's major venues. The two daily newspapers, the *Chicago Sun-Times* and the *Chicago Tribune*, publish an entertainment section in their Friday editions, with movie, music, dance, and theater reviews and listings.

Chicago's **Visitor Information Centers** sell tickets as well as providing entertainment information.

Moviefone provides recorded details of movie show times and theater locations, as well as brief descriptions of the movies.

Hot Tix, a ticket agency run by the League of Chicago Theatres, provides half-price tickets to more than 125 Chicago-area theaters on the day of performance.

Most hotels carry a wide selection of entertainment brochures, and hotel staff will help orient you and may arrange for tickets. The **Mayor's**

Office of Special Events also provides information on local events, including the numerous neighborhood festivals that take place during summer.

Buying Tickets

Tickets for most major entertainment events are sold through **Ticketmaster**. You can buy tickets by phone or at one of its locations. You may be able to buy tickets for sold-out events from a ticket broker (see listings in the yellow pages of the telephone directory), but the price may be astronomical. Be wary of buying tickets from "scalpers" (ticket hawkers) on the street. Some try to sell tickets that are expired or counterfeit.

Many of the major concerts, plays, and musicals are reviewed in the national press, which can lead to them selling out weeks in advance. It is best to buy tickets through a ticket agency or the venue's box office before your trip. Most people buy movie tickets at the theater. Prices range from $1.50 per

The Civic Opera House, home to the Lyric Opera of Chicago

ticket for second-run movies to $10 for first-run movies. You can buy tickets using a major credit card through **Moviefone**. This saves standing in line at the theater, but the tickets are nonrefundable and a surcharge of $1 to $2 is added to the price of each.

Discount Tickets

Half-price tickets for shows on the day of performance are available from **Hot Tix**. These tickets must be purchased in person and paid for in cash or by credit card.

CityPass Traveler packages admissions to five of the top attractions in Chicago, saving you both time and money. The passes can be purchased through its website or at the participating venues.

Explore Chicago, in addition to serving as a primary resource for planning trip activities, offers discounts on attractions, shopping, entertainment, and dining.

Travelers with Disabilities

Many theaters and concert halls in Chicago are fully wheelchair accessible. Some of the smaller theaters and clubs try hard but are less than adequate when it comes to serving patrons with special needs. Even though a venue has the required seating area for persons in wheelchairs, the building may still be difficult to get around in.

Major theaters and halls provide amplifying head-phones for people with hearing impairments.

The **Mayor's Office for People with Disabilities** provides details on which venues are accessible for people with disabilities.

Free Events

Accomplished young musicians play every Wednesday as part of the Dame Myra Hess series of free noontime recitals at the **Chicago Cultural Center** *(see p54)*. This hub for free events hosts live music almost every day of the week as well as dance and theater performances. Art exhibitions shown here are also free. Harold Washington Library Center *(see p84)* also hosts concerts, many free, as well as film screenings, seminars, author events, and childrens' story time activities.

The best free seats in the city are in Grant Park and in Millennium Park *(see p55)*. The Grant Park Orchestra and Chorus give evening concerts, mid-June to mid-August, Wednesday and Friday, in Millennium Park. (see page 158 for details on other free music events.)

The first-rate Grant Park Music Festival in Millennium Park hosts daytime and evening performances June through mid-September. Monday evenings are usually set aside for indie rock acts and experimental sounds, Thursdays in June and July are devoted to world music, and the month of August is devoted to jazz. Classical music performances are also held from June to August.

Concert in Preston Bradley Hall at the Chicago Cultural Center

Sidewalk signs in the Loop's theater district

The season kick-off is the world renowned Blues Festival. In the first weekend of July, Grant Park hosts Taste of Chicago, which includes special days devoted to music: gospel, Latin, and country. The local government also hosts Chicago SummerDance in Grant Park. This program takes place multiple evenings of the week for 11 weeks in the summer. Professional instructors give 1-hour dance lessons in styles ranging from tango to two-step, followed by a 2-hour session of music and dancing. Live bands play salsa, soul, R&B, gypsy, and country to accompany the dancing.

Throughout the summer, dozens of Chicago's neighborhoods block off streets to traffic and hold weekend festivals and block parties. Most are free or require a minimal entrance fee. Vendors sell refreshments, artists show arts and crafts, and local bands perform. You can hear great salsa, gritty rock and roll, country music, blues, or jazz – sometimes on the same day. These festivals allow visitors to experience Chicago's neighborhoods.

Visit http://chicagofree.info for up-to-date listings of free events happening in and around the city.

Buddy Guy, one of the world's greatest blues guitar soloists

DIRECTORY

Useful Numbers

Chicago Cultural Center
Tel 312-744-6630,
312-346-3278.
w chicagoculturalcenter.org

City Helpline
Tel 311 (event information).

Mayor's Office for People with Disabilities
Tel 312-744-6673.
w cityofchicago.org/disabilities

Mayor's Office of Special Events
Tel 312-744-3315.
w explorechicago.org/specialevents

Performance Hotline
Tel 312-987-1123.

Visitor Information Centers
Tel 877-244-2246.
163 E Pearson St.
Map 2 D4.
77 E Randolph St.
Map 4 D1.
w cityofchicago.org and
w choosechicago.org

Ticket Agencies

CityPass Traveler
w citypass.net

Hot Tix
163 E Pearson St.
Map 2 D4.
72 E Randolph St.
Map 4 D1.
Tel 312-751-1876.
Closed Mon.
w hottix.org

Moviefone
Tel 312-444-3456.
w moviefone.com

Ticketmaster
Tel 312-559-1212.
w ticketmaster.com

Free Events

Chicago Free
http://chicagofree.info

Chicago Summer Dance
w chicagosummerdance.org

Performing Arts, Film, and Sports

When it comes to entertainment, Chicago is second to none. The Chicago Symphony and the Lyric Opera are both world-class, while Steppenwolf Theater grew from its beginnings in a basement to become one of the leading theater troupes in the country. Chicago also has its share of art film houses. Many events take place at the city's thousand-odd parks and playgrounds. Ravinia Festival, in Highland Park, showcases music and dance throughout the summer. Spectator sports, especially baseball, are also enormously popular in Chicago, the numerous teams providing year-round entertainment.

Music

The guiding light of classical music in Chicago is the **Chicago Symphony Orchestra**. From September through June, it performs at **Symphony Center**. During the summer, it performs at the **Ravinia Festival**.

The highly acclaimed **Lyric Opera of Chicago** presents lavish productions and brings international stars to **Civic Opera House** during its September-to-March season.

Music of the Baroque is Chicago's leading early-music ensemble. A consortium of Chicago's finest musicians, **Chicago Chamber Musicians** presents a series of free concerts throughout the year at the **Chicago Cultural Center**, held on the first Monday of each month.

Mandel Hall at University of Chicago hosts folk, jazz, and classical groups. Northwestern University presents concerts by leading touring ensembles at **Pick-Staiger Concert Hall**.

Dance

The unique blend of jazz, ballet, and modern dance that **Hubbard Street Dance Chicago** offers will transport you to new places in entertainment. Performances take place at the Music and Dance Theater.

Each season, **Joffrey Ballet of Chicago** presents four performances of classical ballet with a contemporary edge, reflecting the dance company's mandate to present the works of 20th-century American artists.

Theater

Chicago has a vibrant theater scene. **Goodman Theatre**'s home is located in the Loop's theater district. The troupe presents contemporary plays as well as the classics directed with a fresh approach. Productions often star well-known stage and screen actors.

Broadway in Chicago is a theatrical production company which performs touring Broadway productions in the city. The **Chicago Theater** is a multi-purpose venue that presents concerts and theater. The **Auditorium Theatre** (see p46) hosts mainstream musicals such as *Les Miserables* and *Showboat*, as does the **Bank of America Theater**.

Since its inception in a church basement, **Steppenwolf Theater Company** has gained a national reputation for staging avant-garde plays. Although many of the actors who started at Steppenwolf, such as John Malkovich and Laurie Metcalf, have left, they frequently return to perform with the company or direct.

Shakespeare Repertory Company stages three productions a year in **Chicago Shakespeare Theater**, its striking courtyard-style theater at Navy Pier.

Many notable theaters are located near Lincoln Park and in Lakeview, among them the **Royal George** and the **Victory Gardens Theater**.

The **League of Chicago Theaters** shares information on 200 small, mid-sized, and large theaters, which put on performances ranging from cutting-edge drama and Broadway musicals to puppetry.

Summer Performances

The Chicago String Quartet performs frequently at the **DePaul University Concert Hall**. You'll also find them on summer evenings performing in Millennium Park.

In the summer, Chicago's performing arts scene moves to the idyllic Highland Park, 25 miles (40 km) north of the city, for the internationally celebrated **Ravinia Festival**. Chicago Symphony Orchestra performs here, as do leading jazz ensembles, pop and folk acts, children's performers, and dance troupes, including Hubbard Street Dance and the Joffrey Ballet of Chicago.

The park's sound system is excellent. Reserved seats in the pavilion usually cost from $25 to $60. General lawn seat admission to the park costs about $10.

Although Highland Park has several good restaurants, most people buy general-admission tickets, bring a picnic dinner (some, lavish spreads with candles, crystal, and fine wine), and sit on the lawn to enjoy the performances.

Film

Like most cities, Chicago has a cinema multiplex in almost every neighborhood showing first-run movies. There are also several art film houses in the city.

The **Harold Washington Library Center** screens a diverse selection of films. **The Music Box** is a fully restored 1929 movie palace designed to look as though you are outdoors at night. It shows an eclectic mix of foreign, American independent, and classic films. An organist entertains with vintage popular music during intermission on weekend evenings.

The **Gene Siskel Film Center** presents a wide range of standard-setting international cinema. Panel discussion and lectures provide context for the films.

Facets Multimedia has a small screening room where current innovative films from around the world – from South America to Eastern Europe to Africa – are shown. The theater also hosts retrospectives of great directors such as Alfred Hitchcock and Jean-Luc Godard. Facets has the

country's largest collection of videos for rent or sale.

Spectator Sports

Chicago boasts several professional sports teams, including two baseball teams. The **Chicago White Sox** play for the American League at the **US Cellular Field** on the city's South Side. The much-loved-but-often-disappointing **Chicago**

Cubs of the National League play in **Wrigley Field**, a marvelous inner-city stadium on the North Side of Chicago *(see p116)*.

The **Chicago Bulls**, winners of five world championships in the 1990s, play basketball at the **United Center**, as does Chicago's championship hockey team, the **Chicago Blackhawks**. The inimitable **Chicago Bears** play football at **Soldier Field**.

DIRECTORY

Music

Chicago Chamber Musicians and String Quartet
Tel 312-225-5226.

Chicago Cultural Center
78 E Washington St.
Map 4 D1. Tel 312-346-3278.

Chicago Symphony Orchestra
See Symphony Center.

Civic Opera House
20 N Wacker Dr. Map 3 B1. Tel 312-419-0033.

Lyric Opera of Chicago
See Civic Opera House.

Mandel Hall
University of Chicago, 1131 E 57th St. Map 7 C4. Tel 773-702-8068.

Music of the Baroque
Tel 312-551-1414.

Pick-Staiger Concert Hall
Northwestern University, 50 Arts Circle Dr., Evanston.
Tel 847-491-5441.

Symphony Center
220 S Michigan Ave.
Map 4 D2.
Tel 312-294-3000.

Dance

Hubbard Street Dance Chicago
1147 W Jackson Blvd.
Tel 312-850-9744.

Joffrey Ballet of Chicago
10 E Randolph.
Tel 312-739-0120.

Theater

Auditorium Theatre
50 E Congress Pkwy.
Map 4 D3. Tel 312-922-2110.

Bank of America Theater
18 W Monroe St.
Map 3 C2. Tel 312-977-1700.

Broadway in Chicago
Tel 312-977-1700.

Chicago Shakespeare Theater
800 E Grand Ave. Map 2 F5. Tel 312-595-5600.

Chicago Theatre
175 N State St. Map 4 D1.
Tel 312-462-6300.

Goodman Theatre
170 N Dearborn St. Map 3 C1. Tel 312-443-3800.

League of Chicago Theaters
Tel 312-554-9800.

Royal George
1641 N Halsted St.
Map 1 A1.
Tel 312-988-9000.

Shakespeare Repertory Company
See Chicago Shakespeare Theater.

Steppenwolf Theatre Company
1650 N Halsted St., Lincoln Park.
Tel 312-335-1650.

Victory Gardens
2433 N Lincoln Ave., Lincoln Park.
Tel 773-871-3000.

Summer Performances

DePaul University Concert Hall
800 W Belden Ave., Lincoln Park.
Tel 773-325-7444.

Ravinia Festival
Green Bay & Lake Cook Rds, Highland Park.
Tel 847-266-0641.

Film

Facets Multimedia
1517 W Fullerton Ave., DePaul. Tel 773-281-9075.

Gene Siskel Film Center of the Art Institute of Chicago
164 N State St. Map 3 C1.
Tel 312-846-2600.

Harold Washington Library Center
400 S State St. Map 3 C2.
Tel 312-747-4300.

The Music Box
3733 N Southport Ave., Lakeview.
Tel 773-871-6604.

Spectator Sports

Chicago Bears
Halas Hall, 1000 Football Dr. Lake Forest.
Tel 847-615-2327.

Chicago Blackhawks or Bulls
United Center.
Tel 800-745-3000.

Chicago Cubs
Tel 773-404-2827; (800) 843-2827 (tickets).

Chicago White Sox
Tel 312-674-1000.

Soldier Field
425 E McFetridge Dr.
Map 4 E5.
Tel 312-235-7000.

United Center
1901 W Madison St., Near West Side.
Tel 312-455-4500.

US Cellular Field
333 W 35th St.
Map 5 B5–C5.
Tel 312-674-1000.

Wrigley Field
1060 W Addison Ave., Lakeview.
Tel 773-404-2827.

Taverns, Nightclubs, and Live Music

Chicagoans have a reputation for working hard and playing hard. Nowhere is the latter more evident than in the city's night life. The blues are a Chicago institution, but jazz, country, folk, and rock music thrive here as well. Acts both big and small play almost nightly, and many music venues are open into the early hours of the morning. Chicago night-life establishments tend to be clustered together. Singles' bars are gathered at the corner of Division and State streets, bars frequented by the college crowd abound on Lincoln Avenue. Clark Street near Wrigley Field, on Chicago's North Side, has numerous sports bars. The gay scene is concentrated in the Lakeview neighborhood; Wicker Park offers a variety of alternative-music nightclubs.

Bars and Taverns

Bars and taverns are tucked into every neighborhood of Chicago. Some are rather basic drinking places, but others offer a glimpse into neighborhood life. Most bars in Chicago have limited food choices. Taverns, on the other hand, are serious about food. The American version of European pubs and bistros, taverns are relaxed places where locals go to eat, drink, and socialize.

The most venerable of the downtown taverns is **The Berghoff**. This establishment was the first in Chicago to be issued a liquor license once Prohibition ended. A casual dining spot, it features signature German dishes and beers. Two other notable downtown pubs are **Monk's Pub** and **Exchequer Restaurant & Pub**. Both succeed in maintaining a neighborhood atmosphere while catering to a good number of tourists.

Near the Magnificent Mile is **Disotto Enoteca**, a cozy subterranean wine bar. Or head to **Pippin's Tavern** for American sports on the screen, a range of beers on tap, and a jukebox.

Butch McGuire's has a major presence on the bar-lined block of Division Street near the Gold Coast. Its atmosphere is pub-like, and the food is good (especially the brunch). When the city celebrates a sports victory, fans celebrate in the many singles and sports bars near Division, Dearborn, and Rush streets. Summer in Chicago is a great time to sit outside, enjoy a drink, and people-watch. There are several good beer gardens and patios in Lincoln Park. **John Barleycorn's** and **Small Bar** are good bets. **Castaways**, which is located on North Avenue Beach, opens for summer and is an escape from the city for a young, lively crowd. **Goose Island Brewpub** sells brews made on the premises, some of the finest in town.

Nightclubs

Chicago offers a variety of nightclubs: there is sure to be one to suit your taste. Expect to pay an admission charge, though some clubs may impose a drink-order minimum instead.

Castle Chicago is perhaps the most mainstream club in the city. Pool tables and video games fill the first floor; the dance floor is upstairs, where retrospective music is played.

The Hideout, a true Chicago institution, is located in a 100-year-old balloon frame house behind a CTA bus refueling station. Rock, folk, country, and just about anything else can be heard here.

The Underground, located near Mag Mile, hosts international DJs and the city's varsity scene. For a more laidback dance scene, try **Club Foot** near the Ukranian Village.

Jazz

Jazz Showcase is Chicago's longest-running live jazz club. It has changed location many times, but the quality of the performers remains high. The **Green Mill** may not be impressive from the outside, and its Uptown neighborhood may be slightly run-down, but it is one of the city's coolest jazz clubs.

Andy's is one of Chicago's most respected clubs and has been going for over 25 years.

Blues

Major blues acts play at the **House of Blues**, a 1,500-seat venue with superb acoustics.

More intimate blues venues include **B.L.U.E.S.**, a small, busy bar with a friendly atmosphere that offers live music every night of the week. **Kingston Mines** also features nightly live blues on its two stages. Both stay open into the early morning hours.

Buddy Guy's Legends brings the big-name acts downtown. Guy himself plays here each January.

Folk and Country Music

The city's leading venue for folk music is the **Old Town School of Folk Music**. The **Abbey Pub** features local and touring groups, favoring Irish bands. It also offers barn dancing every Monday night.

Heartland Cafe is a throwback to the 1960s. It is a healthfood restaurant that also presents poetry readings, storytelling, and live music. **Schubas** is a neighborhood gem showcasing live folk, country music, and rock.

Although most of the line-dancing and two-stepping action is in the suburbs, it surprisingly can also be found in the city, at **Charlie's**. A gay bar serious about country music, Charlie's always welcomes straight folks.

Rock Music

Rock music is alive and well in Chicago. **Empty Bottle** is known for its eclectic calendar of cutting-edge underground acts and experimental jazz, as well as breaking up-and-coming artists.

House of Blues presents big-name rock stars. **Cubby Bear**, across from Wrigley Field (see p116), is a huge sports bar that presents local bands and touring talents, whereas **Metro**, also in Wrigleyville (see p116), is an independent-rock and dancing mecca. Wicker Park's (see p116) intimate **Double Door** is an excellent place to see live music. Many famous groups, such as the Smashing Pumpkins and the Rolling Stones, have played here under fictitious names, to the delight of unsuspecting patrons.

Reggie's Rock Club, near Southside, offers nightly musical shows with state-of-the art sound and above-average bar fare.

Comedy Clubs

For well-known stand-up comedy acts, visit **Zanies**. Comedians Jerry Seinfeld and Jay Leno have entertained here.

Second City, the celebrated venue that produced many of the comedians who went on to *Saturday Night Live* fame, offers a mix of social-satire sketches and improvisation. Dinner-theater packages are available. Another smaller theater in the same building, **Second City E.T.C.**, presents comedy revues.

DIRECTORY

Bars and Taverns

The Berghoff
17 W Adams St.
Map 3 C2.
Tel 312-427-3170.

Butch McGuire's
20 W Division St.
Map 1 C3.
Tel 312-787-4318.

Castaways
1603 N Lake Shore Dr.
Map 1 D1.
Tel 773-281-1200.

Disotto Enoteca
200 E Chestnut St.
Map 1 D3.
Tel 312-482-8727.

**Exchequer
Restaurant & Pub**
226 S Wabash Ave.
Map 4 D2.
Tel 312-939-5633.

**Goose Island
Brewpub**
1800 N Clybourn Ave.
Map 1 A1.
Tel 312-915-0071.
One of two locations.

John Barleycorn
3524 N Clark St.,
Wrigleyville.
Tel 773-549-6000.
One of two locations.

Monk's Pub
205 W Lake St. **Map** 3 C1.
Tel 312-357-6665.

Pippin's Tavern
806 N Rush St. **Map** 1 C4.
Tel 312-787-5435.

Small Bar

2049 W Division St.,
Wicker Park.
Tel 773-772-2727.
One of several locations.

Nightclubs

Castle Chicago
632 N Dearborn St.
Map 1 C4. **Tel** 312-266-1944.

Club Foot
1824 W Augusta,
Ukrainian Village.
Tel 773-489-0379.

The Hideout
1354 W Wabansia Ave.
Tel 773-227-4433.

The Underground
56 W Illinois. **Map** 1 C5.
Tel 312-644-7600.

Jazz

Andy's
11 E Hubbard St. **Map** 2
D5. **Tel** 312-642-6805.

The Green Mill
4802 N Broadway Ave.,
Uptown.
Tel 773-878-5552.

Jazz Showcase
806 S Plymouth Ct.
Map 3 C3.
Tel 312-360-0234.

Blues

B.L.U.E.S.
2519 N Halsted St.,
Lincoln Park.
Tel 773-528-1012.

Buddy Guy's Legends
754 S Wabash Ave.
Map 4 D3.
Tel 312-427-1190.

House of Blues
329 N Dearborn St.
Map 1 C5. **Tel** 312-923-2000.

Kingston Mines
2548 N Halsted St.,
Lincoln Park.
Tel 773-477-4646.

Folk and Country Music

Abbey Pub
3420 W Grace St.,
Northwest Side.
Tel 773-478-4408.

Charlie's
3726 N Broadway Ave.,
Lakeview.
Tel 773-871-8887.

Heartland Cafe
7000 N Glenwood Ave.,
Rogers Park.
Tel 773-465-8005.

**Old Town School of
Folk Music**
4544 N Lincoln Ave.,
Lincoln Square.
Tel 773-728-6000 (tickets and classes).

Schubas

3159 N Southport Ave.,
Lakeview.
Tel 773-525-2508.

Rock Music

Cubby Bear
1059 W Addison Ave.,
Wrigleyville.
Tel 773-327-1662.

Double Door
1572 N Milwaukee Ave.,
Wicker Park.
Tel 773-489-3160.

Empty Bottle
1035 N Western Ave.,
Ukrainian Village.
Tel 773-276-3600.

House of Blues
329 N Dearborn St. **Map** 3
C4. **Tel** 312-923-2000.

Metro
3730 N Clark St.,
Wrigleyville.
Tel 773-549-4140.

Reggie's Rock Club
2109 S State St. **Map** 5 C1.
Tel 312-949-0120.

Comedy Clubs

Second City
1616 N Wells St. **Map** 1
C2. **Tel** 312-337-3992 or
877-778-4707.

Second City E.T.C.
1608 N Wells St.
Map 1 C2. **Tel** 312-337-3992 or 877-778-4707.

Zanies
1548 N Wells St.
Map 1 C1. **Tel** 312-337-4027.

SURVIVAL GUIDE

LAKE STREET

PRACTICAL INFORMATION

With its easy-to-follow grid street numbering system, and a comprehensive network of tourist information, helplines, and Internet resources, Chicago is a user-friendly city. Thousands visit each year, whether to enjoy its beautiful lakefront, dynamic cultural life, celebrated architecture, Michigan Avenue shopping, or world-class dining. This section includes suggestions for Internet and mobile communications *(see p178)*, safety precautions and emergency medical resources *(see pp174–5)*, and advice for traveling to, around, and beyond the Windy City *(see pp180–87)*. You'll also find tips for responsible and green travel *(see p173 & p184)*.

Visitor information center located in the historic Water Tower *(see p65)*

Visas and Passports

A passport, valid for at least six months after the date of travel, is required for all travelers to the US. Foreign nationals of countries affiliated with the visa waiver program (including EU passport holders) must apply for entry clearance online via the Electronic System for Authorization (ESTA), at least 72 hours prior to travel (http://esta.cbp.dhs.gov). Canadians only need a passport; Mexican citizens require a border crossing card. All other travelers must obtain a visa from their nearest US Consular office. Visitors should always check with their nearest US embassy. Strict security checks (fingerprinting and facial recognition scans) are in place for arrivals to the US.

Customs Information

Customs allowances per person entering the US are: 200 cigarettes; 50 cigars or 4.4 lb (2 kg) of tobacco; no more than 2 pints (1 liter) of alcohol; and gifts that are worth no more than $100. Many foods, including meat, seeds, cheeses, and fresh fruit, are prohibited. Travelers must by law claim currency in excess of $10,000.

Tourist Information

The official Chicago tourism site, www.choosechicago.org, has lots of helpful information. Visit one of the two **Visitor Information Centers** for maps, tour brochures, tickets, public transportation passes, and general information.

Admission Prices and Opening Hours

Business hours in Chicago are usually 9am–5pm, Monday–Friday. For information on opening times of banks *see p176*. Most major museums are open daily from 9am–5pm, with later hours one night per week (check their websites for details). Major museums charge an admission fee, with extra charges for special exhibits. Smaller museums may have more limited hours, and charge a lower "suggested donation" for admission. The Museum Campus, located in the southern end of the downtown area, houses three of Chicago's most popular tourist destinations: The Field Museum *(see pp88–91)*, The Shedd Aquarium *(see pp98–9)*, and the Adler Planetarium *(see pp94–5)*. The **Go Chicago Card** and the **Chicago City Pass** offer discounted admission to a number of worthwhile tours and sights, including the above museums. The Go Chicago card includes 28 different tours and sites, and costs $79.99 (subject to change) for a 1-day pass to $152.99 for a 5-day pass (with reductions for children). The Chicago City Pass, which includes admission to five must-see sites, costs $94 ($79 for children) and is valid for nine days. Both cards can be bought at tourist centers and major sites.

Etiquette

Smoking is prohibited in public buildings (including stadiums and shopping centers), bars, restaurants, and taxis. Many bars provide outdoor spaces where smoking is allowed. On escalators downtown, stand to the right and walk on the left.

Shedd Aquarium on the Museum Campus *(see pp98–9)*

◄ A train crosses the two-tiered Lake Street Bridge above the Chicago River

Taxes and Tipping

Tipping is integral to Chicago's service industry, especially in restaurants (*see p147*). Tip $1 per coat checked; taxi drivers, hairdressers, and bartenders, from 10 to 15 per cent. Tip airport or hotel porters up to $1 per bag, and valet-parking attendants $1 after they bring you your car. Tip tour drivers between $2 and $3 per group member. If a concierge was especially helpful, acknowledge it by tipping between $5 and $10.

Travelers with Special Needs

All municipal facilities are fully accessible for disabled visitors, and most attractions and public buildings (including restaurants) are equipped for easy access. However, small entertainment venues may not be. An increasing number of CTA trains and stations, as well as CTA buses, are completely accessible. Many major stops on other train lines have facilities for the disabled; check www. transitchicago.com for details. Accessible taxis can be ordered by calling a dispatch number managed by **Yellow Cab**. Parking spaces reserved for vehicles with disabled permits are marked by the handicapped symbol either on a sign or painted on the concrete.

Traveling on a Budget

Accommodations in Chicago can be expensive. Be wary of hotels with very low rates, as many are SRO (single-room occupancy) transient housing. There is a good network of youth hostels; the **Chicago Getaway Hostel** is located in a good area in Lincoln Park and **Hosteling International** has a convenient South Loop spot. Many major sites (and even some restaurants), offer discounts for students and seniors over 65. For seniors, proof of age may be required. Students will need a valid student ID.

Chicago Time

Chicago is on Central Standard Time (CST). It is 1 hour behind Eastern Standard Time (EST) and 6 hours behind Greenwich Mean Time (GMT). Daylight saving time begins on the second Sunday in March, when clocks are set ahead 1 hour. It ends on the first Sunday in November, when clocks are set back 1 hour.

Responsible Tourism

Chicagoans are increasingly aware of environmental issues. The city's recycling program is improving and there are separate sorting bins available in many public parks and at popular attractions.

There are numerous markets across Chicago selling locally grown and organic produce. The **Green City Market**, at the south end of Lincoln Park is one of the best. It opens on Wednesday and Saturday mornings from early May through late October. During winter, it is held on Saturday mornings only at the Peggy Notebaert Nature Museum (*see p125*).

Green City Market selling locally grown and organic produce

DIRECTORY

Embassies and Consulates

Australia
123 N Wacker Dr., Suite 1300. Map 3 B1. **Tel** 312-419-1480. **W** dfat.gov. au/missions/countries/ usch.html

Britain
625 N Michigan Ave., Suite 2200. **Map** 2 D4. **Tel** 312-970-3800. **W** gov.uk/government/ world/organisations/ british-consulate- general-chicago

Canada
2 Prudential Plaza, 180 N Stetson Ave., Suite 2400. **Map** 4 D1. **Tel** 312-616-1860. **W** can-am.gc.ca/ chicago/menu.aspx

Ireland
400 N Michigan Ave., Suite 911. **Map** 2 D5. **Tel** 312-337-1868. **W** irishconsulate.org

New Zealand
8600 W Bryn Mawr Ave., Suite 500 N. **Tel** 773-714-8669. **W** nzembassy.com/usa

Tourist Information

Visitor Information Centers
Chicago Cultural Center 77 E Randolf St. **Map** 4 D1. **Tel** 312-346-3278.

Chicago Water Works 163 E Pearson St. **Map** 2 D4. **Tel** 312-744-2400. **W** choosechicago.org

Admission Prices

Chicago City Pass
Tel 888-330-5008. **W** citypass.com/ chicago

Go Chicago Card
Tel 866-628-9031. **W** smartdestinations. com/chicago

Travelers With Special Needs

Yellow Cab
Central Cab Dispatch for Accessible Taxi Cabs: **Tel** 800-281-4466.

Traveling on a Budget

Chicago Getaway Hostel
616 W Arlington Pl. **Tel** 773-929-5380. **W** getawayhostel.com

Hosteling International
J. Ira and Nikki Harris Family Hostel, 24 E Congress Pkwy. **Tel** 312-360-0300. **W** hihostels.com

Responsible Tourism

Green City Market
Tel 773-880-1266. **W** greencitymarket.org

Personal Security and Health

Chicago is a friendly city, and most visitors do not encounter any problems. However, it is always best to take common-sense precautions and be aware of your surroundings. If you don't feel safe, you probably aren't. Public transportation is generally safe during the day, but after dark you may feel more comfortable taking a taxi. The best source of information is often your hotel concierge. Don't hesitate to ask if you think your destination or day's itinerary might take you into unsavory neighborhoods. Bear in mind that parks and the paths along the lakefront are populated during the day but are often fairly deserted at night.

Chicago Fire Department on early-morning firefighting duty

Police

The Chicago Police Department has Segway, car, bicycle, motorcycle, and foot patrols across the city, day and night. There is always a strong police presence at major community and cultural events. Police officers carry handguns and other weapons, and should always be treated with respect and courtesy. They are usually very helpful if approached, but be mindful: they are not tour guides.

Parking-enforcement and traffic officers make their rounds either on foot or in small vehicles. Airports, stores, and even hotels employ their own uniformed and plain-clothes staff who provide security services.

To report a crime, call 911 or visit a local **Police Precinct** office. Should you require legal assistance, contact your nearest embassy or consulate (see p173).

What to be Aware of

Most tourists in Chicago enjoy their stay without incident. However, like all large urban centers, the city has its share of thieves and scam artists. To avoid being a target, always be alert and walk confidently. Conceal your valuables and money, use your hotel safe, and practice particular caution around ATMs. Do not keep all of your credit cards and money in one place.

"L" trains (see p186) are fertile ground for pickpockets and purse snatchers. An increasingly common crime is snatch-and-dash cell phone theft. Scammers often work in pairs, with one playing the role of a random stranger.

Homeless people tend to congregate around Union Station and tourist areas in order to panhandle. Most are benign and genuinely grateful for any donations, but some can be aggressive.

Much of Chicago's West Side and South Side are considered to be unsafe. Exceptions are Little Italy, Chinatown, Hyde Park, and Pullman. Some safe North Side neighborhoods are next to troubled areas. In any neighborhood, stick to well-lit, populated spaces after dark.

In an Emergency

Call 911 for emergencies requiring medical, police, or fire services. Hospital emergency rooms and city hospitals are in the Yellow Pages of the telephone directory. Most Chicago hospitals have 24-hour emergency rooms. Your hotel concierge will know the one closest to the hotel.

For non-emergency police situations, you should dial 311 to reach the **City Helpline**.

For dental emergencies, call the **Chicago Dental Society**, which provides referrals 24 hours a day, every day.

Lost and Stolen Property

You should report all lost or stolen items to the police. Keep a copy of the police report if you plan to make an insurance claim. The Chicago Police Department has branches at **O'Hare** and **Midway** airports; call if you have misplaced something at the airport other than at a restaurant or on a plane. For lost or stolen credit cards, contact the issuing company's office (see p177). If you happen to lose your passport, contact your embassy or consulate immediately (see p173).

Chicago police officers patrolling on bicycles

Fire engine

Ambulance

Police car

Hospitals and Pharmacies

There are many 24-hour walk-in clinics in Chicago that treat minor injuries and ailments, although waiting times can be lengthy. **Physicians Immediate Care** provides urgent medical help without an appointment for illnesses and injuries such as colds, cuts, and sprains. At select pharmacies, **CVS Minute Clinics** offer a clinic where licensed nurse practitioners diagnose and treat minor ailments on a first-come first-served basis. For more serious conditions, there are 24-hour hospital emergency rooms. **Northwestern Memorial Hospital** has an emergency room convenient to both downtown and North Side visitors, and also provides a physician referral service. The **Bernard A. Mitchell Hospital**, at the University of Chicago, serves Hyde Park.

Anyone taking a prescription drug should ask their doctor for an extra supply to take with them and a copy of the prescription in case more is needed. Like medical care, prescription drugs can be very costly, although pharmacies will often offer a generic substitute, at a much lower price. Both **CVS Pharmacy** and **Walgreen's** have pharmacies open 24 hours daily. Call them to find the location nearest to you.

Travel and Health Insurance

Medical insurance and/or travel insurance with provision for health care is highly recommended. If traveling from another country, make sure your medical insurance plan covers care in the United States, as medical care is very expensive. In the case of a medical emergency, the last thing you need is the added stress of sky-high doctor bills. There are many affordable travel insurance programs available on the Internet; **World Nomads** is a reputable and socially-conscious Australian-based service that offers online quotes and travel insurance for the citizens of 150 countries. The website **InsureMyTrip.com** allows users to compare rates and services from several major insurance companies.

In addition to medical and dental expenses, check that your travel insurance covers the cost of trip cancellation, lost or stolen baggage and travel documents, and accidental dismemberment or death. Make sure you travel with all relevant insurance cards (keep a copy in your hotel room and another with a reliable friend or family member back home), and, itemize any valuables you are traveling with.

DIRECTORY

Police

Police Precincts
13th District Office (Chicago Loop), 100 S Racine. **Tel** 312-746-8309. 18th District Office (Near North), 1160 N Larrabee. **Map** 1 A3. **Tel** 312-742-5879.

In an Emergency

All Emergencies
Tel 911 for police, fire, and medical services.

City Helpline
Tel 311 for non-emergency police situations and City services.

Chicago Dental Society
Tel 312-836-7300.

Lost and Stolen Property

Midway Airport Police
Tel 773-838-3003.

O'Hare Airport Police
Tel 773-686-2385.

Hospitals and Pharmacies

Bernard A. Mitchell Hospital
5815 S Maryland Ave. **Map** 7 B4. **Tel** 773-702-1000.

CVS Pharmacy
Tel 800-746-7287.
W cvs.com

CVS Minute Clinics
Central Loop: 137 S State St. **Map** 3 C2. **Tel** 312-609-1215.
Near North Side: 1165 N Clark St. **Map** 1 C3. **Tel** 312-282-2828.

Northwestern Memorial Hospital
251 Huron St. **Map** 2 D4. **Tel** 312-926-2000.
Physicians Referral Service:
Tel 312-926-8400; 877-926-4664.

Physicians Immediate Care
West Loop: 600 W Adams St. **Map** 3 C2. **Tel** 312-506-0900.
South Loop: 811 S State, Suite B. **Map** 3 C3. **Tel** 312-566-9510.

Walgreen's
Tel 800-25-4733.

Travel & Health Insurance

InsureMyTrip.com
W insuremytrip.com

World Nomads
W worldnomads.com

Banking and Local Currency

Most national and international banks have branches in Chicago, and foreign currency exchange is available at the main branches of most large banks. The cheapest and most convenient exchange, however, is usually offered on your credit or debit card, which can be used at most ATMs. It is a good idea to arrive in the city with about $100 cash in US currency, in denominations of $20 or lower and including a few dollars in coins, to cover incidental costs such as tips and taxis until you are able to withdraw or exchange some money.

Facade of the Federal Reserve Bank of Chicago

Banks and Bureaux de Change

Banks are generally open 9am–5pm Monday to Friday. Some, however, open as early as 8am and close as late as 6pm, and many are open from 9am to early afternoon on Saturday. The major consumer banks in Chicago include **Chase**, **Citibank**, **Bank of America**, and **Harris Bank**. Many charge fees for non-members to use a teller for routine matters such as withdrawing money; always ask if any fees apply before making a transaction.

Exchange rates are printed in the daily newspapers and posted where exchange services are offered. Don't be fooled by the ubiquitous and misleadingly named currency exchanges; they cash checks and wire money but do not actually exchange currency.

Foreign exchange brokers in Chicago are few. **Travelex** is the most common, and **American Express**'s Traveler Service Center will also exchange money. Two exchanges can be found at O'Hare Airport, in terminals 3 and 5 (open daily); there are no currency exchanges at Midway Airport.

ATMs

There is no need to carry large amounts of cash as plenty of ATMs can be found throughout the city. They are almost always located in bank lobbies or on an outside wall near the bank's entrance, as well as in most grocery stores and pharmacies. Some bars and fast-food outlets also have ATMs on their premises. Keep in mind that most convenience locations, like bars or corner stores, charge a high fee – up to $3 per transaction – in addition to any bank fees you incur.

US currency, usually in $20 bills, can be electronically withdrawn from your bank or credit card account through an ATM. Ask your bank which American ATM network your card can access in Chicago, and what transaction fees will apply. Cirrus and Plus are common networks in Chicago. Be aware of your surroundings and take care at ATMs by using them in secure conditions and daylight hours. When entering your PIN always shield the numbered keypad.

Credit Cards and Traveler's Checks

Credit cards allow you to carry minimal cash and may offer merchandise guarantees or other benefits. **American Express**, **Diners Club**, **MasterCard**, and **VISA** are all widely accepted throughout Chicago. Before you travel, inform your card provider that you will be abroad, or you may find that your card gets blocked when you start using it.

Most hotels ask for a credit-card number to guarantee a reservation, taking an imprint of the card when you check in. Car rental agencies insist on a credit-card guarantee even if you pay for the rental in cash.

Credit cards are helpful in emergencies, and many hospitals will accept a major credit card as a method of payment.

Traveler's checks issued by American Express and Travelex in US dollars are accepted without a fee by most shops, hotels, and restaurants if accompanied by suitable photographic identification, such as a passport. US-dollar traveler's checks can be cashed at most banks; inquire about commission fees first. Checks in foreign currency can be cashed at a bank branch offering foreign-currency exchange, usually in the bank's main locations. American Express and Travelex will cash their own checks at no fee.

For lost and stolen credit cards *see directory*.

An automated teller machine (ATM) accepting most credit cards

Coins

American coins (actual size shown) come in 1-, 5-, 10-, and 25-cent, as well as $1, denominations; 50-cent pieces are minted but rarely used. Each value of coin has a popular name: 1-cent coins are known as pennies, 5-cent coins as nickels, 10-cent coins as dimes, 25-cent coins as quarters, and 1-dollar coins (and bills) as bucks.

1-cent coin
(a penny)

5-cent coin
(a nickel)

10-cent coin
(a dime)

25-cent coin
(a quarter)

1-dollar coin (a
buck)

Bank Notes (Bills)

Units of currency in the US are dollars and cents, with 100 cents to a dollar. Notes, or "bills," come in $1, $2, $5, $10, $20, $50, and $100 denominations. The $2 bills are rarely seen. Each bank note features a different US President. Security features include subtle color hues and improved color-shifting ink in the lower right hand corner of the face of each note.

1-dollar bill ($1)

5-dollar bill ($5)

10-dollar bill ($10)

20-dollar bill ($20)

50-dollar bill ($50)

100-dollar bill ($100)

Communications and Media

Chicago's communication systems are, for the most part, efficient and reasonably priced. The regular letter service run by the US postal system is reliable, and express services are offered by post offices and independent courier companies. Computer access is available for free or for a nominal fee at libraries, hotels, and Internet cafés. The wide use of cell phones has virtually made pay phones obsolete; mobile phone stores are present across the city. Chicagoans are served by two major newspapers, and several smaller, independent papers.

International and Local Telephone Calls

Chicago phone numbers have eleven digits, beginning with a number one, and including the mandatory three-digit prefix, or area code. Some emergency and public-service numbers, however have only three digits (911, 311, 411). Chicago and its environs use six prefixes: 312 (Downtown Core), 773 (surrounding downtown), 847 and 224 (north and northwestern suburbs), 708 (near western and southern suburbs) and 630 (far western suburbs).

Long distance calls within the US require dialing 1, the prefix or area code, and the number. For calls outside of the US, dial 011, the country code, and then the number. For directory assistance in the US, call 411. Within the US, all numbers with an 800, 866, 877, or 888 prefix are toll-free. Pre-paid international calling cards, which can be purchased at many pharmacies and convenience stores, often offer considerable savings over mobile roaming charges and are available in denominations from $5 to $100. Some cards can be reloaded; check the stipulations for each individual card. Cards can be used with cell phones, land lines or the increasingly rare public pay phone. To use them, dial the phone number associated with the card, enter the pin number, and listen for the dial tone.

T-Mobile pre-paid SIM card

Cell Phones

There are four main GSM frequencies in use around the world, so if you want to guarantee that your phone will work make sure you have a quad-band phone. Notify your phone service provider that you will be traveling as they may have to enable roaming for your phone. Be aware that international roaming charges can be quite steep; you can avoid this by purchasing a local SIM card. **T-Mobile** offers prepaid SIM cards and has store locations throughout the city. Another option is the H2O prepaid SIM card, available at **Best Buy** electronic stores. Packages can run from $10 to $100 or more, depending on individual plans and the types of services needed. Before you can use a temporary SIM card, you will have to make sure your phone is unlocked. Some carriers allow you to unlock your phone electronic-ally; with others, the procedure may be mechanical. Call your servicer to find out more information. Some travelers opt to rent a temporary cell phone for use while traveling. Two reputable Internet-based companies offering phone rentals are **Phone Rental USA** and **Cellhire**.

Internet Access

If you are traveling with a laptop, or a smartphone, most Chicago hotels charge a nominal fee for Wi-Fi service in your hotel room. Many hotels will also have a small business center with computer access, printing, and copying services. The **Harold Washington Library** has a large bank of computers with Internet access available for free on a first-come, first-served basis. Computer stations with Internet service are also available for use at

Wi-Fi access can easily be found in cafés around the city

Useful Dialing Codes

- International direct-dial call: dial 011, followed by country code (UK: 44; Australia: 61; New Zealand: 64; Ireland: 353), then the city or area code, then the local telephone number.
- An 800, 866, 877, or 888 prefix indicates that the call is toll-free. Dial 1 before the prefix.

- Directory assistance for toll-free numbers: dial 1-800-555-1212.
- Directory assistance for outside local area: dial 1-AREACODE-555-1212.
- Local operator assistance: dial 0.
- General directory inquiries: dial 411. There may be a charge.
- Emergencies: dial 911.

Mailbox outside Wrigley Field stadium, home to the Chicago Cubs

FedEx Office stores, which have many locations in the downtown area. The Water Tower Visitor Center (see p172) has one computer with Internet access for use in its small library too. Free Wi-Fi is also available at many cafés throughout the city. Look for a Wi-Fi sign in the window.

Postal Services

Letters and postcards can be mailed from US Post Office branches or free-standing mailboxes located in the lobbies of many public buildings or on occasional street corners. Mailboxes can be recognized by their dark blue color and display of the US Postal Service insignia. Letters can also be mailed at your hotel's concierge desk, which usually sells postage stamps too. Stamps can be purchased at post offices, either at the service window, or through self-service machines,

and at the checkout counter of most Jewel and Dominick's grocery stores.

Packages can be shipped via US Postal Service, or a private courier company such as **UPS**, **FedEx**, or **DHL**. UPS and FedEx Office offer retail stores that handle packaging as well as shipping. All services offer a variety of shipping rates, from next day air mail to ground mail (which averages five to seven days for travel between major cities, longer for more remote areas).

Newspapers and Magazines

Chicago has two major dailies: *Chicago Tribune* and *Chicago Sun-Times*. The *Chicago Defender* is published weekdays, primarily for the city's African-American readership. Business news is found in the weekly *Crain's*. *Streetwise* is a monthly newspaper that

helps support Chicago's homeless population. The *Chicago Reader* is a long-standing independent weekly magazine featuring local news, arts, culture, dining, and nightlife. Most Chicago print media has a comprehensive web presence. For details on entertainment listings, see p164.

TV and Radio

Six major TV networks are broadcast in Chicago: CBS on channel 2, NBC on channel 5, ABC on channel 7, WGN on channel 9, PBS (public television) on channel 11, and FOX on channel 32. AM radio stations include WBBM news (780Hz) and WGN talk/sports (720Hz). FM radio stations include WBEZ Chicago Public Radio, which offers news, current events, and variety programming, and broadcasts BBC World News (91.5M).

Variety of newspaper stands on a Chicago street

DIRECTORY

Cell Phones

Best Buy
875 N Michigan Ave.
Map 2 D3.
Tel 312-397-2146.

Cellhire
National toll-free:
Tel 877-244-7242.
Chicago number:
Tel 877-537-7368.
W **cellhire.com**

Phone Rental USA
Tel 800-335-3705.
W **phonerentalusa.com**

T-Mobile
845 N Michigan Ave. **Map** 2 D3. **Tel** 312-944-9221.
One of many locations.

Internet Access

Harold Washington Library
400 S. State St. **Map** 3 C2.
Tel 312-747-4300.
W **chipublib.org**

FedEx Offices
Loop: 34 S Michigan Ave.
Map 4 D2.
Tel 312-368-1634.

Mag Mile: 540 N Michigan Ave. **Map** 2 D5.
Tel 312-832-0090.
River North: 222 Merchandise Mart Plaza.
Map 1 B5.
Tel 312-755-1088.

Postal Services

Chicago Main Post Office
433 W Harrison St.
Map 3 B3. **Tel** 312-983-7610 or 800-275-8777.

Express and Priority Mail:
Tel 800-222-1811.
Loop Branch:
211 S Clark St.
Tel 312-427-0016.

DHL
Tel 800-225-5345.
W **dhl.com**

FedEx
Tel 800-463-3339.
W **fedex.com**

UPS
Tel 800-742-5877.
W **ups.com**

TRAVEL INFORMATION

Chicago is one of the United States's most important transportation hubs. All major airlines fly into one of its two airports: O'Hare or Midway. O'Hare, the main airport, handles most international flights, and Midway serves many budget carriers. Amtrak trains from across the US and from Canada arrive at Union Station daily.

Two national bus lines, Greyhound and Megabus, provide great value for budget travelers, and several interstate highways run through Chicago, making it easily accessible by car. Within the city, readily available taxis and a comprehensive public transportation system will efficiently get you to your destination.

Terminal 1 of Chicago's O'Hare
International Airport

Arriving by Air

Chicago's largest and busiest airport is **O'Hare International Airport**, located 17 miles (27 km) northwest of the city. **Midway Airport** is much smaller and located about 10 miles (16 km) southwest of downtown. O'Hare manages most international flights and serves all of the major airlines. Midway serves many budget carriers and offers frequent flights to destinations in Mexico and the Caribbean.

Passengers arriving from international destinations will have to clear passport control first. Proceed to baggage claim before passing through US Customs. If arriving via a connecting flight, you must clear customs and immigration at your first port of entry into the United States.

When arriving from destinations within the US, you should follow the signs straight to baggage claim. Directions for taxis, rental cars, airport shuttles, or public transit, are

well posted throughout baggage claim areas.

O'Hare Airport (ORD)

O'Hare International Airport is one of the world's busiest airports, servicing up to 70 million passengers each year. Despite its size, O'Hare is clean, modern, and easy to navigate. Three terminals are used for domestic flights, and one for international flights.

Chicago is the home base for **United Airlines**, and O'Hare is United's main hub. Terminal 1 at O'Hare is dominated by United Airlines, and United's code-share partner, **Lufthansa**. **Continental**, **Air Canada**, and **US Airways** arrive at Terminal 2; **American Airlines** and **Delta** arrive at Terminal 3. There is no Terminal 4.

Most international departures, including **British Airways** and **British Midland**, and all international arrivals, fly to and from Terminal 5.

An Airport Transit System (ATS) shuttles passengers quickly and efficiently between the three domestic terminals, the international terminal, and the parking areas. Facilities throughout the airport include food concessions and ATMs. There are also many upscale stores and kiosks within each terminal. If departing from Terminal 5 (international flights), be aware that the food court is located outside of passport control; once you go through passport

control and security, your choices are very limited. Wi-Fi service is available at designated "hot spots" in all passenger areas. For those traveling with young children, branches of the Chicago Children's Museum (see p67) are located in Terminal 2 and Terminal 5.

Clear, well-posted signs direct passengers to departure gates, ticket counters, baggage claim, restrooms, and ground transport.

Midway Airport (MDW)

Midway airport is located 10 miles (16 km) from downtown Chicago. Considerably smaller than O'Hare, Midway airport primarily serves commuter and budget carriers, and is the main Chicago transport hub for **Southwest Airlines**. Midway is one of the fastest growing airports in the country. Improvements include expanded parking, a shopping concourse with a food court, and the addition of 14 runways (bringing the total number to 43). Midway offers business travelers a number of seated workstations with AC

Southwest Airlines descends on to the runway of
Chicago's Midway Airport

outlets throughout the terminal. Wi-Fi is available in all passenger areas. The CTA Orange Line "L" train is easily accessible from the airport. Taxis are available from exit 5, shuttle buses leave from in front of the main terminal building, and car rental agencies are located inside.

Tickets and Fares

Travel websites such as www.expedia.com, www.orbitz.com, and www.travelocity.com make it easy to compare costs for the best price. Most airline websites offer lowest-price guarantees. Auction sites www.priceline.com and www.skyauction.com allow users to bid on unsold seats, which can save money if you are willing to take the risk of making travel plans at the last minute; however, there may not be any unsold seats offered to your destination. Traveling on Tuesdays, Wednesdays, or Saturdays is generally cheaper than other days of the week. Fridays and Sundays are the most expensive days to travel.

Listed ticket prices in the US do not include additional taxes and fuel surcharges.

Direct tickets may include a stop, but do not require passengers to change planes. Non-stop flights fly directly to the final destination with no stops along the way.

Airport Transit System at O'Hare International airport

Transport from Airport to Town

A convenient, inexpensive way to get into the city from either airport is via **CTA** train (see p186). Blue Line trains run to and from O'Hare Airport, 24 hours daily. The ride to downtown takes about 45 minutes. Orange Line trains run between Midway Airport and downtown 4am–midnight. Allow 35 minutes for the journey. A one-way train fare is $2.25 – you'll need to purchase a CTA fare card at the terminal station. During rush hours, trains can be very crowded, making traveling with luggage difficult. The Blue Line to O'Hare sometimes has delays on Sundays due to maintenance works.

Go Airport Express operates a shuttle service between both airports and downtown hotels. Shuttles operate daily; 6am–11:30pm from O'Hare airport and 6am–10:30pm from

Midway. Prices vary depending on one way or return travel and the number of people. A single, one-way ticket from O'Hare costs from $30, and a return from $51. For groups of three or more, tickets range from $16 for one way and from $29 for a round trip. From Midway, single fares are $25 one way, or $44 return. For a group of three or more, tickets range from $14 one way, and from $24 for a return.

Car rental is available at both airports. For details of rental agencies see p187. It usually takes about 45 minutes to drive from O'Hare to downtown Chicago, and 30 minutes from Midway, but allow up to twice this time during rush hours. Taxis are located outside of the baggage claim areas. Do not accept a ride from a taxi driver outside of the queue system. During off peak hours, a taxi will cost about $30 from O'Hare to downtown and about $35 from Midway to downtown.

DIRECTORY

Arriving by Air

Midway Airport
Tel 773-838-9111.
Ⓦ flychicago.com

O'Hare International Airport
Tel 773-686-2200 or 800-832-6352.
Ⓦ flychicago.com

O'Hare Airport

Air Canada
Tel 888-247-2262.
Ⓦ aircanada.com

American Airlines
Tel 800-443-7300.
Ⓦ aa.com

British Airways
Tel 800-247-9297.
Ⓦ britishairways.com

British Midland
Tel 800-788-0555.
Ⓦ flybmi.com

Continental Airlines
Tel 800-525-0280.
Ⓦ continental.com

Delta
Tel 888-750-3284.
Ⓦ delta.com

Lufthansa
Tel 800-645-3880.
Ⓦ lufthansa.com

United Airlines
Tel 800-241-6522.
Ⓦ united.com

US Airways
Tel 800-428-4322.
Ⓦ usairways.com

Midway Airport

Southwest Airlines
Tel 800-435-9792.
Ⓦ southwest.com

Transport from Airport to Town

Chicago Transit Authority (CTA)
Tel 800-968-7282.
Ⓦ transitchicago.com

Go Airport Express
Tel 888-284-3286.
Ⓦ airportexpress.com

Amtrak train en route to Chicago

Arriving by Train

Chicago is the national rail hub of **Amtrak**, the US's passenger rail line. Fifty trains linking to hundreds of US destinations, as well as those from Canada, arrive at or depart from Chicago's **Union Station** daily. Amtrak also services 34 destinations in Illinois, either through trains or connecting buses.

Amtrak's commuter trains have refreshment cars, and long-distance routes have dining cars and sleeping cars. Reservations are necessary on many routes and advised for travel during peak periods: the summer months and major holidays. Seats can be reserved online, via telephone or in-person. Fares vary considerably based on advance purchase, with the cheapest fares offered for tickets bought at least 90 days ahead of travel. An average-priced one-way ticket from New York to Chicago will cost about $120; from Detroit, $75; from Washington DC, $115. Fares for the 43-hour trip from Los Angeles to Chicago will average about $190.

Amtrak offers discounts to seniors and students. When you book, check the website or ask a ticket sales agent about special promotions.

Although Union Station is just west of the Loop and close to downtown Chicago, it is not an easy walk to hotels or CTA trains when you are carrying luggage. If arriving in Chicago by train, it is probably best to plan on taking a taxi to your hotel. You will find that taxis are plentiful around the station.

Arriving by Long-Distance Bus

The main terminal in Chicago for **Greyhound Bus Line** is in a rather desolate area a few blocks from Union Station. It is not within easy walking distance to hotels in the Loop, so plan on taking a taxi to your final destination.

Although walk-up ticket sales are readily available, Greyhound offers substantial discounts for purchasing tickets online and in advance. For example, a standard fare of $58 one way from Minneapolis will only cost $23 when booked online, even just a day or two in advance. Traveling "the dog" from New York to Chicago will cost between $95 and $125; the journey from Los Angeles to Chicago takes three days and costs between $178 and $225. Most Greyhound trains are equipped with decent legroom, free Wi-Fi, and AC outlets available for passenger use; restrooms are provided on all buses. Greyhound offers

Greyhound
logo

assistance to travelers with disabilities with 48 hours' notice, including priority seating. In some cases, a personal care assistant may travel for free. Call the **Greyhound ADA Assist Line** for details. **Megabus** drops Chicago arrivals at Union Station and offers cheap, no-frills regional direct transport between cities. A one-way Megabus trip from Minneapolis will cost $39 (several arrival times daily), $35 from Memphis or St. Louis.

All buses have restrooms, power outlets, and free Wi-Fi.

Arriving by Car

If you arrive in Chicago from the southwest, on I-55 (Stevenson Expressway), follow the freeway to its end, to Lake Shore Drive, then follow Lake Shore Drive north. Shortly you will pass the city center, and have one of the best views of Chicago's skyline. Several exits lead off Lake Shore Drive into downtown or the North Side, including the Wacker Drive exit. Taking Lake Shore Drive is a good way to traverse the city. The historic Route 66, running from Los Angeles, joins I-55 on the outskirts of Chicago.

I-90 East (Northwest Tollway to Kennedy Expressway) running from the northwest, from O'Hare Airport, will bring you into the city. Take the Ohio Street exit for downtown.

Arriving by car from the west, US Route 20 leads into I-290 East (Eisenhower Expressway),

View from scenic US Route 20, running northwest through Illinois

which becomes Congress Parkway at the southwest edge of Chicago's downtown Loop. From the parkway, drive north for destinations downtown or beyond.

From the south, I-57 leads into the Dan Ryan Expressway and to I-90 and I-94, which converge in the city.

The **Illinois Department of Transportation** has a website which details driving directions as well as information about weather and road conditions. If you suffer a breakdown, call the **American Automobile Association** for help.

| Speed limit (in mph) | Rest area, indicated off an interstate |

Interstates

The several highways running through and around Chicago are of two types: freeways and tollways. Freeways are toll-free public highways. The charge for driving on a state tollway ranges from 15 cents to $2, with 80 cents being the most common toll around the Chicagoland area. Most regular commuters have an I-Go Pass, a micro-chipped permit that allows non-stop passage through toll areas. Everyone else must pay cash at the manned tollbooths; exact

change is not necessary but tollbooth operators cannot change large bills. Credit cards are not accepted.

Interstates are divided multi-lane highways and are the main routes between cities. Most swell to six or more lanes as they near large cities. Interstate numbers are posted on red, white, and blue shield-shaped signs. Main interstate routes have two-digit numbers, with those with even numbers generally running east-west and those with odd numbers generally running north-south. There are exceptions, however. While I-94 runs east-west across the US, it runs north-south in Illinois.

Speed Limits and Fines

The speed limit for vehicles on Illinois' open highways is 65 mph (105 km/h) and 55 mph (88 km/h) on metro highways. The standard speeding fine is $120, with increases for higher speeds

or protected areas. A minimum speed regulation in Illinois means you could also be ticketed for driving too slowly. Roadside tests and fines for drink driving are common.

Getting to McCormick Place

Located one mile (1.5 km) south of downtown Chicago, **McCormick Place Convention Center** is the largest exhibition and meeting facility in North America. Even though it is close to the Loop, the walk is not a practical one. A taxi ride from the Loop to McCormick Place will cost about $7. Large conventions often provide shuttle bus services from major downtown hotels, and sometimes from the airports. The **Metra** Electric line (*see p187*) services the 23rd Street/McCormick Place station. Trains depart from the Randolph Street and Van Buren Street stations.

Trade show in Hall B, North Building, McCormick Place

DIRECTORY

Arriving by Train

Amtrak at Union Station
Tel 800-872-7245.
w amtrak.com

Union Station
225 S Canal St.
Map 3 B2.
Tel 312-655-2066.
w chicagounion station.com

Arriving by Long-Distance Bus

Greyhound Bus Line
630 W Harrison St.
Map 3 A3.
Tel 800-231-2222.
w greyhound.com

Greyhound ADA Assist Line
Tel 800-752-4841.

Megabus
Tel 877-462-6342.
w megabus.com

Arriving by Car

American Automobile Association (Triple A)
Roadside Assistance:
Tel 866-968-7222.
w chicago.aaa.com

Illinois Department of Transportation
Tel 217-782-7820.
w dot.state.il.us

Getting to McCormick Place

McCormick Place Convention Center
2301 S Lake Shore Dr.
Map 6 E1.
Tel 312-791-7000.
w mccormickplace. com

Metra Passenger Information
Tel 312-322-6777.
w metrarail.com

Getting Around Chicago

Although Chicago is a sprawling Midwestern metropolis, many of the city's sights and main cultural centers are centrally located downtown, making it a walker's dream. The city's public transportation is inexpensive and efficient. The train system, known as the "L" for "elevated", is the easiest way to get around, although public bus lines cover more territory. Taxis are affordable, convenient, and readily available (and recommended for traveling late at night). Both public transit and street traffic are extremely busy during the rush hours, which are weekdays from 7–9am and 3–7pm. If possible, you may want to avoid traveling at these peak times.

Cyclist taking advantage of a quiet spell on Chicago's lakefront path

Green Travel

Despite the fact that traffic congestion during rush hours continues to choke the city in fumes, more Chicagoans are becoming conscious of their ecological footprint, and demand for environmentally-friendly alternatives has spurred real change. Public transportation is being redesigned to burn cleaner fuel, and Chicago currently has more than 200 hybrid buses in circulation. The city has added miles and miles of bicycle lanes on many major thoroughfares, including a few dedicated lanes, which are restricted from vehicle traffic. Every CTA bus comes equipped with a bike rack, and, with the exception of rush hours, bicycles are allowed on all "L" trains (up to two per car).

Street Layout and Numbering

Chicago streets are laid out on a grid system. Most streets run north and south or east and west, though some run on the diagonal. The zero point in the city is at Madison and State Streets, in the Loop. Street numbers ascend by 50 or 100 numbers in each block as they radiate out from Madison and State. Most streets in the Loop are one-way streets.

Walking

Shopping areas are only a short walk from each other and streets are relatively flat, so you will not have to tackle hills during your outings.

Traffic lights signal drivers (and pedestrians) to stop (red), go (green), or proceed with caution (yellow). As Chicago drivers tend to be especially aggressive, never rely solely on the traffic lights; look both ways before crossing the street, and watch for cars making right turns or racing through yellow lights. During rush hour, traffic is often controlled by traffic police.

Bicycling

Cycling is a popular form of transport in Chicago. There are more public bicycle racks in Chicago than other city in the US, and most major throughways have designated bike lanes. However, cyclists on the streets must still use extreme caution, obey traffic laws, and wear a safety helmet.

The lakefront offers miles of scenic paths, although it can be busy. Informal rules of the road exist, but it is often difficult for walkers, cyclists, and in-line skaters to co-exist. Saying "on your left" as you overtake another cyclist is common courtesy. The best time to enjoy the path is during business hours when traffic is quieter. **Bike & Roll**, among others, rents out both bicycles and in-line skates.

Guided Tours

Excellent walking, coach, and boat tours are offered by the **Chicago Architecture Foundation (CAF)**. Tour rates run from $10 for a 1-hour walking tour to $75 for a 7-hour coach tour. A fabulous way to get away from the tourist center and discover a few of Chicago's 77 neighborhoods is to take one of the Saturday tours with **Chicago Neighborhood Tours** ($30). **Chicago Trolley Company** sells an all-day hop-on hop-off pass for self-guided tours ($35). **Chicago Detours** offers guided tours with iPads that include interior architecture and a historic pub crawl ($28–32).

Boat tour season is from April to October. Several companies offer Lake Michigan and Chicago River excursions. Lake Michigan cruises depart regularly from Navy Pier, and river tours depart from the Michigan Avenue Bridge. Prices vary, but average about

A Chicago Architecture Foundation (CAF) tour of the city's great buildings

$25–35 per person. Many companies offer discounts when two or more tours per person are purchased; be sure to ask.

Taxis

Taxis come in many colors and models, but all are distinguishable by the taxi light on top of the cab. You will usually be able to flag a vacant taxi on a busy street, or find one waiting outside a hotel. If the taxi's roof light is lit, it is available. In more remote areas of the city, you may have to phone for a taxi.

Taxis charge a base fare of $2.25, plus $1 for a second passenger, and 50 cents for each additional passenger (up to four). When gas prices are high, there is a $1 fuel surcharge. Additionally, a $2 surcharge is added to all airport trips. From that point, rates are 20 cents for each ninth of a mile.

Most Chicago taxi drivers are good drivers. But, as in any city, there are exceptions. For a serious complaint, note the name of the taxi company and the car number (on the side of the taxi) and call **Consumer Services**.

Water Taxis

During summer months, water taxis, operated by **Wendella** and **Shoreline**, run commuter and sightseeing services around the downtown area. Wendella operates one route with stops at Michigan Avenue, LaSalle/Clark, Madison Street, and Chinatown. A single ride costs $2; a single ride including Chinatown costs

$4. All-day passes are priced at $6 and a 10-ride pass costs $16. Operating hours vary but all taxis run 9:30am–5:30pm. Tickets can be bought on board any water taxi, at a Wendella kiosk (located at Madison Street and Michigan Avenue docks), or at the main ticket office at 400 North Michigan Avenue.

Shoreline offers a service every 15–20 minutes 10am–6pm from Navy Pier to the Museum Campus and near Willis Tower (commuter taxis run 7–9:20am and 4–6:30pm). A one-day pass costs $22 for adults, $11 for children, and a two-day pass costs $28 for adults and $14 for children. Other fares range from $4–7 for adults and $2–4 for children. Tickets can be purchased at kiosks located at each taxi stop.

Driving

Vehicles are driven on the right-hand side of the road in the US, except on one-way streets. The Illinois speed limit is 30 mph (48 km/h) on city and residential

Typical pedestrian and vehicular traffic on busy State Street

roads and 55 mph (88 km/h) on metro highways. You must wear a seatbelt, and it is illegal to talk on your cell phone while driving. A right turn on a red light is permitted unless a sign prohibits it. Left turns are not allowed at some intersections during peak times, or are allowed only when the green arrow signal is illuminated.

Driving in Chicago's busiest neighborhoods (downtown, Lincoln Park, Wicker Park) can be a harrowing experience, especially during rush hours and weekends.

Parking

Street parking in Chicago falls into three categories: free, metered, and restricted. Downtown, free street parking is scarce. Metered parking is the most readily available option. Meter boxes accept cash, coins and credit cards; place the printed receipt on your dashboard. Rates vary by location, from $1.50 per hour to $5 per hour, with downtown being the most expensive. Check the fare box for specific details. Free-standing coin meters are sometimes left for locking bikes and no longer function.

Residential streets often require a parking permit, and violators are subject to a $60 ticket. Parking in front of a fire hydrant tallies a $150 fine. In winter months, be careful not to park in snow emergency routes as your car may be towed.

Parking garages and lots in downtown Chicago are plentiful but quite expensive; $40–50 per day is not unusual. Outside of the central downtown area, lots and garages are cheaper but harder to come by. Most are located around popular attractions like sports arenas and shopping districts. If your car is towed off a downtown city street, call **City Services** to locate it. If it is towed from a privately managed lot, a sign nearby will tell you how to reclaim your vehicle. Expect to pay at least $150 to retrieve your car. If it is a rental car, be prepared to show your contract.

Chicago's historic Union Station, served by numerous bus lines

Traveling by Public Trains

The **Chicago Transit Authority (CTA)** operates the "L" train system as well as the public bus system. There are eight train lines: Blue, Brown, Red, Green, Yellow, Orange, Pink, and Purple *(see inside back cover)*. You need a fare card to pass through the turnstile to the train platform; fare card machines are located in every CTA station. Most vending machines only accept cash but in select larger stations, such as Washington and Wells, Jackson, and O'Hare stations, there are machines offering a wider array of transit passes that accept credit cards. The train fare is $2.25, plus 25 cents for up to two transfers. Downtown, you can transfer for free between the Blue Line and Red Line through the station underpass. Transfers are free between all lines that share a track, and additionally at State & Lake (although here passengers must exit the station to transfer between the subway and the elevated tracks; money will not be deducted from your fare card). Train directions are indicated by the last stop on the line in the direction of travel. Use caution when riding the "L" train system late at night.

Traveling by Public Buses

Operated by the CTA, buses run in a straight trajectory along nearly every major thoroughfare. They stop about every two blocks at posted CTA signs that indicate the number and name of the route, but not the direction. Some buses do not travel the entire route; check the destination sign on the front of the bus. To board a bus, hail the driver and remain on the curb until the bus has come to a stop. An adult bus fare is $2.25 if paying with cash, $2 with a fare card; children aged 11 and under pay $1. Buses accept only exact currency (in bills and/or coins), or CTA fare cards (available at CTA train stations, as well as many Walgreens pharmacies, currency exchanges, and Jewel grocery stores). Be aware that drivers do not give change. No transfer is allowed with a cash fare on buses; with a fare card,

CTA transit cards offering cheaper fares than cash

transferring between trains and buses costs 25 cents for up to two additional rides. Transfers must be made within 2 hours of the first journey. Most buses run every 10–20 minutes from dawn to late evening daily. Night buses (indicated with an owl on the bus stop sign) run every 30 minutes 1am–4am daily.

All CTA buses are fully wheelchair accessible, and bus entrances use a hydraulic tilt to accommodate the elderly, infirm, and those with pushchairs. Bike racks are located on the front of all CTA buses, most standard, two-wheeled bikes will fit.

DIRECTORY

Bicycling

Bike and Roll
Tel 866-736-8224.
Millennium Park,
239 E Randolph St.
Map 3 A3.
W bikeandroll.com/
chicago/
chicagobiketours.html

Guided Tours

Chicago Architecture Foundation
224 S Michigan Ave.
Tel 312-922-3432.
Map 4 D2.
W architecture.org

Chicago Detours
Tel 312-350-1131.
W chicagodetours.com

Chicago Neigh-borhood Tours
Tel 312-742-1190.
W chicagoneighbor
hoodtours.com

Chicago Trolley Company
Tel 773-648-5000.
W chicagotrolley.com

Taxis

American-United Cab
Tel 773-248-7600.

Checker Taxi
Tel 312-243-2537.

City of Chicago Department of Consumer Services
Tel 312-744-4006.

Flash Cab
Tel 773-561-1444.

Yellow Cab
Tel 312-829-4222.

Water Taxis

Shoreline
Tel 312-222-9328.
W shorelinewatertaxi.
com

Wendella
Tel 312-337-1446.
W chicagowatertaxi.
com

Parking

City Services
Tel 312-744-7275 to pay tickets by credit card.

Travelling by Public Trains and Buses

Chicago Transit Authority (CTA)
Tel 888-968-7282.
W transitchicago.com

Traveling Outside Chicago

Traveling outside Chicago is most convenient by car, although Pace buses and Metra trains, both operated by the RTA (Regional Transit Authority), comprise an inexpensive and extensive public transportation system to the many suburbs and beyond. Rush hours are the only real obstacle to smooth traveling. At peak times during the day, city dwellers are going to work at industry headquarters located in the suburbs; at the same time, suburbanites are heading into the city to office jobs. Rush hour can start as early as 5:30am and last until 9am. The afternoon rush begins at 3pm and often lasts until past 7pm.

Metra commuter train

Metra

Metra operates a network of 11 commuter train lines that begin in the city center and stretch out like tentacles to the suburbs. The 495-mile (795-km) system has 230 stations in the Illinois counties of Cook, Du Page, Lake, Will, McHenry, and Kane. It also services some cities in Indiana and Wisconsin. Trains run frequently during rush hour and every 1–3 hours at other times.

Metra fares vary based on distance traveled, ranging from $2.25 to $8.50 for a one-way ticket. Buy tickets at a Metra station, or from a conductor on the train. On weekends and holidays, youngsters aged 12 to 17 ride for half fare. Kids under 12 may ride free when accompanied by a fare-paying adult. Weekend passes are also available for unlimited travel on all Metra lines.

Metra trains depart from five stations surrounding the Loop: Union Station, Ogilvie Transportation Center, Randolph Street Station, Van Buren Street Station, and LaSalle Street Station. Union Station is the main Metra station. The Electric Line, which runs to McCormick Place, stops at three stations along Michigan Avenue: at Randolph and Van Buren Streets, and at Roosevelt Road. The Union Pacific North Line runs to Highland Park, stopping just outside the Ravinia Festival gate.

Pace

The suburban bus system, **Pace**, is a division of the **Regional Transportation Authority (RTA)**, which also oversees Metra and the CTA. Pace provides fixed bus routes, Dial-a-Ride services for travelers with disabilities, vanpools, and special-event buses throughout Chicago's six-county suburban region. Pace buses also provide good connections between Metra stations and shopping malls.

Fares start from $1.75 for a standard point-to-point journey (25 cents to transfer) to $4 special fares to premium places such as Wrigley Field, and Six Flags Great America. Children under 7, seniors, and disabled passengers with suitable identification ride free.

Pace bus operating in the suburbs of the city

Rental Cars

To rent a car, you must be at least 25 years old, with a valid driver's license (for foreign visitors, an international driver's license) and a major credit card in your name. Note that a deposit will be required. Before leaving home, check your insurance policy to see if you are covered in a rental car.

All major rental car companies including **Alamo**, **Avis** **Budget**, and **Hertz** are represented at O'Hare and Midway airports (see pp180–81), and most have car rental sites available throughout the city. All US rental cars are automatic and have power steering.

STREET FINDER

Map references given in this guide for sights, hotels, restaurants, shops, and entertainment venues refer to the Street Finder maps on the following pages only (*see How the Map References Work below*). A complete index of the street names and places of interest marked on the maps can also be found on the pages that follow.

The map opposite shows the area of Chicago the eight *Street Finder* maps cover. This includes the sightseeing areas (which are color-coded) as well as the whole of central Chicago. The symbols used to represent sights and useful information on the *Street Finder* maps are listed below in the key.

How the Map References Work

The first figure tells you which *Street Finder* map to turn to.

❶ Willis Tower

233 S Wacker Dr. **Map** 3 B2 **Tel** 875-9696. Ⓜ Quincy. **Open** Mar–Sep: 9am–11pm daily; Oct–Feb: 9am–10pm daily; last adm 30 min before closing. ⏏ ⏏ ⏏

The letter and number give the grid reference. Letters go across the map's top and bottom; figures on its sides.

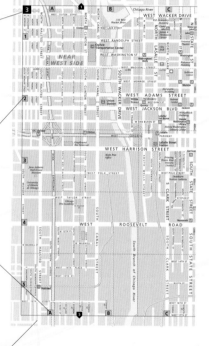

Key to Street Finder

- ▦ Major sight
- ▦ Minor sight
- ▢ Other building
- Ⓜ CTA train station
- Ⓡ Metra train station
- ⓘ Tourist information
- ✚ Hospital with emergency room
- ▥ Police station
- ✝ Church
- ✡ Synagogue
- ⚑ Buddhist temple
- ═ Railroad
- ▤ Highway

The map continues on map 5 of the *Street Finder*.

0 kilometers		2
0 mile	1	

Scale of Maps 1–6

0 meters	500
0 yards	500

Scale of Maps 7 & 8

0 meters	500
0 yards	500

North Side

Downtown
Core

South Loop
& Near
South Side

*Lake
Michigan*

South Side

View of Chicago's skyline, with Willis Tower in
the background

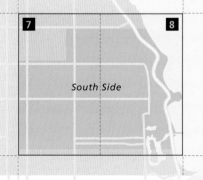

Street Finder Index

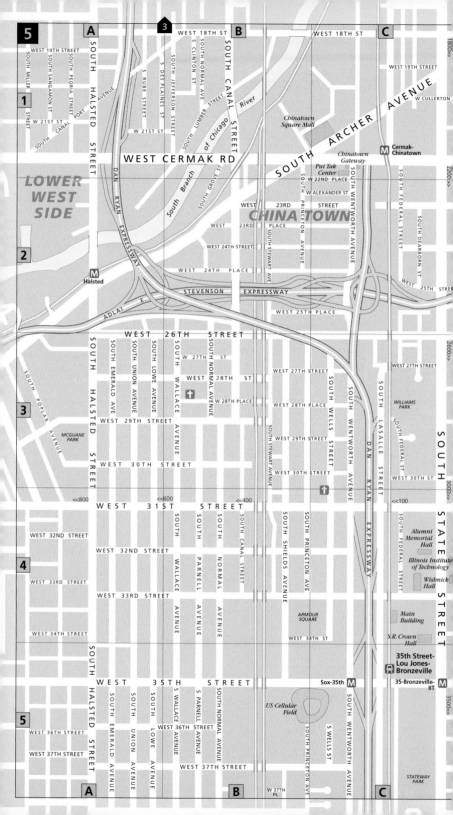

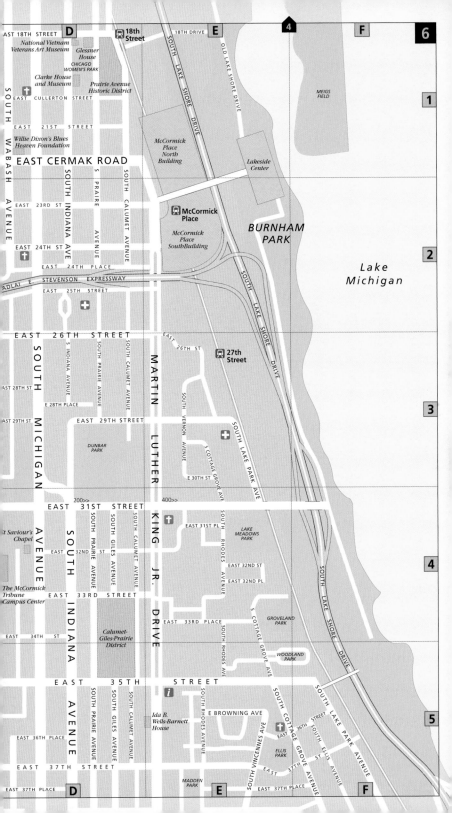

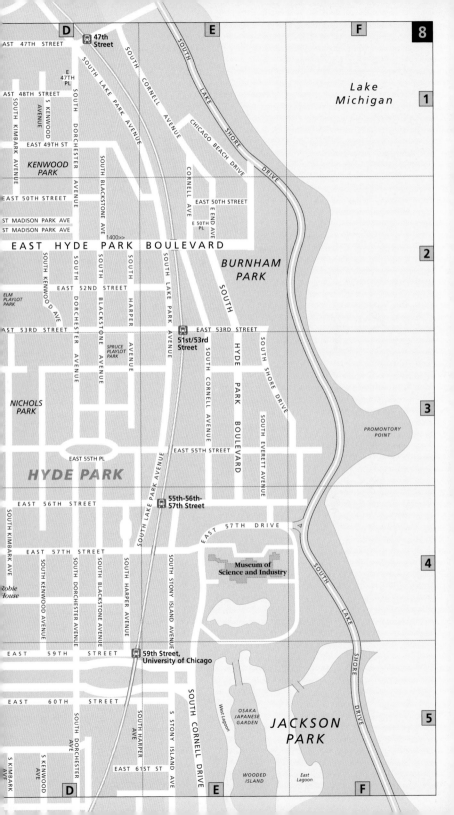

D · 47th Street
E 47TH PL
AST 47TH STREET
AST 48TH STREET
SOUTH KENWOOD AVENUE
SOUTH KIMBARK AVENUE
EAST 49TH ST
KENWOOD PARK
SOUTH DORCHESTER AVENUE
SOUTH LAKE PARK AVENUE
SOUTH CORNELL AVENUE
CHICAGO BEACH DRIVE
SOUTH LAKE SHORE DRIVE

Lake Michigan

EAST 50TH STREET
ST MADISON PARK AVE
ST MADISON PARK AVE
SOUTH BLACKSTONE AVE
1400>>
CORNELL AVE
E END AVE
E 50TH PL
EAST 50TH STREET

EAST HYDE PARK BOULEVARD

BURNHAM PARK

SOUTH KENWOOD AVE
EAST 52ND STREET
SOUTH DORCHESTER AVENUE
SOUTH BLACKSTONE AVENUE
SOUTH HARPER AVENUE
SOUTH LAKE PARK AVENUE
SOUTH
ELM PLAYLOT PARK

AST 53RD STREET
SPRUCE PLAYLOT PARK
EAST 53RD STREET · 51st/53rd Street
SOUTH CORNELL AVENUE
HYDE PARK BOULEVARD
SOUTH SHORE DRIVE

NICHOLS PARK

EAST 55TH STREET
SOUTH EVERETT AVENUE
EAST 55TH PL

HYDE PARK

EAST 56TH STREET
SOUTH KIMBARK AVE
SOUTH LAKE PARK AVENUE
· 55th-56th-57th Street

EAST 57TH DRIVE

EAST 57TH STREET
SOUTH KENWOOD AVENUE
SOUTH DORCHESTER AVENUE
SOUTH BLACKSTONE AVENUE
SOUTH HARPER AVENUE
SOUTH STONY ISLAND AVENUE

Robie House

Museum of Science and Industry

SOUTH LAKE SHORE DRIVE

EAST 59TH STREET · 59th Street, University of Chicago

EAST 60TH STREET
SOUTH DORCHESTER AVE
SOUTH HARPER AVE
S STONY ISLAND AVE
SOUTH CORNELL DRIVE

West Lagoon
OSAKA JAPANESE GARDEN

JACKSON PARK

S KIMBARK AVE
S KENWOOD AVE
EAST 61ST ST

WOODED ISLAND
East Lagoon

D · **E** · **F**

General Index

Acknowledgments

Dorling Kindersley and International Book Productions would like to thank the following people whose contributions and assistance have made the book possible:

At Dorling Kindersley
Managing Art Editor: Jane Ewart *Managing Editor:* Helen Townsend *Senior Publishing Manager:* Louise Lang *Production Controllers:* Marie Ingledew, *Michelle Thomas Cartographers:* Casper Morris, Dave Pugh

Main Contributors
Lorraine Johnson is a freelance writer living in Toronto who has a lifelong fascination with Chicago. She is the author of six books and contributes articles and book reviews regularly to magazines and newspapers.

John Ryan lives in Chicago. A professional musician and former chef, he manages the Elgin Symphony Orchestra in addition to writing regular food columns for America Online.

Additional Contributors
J.P. Anderson, Penney Kome

Special Research
Dana Joy Altman Deanna Cates

Proofreader
Maraya Raduha

Indexer
Barbara Sale Schon

Cartography
Visutronx, Ajax, Ontario, Canada

Additional Photography
Alessandra Santarelli and Joeff Davis

Revisions & Relaunch Team
Tora Agarwala, Emma Anacootee, Jasneet Arora, Claire Baranowski, Kathie Bergquist, Sherry Collins, Conrad van Dyk, Karen Fitzpatrick, Jacky Jackson, Rupanki Kaushik, Laura Jones, Nicola Malone, Sam Merrell, Scarlett O'Hara, Catherine Palmi, Amanda Scotese, Azeem Siddiqui, Susana Smith, Rada Radojicic, Brett Steel, Lauren Viera, Ros Walford, Ed Wright, Tanveer Zaidi.

Additional Picture Research
Ashwin Adimari, Rachel Barber, Marta Bescos, Rhiannon Furbear, Ellen Root

Special Assistance
Particular thanks go to Vanetta Anderson, Chicago Office of Tourism; Norah Zboril, City of Chicago, Mayor's Office, Special Events; Daniel J. Curtin, City of Chicago, Department of Aviation; Jeff Stern, Chicago Transit Authority; Diana Holic and Dawn Kappel, Adler Planetarium and Astronomy Museum; Brigid Murphy, Newberry Library; Mily Anzo, Museum of Science and Industry; Patricia Kremer, Field Museum; Corey Tovian and Gwen Biassi, John G. Shedd Aquarium; Rosemary Haack, City of Lake Forest; Janice Klein, Mitchell Museum of the American Indian; Ms. Chase Ruppert, McCormick Place Convention Center; Stephen Majsak, Chicago Architectural Foundation; Lois Berger, Chicago Public Library, Harold Washington Library Center; Jennifer Swanson, Lincoln Park Zoo; Adam Davies, Chicago Place; Angela Sweeney, Water Tower Place; Kelly Boggs and Michael Rilley, Chicago Theatre; Sarah Hamilton Hadley, Terra Museum of American Art; Karen Irvine, Museum of Contemporary Photography; Zarine Weil, Robie House; Ken Price, Palmer House Hilton Hotel; Michilla Johnson, Goose Island Beer Co.; Jan Berghoff, 17/West; Janet Femarek and David Caruso, Ed Debevic's Restaurant

Photography Permission
Dorling Kindersley and International Book Productions would like to thank everyone for their assistance and kind permission to photograph at their establishments.

Picture Credits
a-above; b-below/bottom; c-centre; f-far; l-left; r-right; t-top.

Works of art have been reproduced with the permission of the following copyright holders:

© ADAGP, Paris and DACS, London 2011: 126bl, © Succession Miro/ADAGP, Paris and DACS, London 2011: 126tr; The work illustrated on 4tr and 105tc has been reproduced by permission of the Henry Moore Foundation *Nuclear Energy* Henry Moore; © Estate of Grant Wood/DACS, London/VAGA, New York 2011: 49cra.

The Publishers are grateful to the following museums, companies, and picture libraries for permission to reproduce their photographs:

© **Adler Planetarium and Astronomy Museum**: 23bl, 94tr, 95crb; Craig Stillwell 11br.

Alamy Images: Chuck Eckert 174bl; Jeff Greenberg 1 of 6 178br; Edward Hattersley 21crb; John Henshall 10cla; Kim Karpeles 11tr, 124cl, 125crb; Russell Kord 112; Linda Matlow 11cl, 124tr; Nikreates 176cla; Peter Ravallo 175tl.

Amtrak:182tl.

The Art Institute of Chicago: All rights reserved – Mary Cassatt, American, 1844–1926, *The Child's Bath*, oil on canvas, 1893, 39 1/2 x 26 inches, Robert A. Waller Fund, 1910.2 – 49tc; India, Andhra Pradesh, Madanapalle. *The Divine General Karttikeya/Shanmukha*, Ganga Period, 12th century. Granite. Restricted Gift of Mr. and Mrs. Sylvain S. Wyler 1962.203 48 tr ; Nepal, Kathmandu Valley, *God Indra*, 16th century, Gilt bronze with gemstones. The James W. and Marilynn Alsdorf Collection 173.1997 48bl; Rembrandt Harmenszoon van Rijn, Dutch, 1606–1669, *Old Man with a Gold Chain*, oil on panel, c.1631, 83.1 x 75.7 cm, Mr. and Mrs. W.W. Kimball Collection, 1922.4467 – 49br; Charles Percier and Alexandre Theodore Brogniart Londonderry Vase, Sevres Manufacture, 1813, hard-paste porcelain with polychrome enamel decoration gilding and ormolu mounts, height: 137 cm, Harry and Maribel Blum Foundation Fund and the Harold L. Stewart Fund, 1987 51cl.

Au Cheval: Kari Skaflen 154bc.

Best Western Hawthorne: 145br.

Buddy Guy's Legends:165bl.

Café Spiaggia: 147tl, 151br.

The Canadian Press/Associated Press AP: 33ca; AP/Wide World Photos Inc. Charles Bennett 174tr.

Chicago Architecture Foundation: Bill Richert 172br, 185tl.

Chicago Firehouse: 152tc.

Chicago Historical Museum: 76bl; ICHi-2212 – 8–9; ICHi-08732 – 17bc; ICHi-30084 – 19cb; ICHi-31412 – 21tl; ICHi-31413 – 33tr; ICHi-31411 – 73br; ICHi- 09440 – 74cla; ICHi-31414 – 74cb; ICHi-14063 Currier & Ives 18crb; ICHi-05836 Leslie's Weekly 19bc; ICHi-27363 Paris Raoul Varin 17cb.

Chicago Park District: Brook Collins 124bl.

Chicago Public Library, Harold Washington Library Center: 84tl; *Events in the Life of Harold Washington* ceramic tile mosaic by Jacob Lawrence 26br; *Sleeping Beauty* sculpture by Alison Saar 82tr.

Chicago Reader: 164cla.

Chicago Transit Authority: 186c.

City of Chicago, Department of Aviation: 20crb, 181tr.

City of Chicago/ GRC: Patrick L. Pyszka 172cla, 189bl; Willy Schmidt 37bl; Peter J. Schultz 23tr, 35br; Chicago Air and Water Show 35cra.

Columbus Association for the Performing Arts: 56b.

Corbis: 20cra, 111cra; Sandy Felsenthal 30cla, 34cla; Mitchell Gerber 32br; Robert Holmes 50br; Layne Kennedy 50cla; Francis G. Mayer, *The Basket of Apples* by Paul Cézanne 51tr, *On the Seine at Bennecourt* by Claude Monet 51br; Robert Harding World Imagery/Amanda Hall 184cl; Derick A. Thomas, Dat's Jazz 32tr; AFP/Corbis 33clb; Bettmann/Corbis 19tl, 31cla, 32cl, 33bc, *A Sunday on La Grande Jatte* by Georges Seurat 49crb, *American Gothic* by Grant Wood, Friends of the American Art Collection. All rights reserved by the Art Institue of Chicago 49cra; 79bl; Hulton-Deutsch Collection 20tl; UPI/Corbis-Bettmann 20bc.

Courtesy of Chicago Department of Cultural Affairs:Chicago Photographic Department 24cr, 43br.

The David and Alfred Smart Museum of Art, The University of Chicago: reproduced with permission 103tc; University Transfer – Dining Table and Six Side Chairs, Frank Lloyd Wright 104cr.

Joeff Davis: 30bc, 123tr, 125tc.

Davis Street Fishmarket: 157tc.

Drake Hotel: 144tc.

Dreamstime.com: Andreykr 40; Footer 95tl, 123bl; Lawrence Weslowski Jr 13tr; Jesse Kraft 38-9; Mramos7637 63ca; Glenn Nagel 2-3; Rover2055 62crb; Rsusanto 128-9; Rudi1976 60; Peter Tambroni 42cl.

Courtesy of the Field Museum: 88cl, 88tr, 89tc, 91bl; John Weinstein © 1998 – 25ca; George Papadakis © 1998 – 89ca, 89crb.

Flickr.com: www.flickr.com/photos/solarwind-chicago/3605736668/ 79cr.

Getty Images: 180br, Scott Boehm 179tl; Carl Larson Photography 12br, Photographer's Choice RF/Bruce Leighty 170-1.

Glowimages: Michael Weber 180cla.

Goose Island Beer Company: © Daniel J. Wigg 147br.

The Granger Collection, New York: 16.

Green City Market.org: Kate Gross Photography 173cr.

Greyhound Lines, Inc:182c.

.Courtesy of Hershey's Chicago: 65tl.

Hilton Worldwide: 138-9.

Hot Doug's: 153br.

Hotel Monaco: 142br.

House of Two Urns B&B: 143tr.

Hugo's Frog Bar and Fish House: 150tl.

International Museum of Surgical Science, Chicago: 24clb; *Hope and Help* sculpture by Edouard Chaissing reproduced with permission 77c.

Jane Addams' Hull-House Museum, University of Illinois at Chicago :118tl.

John G. Shedd Aquarium: 98cl, 99cra; © Edward G. Lines 98tr, 98br, 99tlc 99bc, 99crb..

Kimpton Group: 140cl, 141tl.

Lincoln Park Zoo, Chicago: 114bc, 115tc, 115crb; © Grant Kessler 23crb; Greg Neise 122bl.

McCormick Place Convention Center: 183crb.

Millennium Park Project: Skidmore, Owings & Merrill LLP 55t.

Mitchell Museum of the American Indian: 133tl.

Museum of Contemporary Photography, Columbia College Chicago: Tom Nowak 83tl, 86tl.

Museum of Science and Industry: 108cla, 108clb, 108tr, 109cr; © 2000 Dirk Fletcher 25br, 109tl, 110bl, 111tl; J.B. Spector 109cb.

The Newberry Library: 69br.

North Pond Restaurant: 146bl, 156tl.

Palmer House Hilton Hotel: 5tr, 140br.

Pastoral: 148bc.

Pictures Colour Library: Clive Sawyer 10br.

The Publican: 155tr.

Quartino: 149tr.

The Richard H. Driehaus Museum: Steve Hall 28bl.

Russian Tea Time: 149tr.

Spertus Museum (Spertus Institute of Jewish Studies): 24br; *Flame of Hope* by Leonardo Nierman, 1995. Collection of Spertus Museum 83tc.

The Sullivan Center: 52bl.

SuperStock: imagebroker.net 13bc; James Lemass 67b.

Takashi: 156bc.

Courtesy of Water Tower Place: 159tl; Solari Photography 63t.

Frank Lloyd Wright Home and Studio Foundation: Courtesy of Henrich Blessing and the Frank Lloyd Wright Home and Studio Foundation 27br.

Wrigley Building: The Wrigley Building and design are registered trademarks of the Wm. Wrigley Jr. Company, used by permission 63br, 64tl.

Front Endpaper : Alamy Images: Russell Kord Lclb; Dreamstime.com: Andreykr Rtr; Rsusanto Lbr; Rudi1976 Lcr.

Map Cover

Getty Images: Panoramic Images.

Jacket

Front main and Spine Getty Images: Panoramic Images; Front bl Courtesy of the Chicago Cultural Center.

All other images © Dorling Kindersley. See www.dkimages.com for more information.